**Determann's Field Guide to
Data Privacy Law**

# Elgar Compliance Guides

**Series Editor:** James Fanto, *Brooklyn Law School, USA*

# Determann's Field Guide to Data Privacy Law

## International Corporate Compliance

### Third Edition

LOTHAR DETERMANN

*Baker & McKenzie LLP, USA, Freie Universität Berlin, Germany, UC Berkeley School of Law and Hastings College of the Law, USA*

**Elgar Compliance Guides**

Edward Elgar
PUBLISHING

Cheltenham, UK • Northampton, MA, USA

Published by
Edward Elgar Publishing Limited
The Lypiatts
15 Lansdown Road
Cheltenham
Glos GL50 2JA
UK

Edward Elgar Publishing, Inc.
William Pratt House
9 Dewey Court
Northampton
Massachusetts 01060
USA

A catalogue record for this book
is available from the British Library

Library of Congress Control Number: 2017941914

This book is available electronically in the **Elgar**online
Law subject collection
DOI 10.4337/9781786438690

MIX
Paper from
responsible sources
FSC® C013604

ISBN 978 1 78643 868 3 (cased)
ISBN 978 1 78643 870 6 (paperback)
ISBN 978 1 78643 869 0 (eBook)

Typeset by Servis Filmsetting Ltd, Stockport, Cheshire
Printed and bound by CPI Group (UK) Ltd, Croydon, CR0 4YY

# Content overview

Table of contents      vi
About this third edition, contributors and the author      ix
Introduction      xi
Key terms      xiii
Key concepts      xv

## The Field Guide

1. Starting a compliance program      1

2. International data transfers – selecting
   compliance mechanisms      28

3. Drafting documentation      59

4. Maintaining and auditing compliance programs      102

5. Data privacy A to Z      106

Checklist      188
Resources      192
Abbreviations      194
Index      197

# Table of contents

About this third edition, contributors and the author     ix
Introduction     xi
Key terms     xiii

**Key concepts**     xv
    The field: data protection, privacy and security     xv
    The territory: Europe, U.S. and ROW     xvii
    The species: personal data, PII and sensitive data     xx
    Activities encountered: transfers and other forms of
      processing     xxiii
    The observed: data controllers, processors     xxiv
    The game wardens: data protection authorities,
      officers     xxv

## The Field Guide

**1. Starting a compliance program**     1
    Taking charge     1
    Working with internal stakeholders and outside
      advisors     3
    Appointing a privacy officer     4
    Preparing a task list     11
    Executing tasks     27

**2. International data transfers – selecting
compliance mechanisms**     28
    Three hurdles     30
    Options to clear hurdle 3 – prohibition of
      international transfers     35
    Compliance mechanisms compared     39
    Implementation     51
    Data transfers from other jurisdictions     56

3.  Drafting documentation                                      59
        Why are you creating the document?                      59
        Who is your audience?                                   62
        Categories and examples of documentation               64
        Notices                                                 68
        Consent                                                 78
        How to obtain valid consent                            80
        Opt-in, out and in between                             82
        Above and beyond opt-in consent                        86
        Other considerations for consent drafting              88
        Agreements                                              90
        Protocols                                               96
        Questionnaires and data submission forms               97
        Documenting decisions and compliance efforts           98
        Government notifications, approvals                     99

4.  Maintaining and auditing compliance programs               102

5.  Data privacy A to Z                                        106
        Advertising                                            107
        Brexit, GDPR, ePrivacy and Privacy Shield              109
        Cloud computing                                        111
        Data retention and residency requirements              124
        Employee data and monitoring                           128
        Financial information                                  139
        Government investigations, information requests        140
        Health information                                     143
        Internet of Everything, big data and data brokers      145
        Jurisdiction                                           148
        K – Contracts                                          151
        Location data                                          152
        Minors                                                 153
        Notification of data security breaches                 154
        Ownership                                              158
        Privacy by design                                      159
        Questionnaires                                         160
        Rights, remedies, enforcement                          161
        Social media                                           166
        Tracking                                               168
        Unsolicited communications (spam email,
            cold calls, etc.)                                  173
        Vendor management                                      178

Wiretapping                                                    180
X-ray, genes, fingerprints, faces – biometric data            181
Y – Why protect data privacy?                                 183
ZIP codes, IP addresses and other numbers                     186

Checklist: Data privacy and security compliance program       188
Resources                                                     192
Abbreviations                                                 194
Index                                                         197

# About this third edition, contributors and the author

Since the second edition of this Field Guide went to print in 2015, global privacy laws changed significantly. The European Union finally updated its data protection laws for the first time in more than 20 years. In 2016, the EU enacted its General Data Protection Regulation, which will become effective in 2018. The EU Court of Justice invalidated the adequacy decision regarding data transfers to the United States under the Safe Harbor Program in 2015 and the EU Commission approved a successor program in 2016, the EU-U.S. Privacy Shield. Meanwhile, data protection authorities have increased their data protection audit and enforcement activities. Russia, Kazakhstan Indonesia, China and Germany enacted laws according to which companies are required to store personal data locally within better reach of local government agencies. In the United States, plaintiffs' lawyers have brought numerous class action lawsuits based on data privacy and security claims against companies and the government; the U.S. Federal Trade Commission successfully defended in court its creation of data privacy and security law through complaints and consent decrees that the Commission based on general unfair competition laws; and the State of California, where most major information technology companies are headquartered, has been actively passing new laws in response to perceived new threats and abuses. These developments required numerous edits to this Field Guide even though much of the practical guidance and the general direction remain steady. The author is grateful for the interest and feedback regarding the first and second editions of this book and looks forward to continued dialogue with users of this Field Guide.

The author thanks Bethany Lewis, CIPP/US, CIPP/E, Privacy Project Manager, The Nielsen Company, for valuable edits and contributions to the third edition of this Field Guide, and all contributors to previous editions, including Dr. Ron A. Dolin, Diana Francis, Prof. Susan Freiwald, Emmanuel Fua, Sarah Jain, Dr. Sebastian Kraska and Dr. Christoph Rittweger. The author takes sole responsibility for any errors and omissions.

Lothar Determann practices and teaches international data privacy, commercial and intellectual property law. He is admitted to practice law in Germany and California and a partner with Baker & McKenzie LLP in San Francisco and Palo Alto, California. He has been a member of the Association of German Public Law Professors since 1999 and teaches Data Privacy Law, Computer Law and Internet Law at Freie Universität Berlin (since 1994), University of California, Berkeley School of Law (Boalt Hall, since 2004), Hastings College of the Law (since 2010), Stanford Law School (2011) and University of San Francisco School of Law (2000 to 2005). He has authored more than 100 articles and treatise contributions and four other books, including California Privacy Law – Practical Guide and Commentary (2nd E. 2017).

# Introduction

This Field Guide is not about 'roughing it'. This book guides you 0.01
through an increasingly complex field of laws, regulations and technology. Generalists in corporate legal departments and private practice, privacy officers, information technology product developers, marketing managers and others are confronted with data privacy and security issues more and more frequently. Tons of information is publicly available, much of which is free of charge. Still, it can be difficult to get a handle on a practical problem quickly without getting lost in details.

This is where this Field Guide is meant to come into play. It is designed 0.02
to help identify issues, provide a brief practical overview, shape questions and lead to solutions. Where the Field Guide cannot provide an answer that is detailed enough, it contains directions to further resources that are easily accessible – by providing key terminology that can be easily looked up. Footnotes with citations in 'Bluebook format' have consciously been omitted; this book is for use in the field, not in a library.

For example, in this Field Guide you will find checklists with key com- 0.03
pliance requirements and practical suggestions on how to go about satisfying them in an efficient manner. You will also be presented with examples of jurisdiction-specific details that global companies are most likely to encounter in the field, selected for illustrative purposes, but never for all 190+ countries. Once you have your bearings and you want to determine applicable details by country and situation, for example, whether you have to appoint a data protection officer in China, this Field Guide will refer you to other resources, listed at the back of the book, including Baker & McKenzie's Global Privacy Handbook (available free of charge, the 2017 Edition covers 60+ jurisdictions).

Consider a few suggestions on how to use the Field Guide: If you got 0.04
this book because you are tasked with designing or implementing a new data privacy compliance program, you could start with the

following overview of 'Key Terms' and 'Key Concepts' for orientation, and then use the main five Chapters of the Field Guide for navigation. If you just want to get a quick read on a particular issue, you could look up buzz words in the Index at the end of the book to zoom in on a topic that concerns you. Or, if you are faced with a particular task, you could also try one of the following paths:

| Task or issue | Guidance |
| --- | --- |
| Draft a privacy policy | Ch. 3.1–3.8 |
| Respond to data security breach | Ch. 5 – Breaches of Data Security |
| Buy or sell cloud computing services | Ch. 5 – Cloud Computing; Vendors Ch. 3.9 – Agreements |
| Appoint data privacy officer | Ch. 1.1–1.2 |
| Achieve compliance re. international data transfers | Ch. 2 |
| Prepare filings for data protection authorities | Ch. 3.12 |
| Conduct due diligence on M&A targets, vendors | Ch. 4 |
| Select network/employee monitoring tools | Ch. 5 – Employee Data and Monitoring; Wiretapping |
| Deploy cookies, tracking technologies legally | Ch. 5 – Advertising, Tracking |
| Comply with anti-spam laws | Ch. 5 – Unsolicited Communications |
| Develop product, process or service | Ch. 5 – Privacy by Design |
| Gather management support | Ch. 5 – Rights, Remedies, Enforcement; Y – Why Protect Privacy? |

# Key terms

Every discipline coins its own special terms, acronyms, other abbrevia- 0.05
tions and jargon. Data privacy law is no different in this respect. In the
interest of serving as a quick reference and easy read, this Field Guide
minimizes the use of jargon and abbreviations and employs everyday
language whenever practical. But, seven key terms are used throughout
the guide, because you have to know them. These terms are omnipresent in data privacy literature and hard to avoid:

| | |
|---|---|
| **Personal Data** | Information that relates to an individual 0.06 person who can be identified, including identifying information (name, passport number, etc.) and any other data (*e.g.*, photos, phone numbers, etc.). European data protection laws tend to cover all personal data, but U.S–style data privacy laws are often more limited and focused on particularly sensitive data categories |
| **Processing** | Any activity relating to data, including col- 0.07 lection, storage, alteration, disclosure and destruction |
| **Data Subject** | The individual person to whom data relates 0.08 |
| **Data Controller** | A company that determines the purposes 0.09 and means of the data processing, *e.g.*, an employer with respect to employee data |
| **Data Processor** | A company that processes personal data on 0.10 behalf of a data controller, *e.g.*, an accountant or payroll service provider that assists an employer |
| **Transfer** | Transmitting data to, or making data avail- 0.11 able for access by, another organization or in another country, *e.g.*, via remote Internet access |

| | | |
|---|---|---|
| 0.12 | **Data Privacy Law** | Laws intended to protect an individual data subject's ability to control information about him or herself, including European-style data protection laws (regulating any processing of any personal data) and common law privacy laws (protecting reasonable expectations of being left alone by other individuals, organizations and governments) |

More detailed definitions follow in the next Section on 'Key Concepts'. Abbreviations are defined at the end of the book.

0.13   A few other key terms should perhaps be used more sparingly and carefully. Information technologists and marketers tend to be so excited about 'the cloud' and 'big data' that they overuse these labels, extend their meaning to products on the periphery and overlook all negative connotations. When software-as-a-service providers and users talk about 'the cloud', they think about dynamic usage of computing capacity, cost savings, follow-the-sun support, connectivity, mobility and other benefits. The term 'cloud' originates from the symbol that designers of technical charts use to refer to the Internet, a global net of servers, cables, satellite connections, routers, switches and other telecommunication equipment. In Silicon Valley, where most major 'cloud' providers are headquartered, the term 'cloud' comes with positive associations, given the fact that California notoriously suffers from lack of rain. When data protection officers and politicians in Europe, where it rains too much, hear 'the cloud', however, they seem to think about bad visibility into where data resides and who has access to it. Similarly, when researchers get excited about opportunities concerning 'big data', they seem to forget the relatively low public preference for *big* government, *big* business, banks too *big* to fail, etc. If you are trying to sell services, features and opportunities, be mindful of your audience before resorting to these buzzwords.

# Key concepts

Before entering the field, it is helpful for orientation to scope out or recall key concepts and terminology. Acronyms and abbreviations are also summarized at the back of this book.

## The field: data protection, privacy and security

The terms 'data privacy' and 'data protection' are often used inter- 0.14 changeably, in particular in the context of comparisons of Anglo-Saxon data privacy laws and continental European data protection laws. Actually, the two terms and legislative concepts have quite different origins and purposes. Here is a simplified overview:

*Data protection:* Data protection is about protecting information con- 0.15 cerning persons. Immediate focus is not the individual person, but data about a person. By protecting personal data, laws are intended to protect persons (the data subjects) from the effects of automated data processing. When you try to understand or comply with European data protection laws, keep in mind that the default rule is "verboten" (German for: forbidden). Businesses and other organizations are generally prohibited from processing personal data, unless they obtain consent from the data subjects or they find an applicable statutory exemption. European data protection laws are first and foremost intended to restrict and reduce the automated processing of personal data – even if such data is publicly available. My home state, the German State of Hessen, enacted the first data protection law in 1970 due to growing concerns regarding dangers of automated data processing for individual freedoms. Citizens and politicians were concerned that George Orwell's forecast for 1984 could become reality: where 'glass citizens' are observed and controlled by an omniscient 'big brother' – the government. More recently, these concerns were joined by fears regarding 'little brothers,' namely private companies that amass data and databases for commercial purposes, which can then be conveniently (ab)used by governments or criminals.

Due to these concerns, legislatures decided to regulate automated data processing like other dangerous activities. The Hessian data protection law – and laws of other German states and European countries – established a general prohibition and regulatory regime regarding the processing of personal data. One key feature of European-style data protection laws is a data minimization requirement: companies are prohibited from collecting, using and retaining data, unless they obtain consent or have another compelling reason to process the data. And, companies are required to minimize the amount of data they collect, the instances of processing, the people who have access and the time periods for which they retain data. In practice, many companies in Europe collect and process personal data as much as their competitors in other parts of the world. European data protection laws provide for exemptions and data subjects grant consent to allow this. But, the principal hostility to personal data processing and databases in European data protection laws is important to keep in mind for purposes of understanding and applying European data protection laws. And, this hostility is probably one reason why that European companies do not lead in information-driven economy sectors such as electronic commerce, cloud computing, software-as-a-service and social networking, where much of the innovation and market leaders come from the United States and increasingly also Asia.

0.16   *Data privacy:* The United States and other countries outside of Europe, by contrast, generally allow data processing. Data privacy laws are primarily intended to protect individuals from intrusion into seclusion and interception of confidential communications. Given this focus, individuals are usually not protected, unless they have a reasonable expectation of privacy in a particular situation. Companies can – and frequently do – destroy such expectations of privacy by notifying individuals of the companies' data collection and processing activities, for example, in employee handbooks, website privacy statements and in-store warnings about security cameras. Individuals receive some protection in the sanctity of their homes, but communications and activities outside the home receive little or no protection, *e.g.*, information in public records, assembling in the open, calls on cell phones in public, postings on the Internet or via social networking platforms, etc. Instead of enacting one comprehensive data protection law, the United States has enacted numerous sector- and threat-specific laws on the Federal and State level to address specific concerns narrowly and without too much collateral damage to freedom of information and technological progress.

*Data security:* More recently, legislatures around the world have 0.17
started to supplement data privacy laws with sectoral data security laws. These laws aim to protect individuals from specific harm resulting from unauthorized access to personal information, in particular identity theft (*e.g.*, criminals using someone's personal data to acquire or charge credit cards). Examples include data security breach notification laws (California passed the first law in 2003, with most U.S. states and many countries following suit thereafter), detailed prescriptions regarding technical and organizational measures to protect health information in HIPAA and U.S. state laws in California, Massachusetts, Nevada and New York requiring encryption of certain data in certain circumstances.

*Data privacy as umbrella term:* In line with common language usage 0.18
and in the interest of simplicity, this Field Guide will use the term 'data privacy' collectively for data protection, data privacy and data security, except where differentiation matters.

## The territory: Europe, U.S. and ROW

Most companies are dealing with data privacy issues in more than one 0.19
jurisdiction, given the global nature of the world economy. But while businesses have to solve global problems, the laws they have to comply with remain territorial. On the Internet, companies can reach more than 190 countries instantaneously – and each country has its own laws. In the United States alone, you are dealing with laws made by 50 states plus federal laws enacted by the U.S. Congress. In Europe, you will find some harmonization due to the EC Data Protection Directive of 1995, which has been implemented in the 31 member states of the European Economic Area (EEA) and closely followed by Argentina, Colombia, Israel, Switzerland, Russia, Uruguay and some candidates for EU membership.

In May 2018, the new EU General Data Protection Regulation (GDPR) 0.20
will enter into effect in all EEA Member States with direct and immediate effect on companies within the EEA. Many companies outside the EEA will also be subject to the GDPR, if, for example, they collect personal data via online services from consumers in the EEA or via an establishment in the EEA. The GDPR is the first significant update of EU data protection laws since 1995, provides for draconian fines, and brings many major changes for companies, including the following:

• Companies must document all data processing activities and compliance efforts to demonstrate how they comply with data protection laws; they must conduct impact assessments for high risk activities and prepare records describing all data processing and compliance measures, including categories of data and data subjects, purposes of processing, recipients, international transfers and suitable safeguards, time limits for erasure, technical and organizational security measures (Art. 30, 35)

• Companies must designate a data protection officer for each of their establishments, subject to exemptions for small and low risk presences and an option that one data protection officer can watch over several companies and offices so long as she is accessible and accountable for each establishment

• Companies outside the EEA must designate a representative within the EEA

• Companies must implement robust data retention and deletion programs to comply with more stringent rules regarding data access, rectification and erasure

• Companies must provide more detailed privacy notices to data subjects, disclosing identity and contact details of the data controller (and representative in the EEA for foreign companies); contact details of the data protection officer; purposes of data processing; legal basis for processing; legitimate interests pursued by the controller or a third party, if that is the basis for justifying the processing; recipients or categories of recipients; in case of international data transfers, the existence or absence of an adequacy decision by the Commission and information on safeguards, including the means by which to obtain a copy of them; and many other details. At the same time, companies are required to present this information in a "concise, transparent, intelligible and easily accessible form, using clear and plain language" (Art. 12, 13)

• Companies must establish processes to ensure that they can report data security breaches within 72 hours to data protection authorities and data subjects

Besides the GDPR, companies will have to continue complying with national data protection laws. Unlike the Data Protection Directive of

1995, the GDPR applies directly to companies and does not have to be implemented into national law. But, national laws can provide for additional or stricter rules in some respects and will remain effective until affirmatively revoked.

The GDPR is intended to create even greater harmonization in European data protection laws than the Data Protection Directive and it has the potential to achieve this if EEA Member States withdraw their existing national laws in favor of the new GDPR. It is not unlikely, however, that some EEA Member States will keep existing laws around and thus create uncertainties regarding the degree of preemption and harmonization. Another factor adding uncertainty in Europe is the UK's exit from the EU, which could result in the introduction of different privacy laws in one of the most important jurisdictions in Europe by the size of its population and economy.

Given the level of harmonization in Europe, this Field Guide can occasionally refer to general principles of 'European laws'; but this should not obscure the fact that companies have to comply with each individual European country's laws, when applicable, in addition to the GDPR, and possibly also additional laws of states, provinces and other subsections within a European country.

This Field Guide is intended to provide you with guidance for all territories and help you identify globally recurring themes and pitfalls to watch out for. For illustrative purposes, you will see examples mostly from Europe and the United States. Europe and the U.S. have had data privacy laws, litigation and regulatory proceedings for the longest time and so they are the most charted territories with respect to many issues. Also, Europe and the U.S. lend themselves well to illustrations because they are frequently on the opposing end of the spectrum of regulatory approaches: Europe tends to be more protective/paternalistic with respect to individuals and leans towards imposing heavy regulatory burdens on companies, including requirements to obtain prior approvals, submit filings and comply with various formal requirements. The United States on the other hand has consciously passed on European-style omnibus data protection legislation and instead enacted sector-specific, narrowly framed laws, providing for a private right of action, in response to concrete threats to particular aspects of individual privacy. Once you have familiarized yourself with the U.S. and European position on a particular question, you can often navigate other countries (charmingly referred to as "ROW" for "Rest Of World") by grouping

0.21

them closer to the U.S. or European position. This is particularly effective when you have to implement global systems or processes and your organization or technology can accommodate only a limited number of options.

Please keep in mind that you are looking at approximation and high-level themes when the Field Guide refers to European or U.S. laws for orientation purposes. Some states within and outside the U.S. and EEA have different laws or interpretations of laws, many countries do not have any specific laws yet and there is little harmonization in other continents and regions (*e.g.*, Asia-Pac, Latin America, Middle East and Africa).

## The species: personal data, PII and sensitive data

0.22   When you encounter terms like 'personal data' and 'personally identifiable information' in laws or contracts, you must check the applicable definitions to determine the impact of a particular provision. When you draft a website privacy statement, notice or contract clause, you can either assume a very broad range of application or include an express, limiting definition yourself.

0.23   *Personal data:* For the purposes of European data protection laws, personal data is any information that relates to an identifiable human individual. For example, a person's name, photo, address or birth date would be considered 'personal data.' It is not necessary that the data by itself allows identification of the data subject. It is sufficient that the data relates in a meaningful manner to an individual person who could be identified.

0.24   For example, a company phone number that can be answered by a number of persons does not constitute 'personal data,' but an individual extension that is permanently allocated to an individual person does. Also, a general company phone number can become part of 'personal data' in combination with other information, such as the time of a particular call whose participants can be determined. An Internet Protocol (IP) address of a router or other device can constitute personal data if it relates to an individual user (*e.g.*, single person household). But, an IP address does not constitute personal data if it relates to a large business without a reasonable connection to an individual person. The question whether IP addresses and phone numbers constitute personal data has been hotly debated for years by academics and even legal practitioners, but if you take a close look, it often does not matter to a company: If some of the data that your company processes can be linked to an individual, then you have to either treat all of the data as personal data or differentiate and separate. But, differentiation is usually impractical or too expensive to implement. For example, if you implement cookie technology to analyze website visitor conduct and you log IP addresses in the process, you will inevitably gather some IP addresses that can be linked to an individual and for compliance purposes, it does not matter whether the large majority of IP addresses could be excluded from the scope of data privacy laws.

Data can cease to qualify as 'personal data' if it is redacted or aggregated   0.25 in a manner that destroys the connection to an individual. Encryption and partial redaction do not do the trick, as long as someone holds the key and could re-identify the data subject. Thus, for the most part, you still have to treat encrypted data as 'personal data' under data protection laws. On the other hand, true aggregation can remove data from the scope of data protection laws. For example, if you take information on video rental habits of a thousand randomly selected individuals, and you merge the information to create statistical information about less than all one thousand individuals, the resulting aggregate data (*e.g.*, 20% of video renters watch less than 20 hours a month) is no longer 'personal data' (while the raw data on individual habits continues to be personal data). Theoretically, you could also redact data relating to an individual by removing names and all identifiers from a profile. But, this is harder than one would think in practice. If the redacted data sets retain any information that allows the reversal of the redaction process (*e.g.*, an address, birth date/place, etc.), then the data will typically continue to qualify as 'personal data' under European data protection laws. Reversible redaction is also referred to as "pseudonymization." It does not remove data from the scope of European data protection laws, but is recognized as a legitimate data security measure and an effort to protect the privacy of the individual.

*PII – Personally identifiable information:* In stark contrast to the broad   0.26 concept of 'personal data' under European laws, many other countries use slightly different terms and define them much more narrowly. For example, the California Civil Code uses the term 'personally identifiable information' in many statutory sections and defines the term narrowly and differently each time, depending on each section's context and purpose. Other California laws, as well as federal law and the laws of other states, use different definitions. Often only particularly sensitive types of information are covered (*e.g.*, credit card numbers, social security numbers, etc.).

0.27 *Sensitive data:* Most jurisdictions and laws apply higher standards to certain categories of personal data. Reasons and covered categories vary from jurisdiction to jurisdiction. For example, laws in the United States protect social security numbers and credit card information in particular because consumers are exposed to high identity theft risks due to relatively lax authentication procedures by banks and merchants. Identity theft is less of a concern in Europe, but under European laws, companies generally have to observe special restrictions regarding personal information relating to:

• political opinions,

• trade union membership,

• medical or health conditions (*e.g.*, employee sick days, prescriptions, clinical trial data – even if stored by impersonal IDs without patient names),

• racial or ethnic origin (*e.g.*, place of birth, photos showing skin color),

• religious or philosophical beliefs (*e.g.*, German church tax status in payroll systems),

• information relating to sexual orientation (*e.g.*, marital status in jurisdictions that do not recognize same sex marriages), and

• certain types of criminal records.

0.28 Some limited exceptions apply in Europe, particularly for collection and local processing of sensitive data by employers as required by law. Companies need to obtain express consent, however, before transferring any sensitive data outside the European Economic Area (see Chapter 2).

0.29 International conflicts between national laws are possible. For example, a company might be required to produce certain sensitive data in U.S. litigation or government investigations, which the company is prohibited from sharing under European laws. But, upon closer review, you can avoid many apparent conflicts. For example, U.S. export control compliance programs can require collection of certain information on citizenship and residency of foreign workers with access to controlled U.S. technology, but information on racial or ethnic origin (which would constitute 'sensitive personal data' under European laws) is usually not required.

Laws in the United States and other jurisdictions also differentiate o.30 between various categories of personal data with respect to particular scenarios. There are hardly any common themes beyond what common sense would suggest, so companies must survey their data collection practices in each relevant jurisdiction separately.

## Activities encountered: transfers and other forms of processing

European data protection laws regulate any processing of personal o.31 data and define the term 'processing' very broadly to include any activity relating to personal data. Processing includes collection, recording, organization, storage, adaptation or alteration, retrieval, consultation, use, disclosure by transmission, dissemination or otherwise making available, alignment or combination, blocking, erasure and destruction, whether by manual or automated means. Even as you are redacting personal data – making it anonymous – you are processing the personal data under European laws and you trigger the same general prohibitions and data minimization requirements.

Under U.S. and other countries' laws, however, data privacy laws tend o.32 to pertain to particular activities. In most jurisdictions, people and data privacy laws tend to be particularly sensitive with respect to one form of processing: data transfers. A transfer occurs when one company sends data to another company or country via email, mail or otherwise, but also if someone in the other company or country can remotely access data via the Internet or other technologies. Thus, if a company posts an employee directory for all employees worldwide to access, that constitutes a data transfer to all jurisdictions where such data is available. If you post information on the Internet, you transfer such information everywhere. Therefore, a 'transfer' in the broadest sense of the word occurs every time you allow someone else to access data – regardless of the technical means or commercial context.

0.33    Conceptually, however, an important distinction applies with respect to transfers within an organization and its circle of service providers (*i.e.*, data processors, which often include the parent company providing IT infrastructure-as-a-service as well as unaffiliated providers of payroll processing, Internet access and physical security services). Companies do not typically have to explain details regarding data sharing with data processors in privacy notices or government filings and data subjects typically do not have a choice in this respect. To be on the safe side, you should draw the net wide and consider restrictions under data privacy laws each time you make data available to someone else. But, you should also keep in mind that transfers to mere data processors are often less restricted than transfers to data controllers, *i.e.*, those who use data for their own purposes. The rationale for this is that what matters to the data subject is that the company he or she entrusts with personal data stays responsible and that any individuals who act for this company comply with all of the company's privacy promises and applicable law – regardless of the employment status of such individuals. Companies are legal fictions that do not themselves act except through employees, individual independent contractors and employees of corporate service providers. Which individuals a company chooses to process personal data – its own employees, individual independent contractors, employees of corporate contractors or subcontractors – does not usually affect the data subject's privacy interests. Therefore, companies are usually permitted to share personal data with individual and corporate service providers (*i.e.*, data processors) without notice to or consent from data subjects, so long as they execute a written data processing agreement that clearly documents the limited discretion of the service provider regarding data usage.

## The observed: data controllers, processors

0.34    European data protection laws differentiate between 'data controllers' – who use data for their own purposes and at their own discretion – and 'data processors' – who process data only on behalf of a data controller as a service provider. Data controllers are the ones who are primarily obligated to comply with data protection and privacy laws. Data processors are obligated to comply with instructions from the data controller, keep data secure and refrain from using data for any purposes other than as instructed by the data controller. Data processors are also referred to as 'agents' or service providers in many laws and privacy statements. A company can qualify as data controller with respect to some activities (*e.g.*, processing of employee and customer relationship information) and as a data processor with respect to other activities (*e.g.*, assisting its subsidiaries with payroll processing and customers with respect to computer maintenance).

Service providers that gain physical custody and technical access, but that are not allowed or expected ever to access data under any circumstances, refer to themselves as 'data handlers' or 'mere conduits' in order to excuse themselves from any direct obligations under data privacy laws. Some types of providers have a compelling case, for example telecommunications companies that are not allowed or expected to know whether their systems are used to communicate health or other information. Also, colocation providers (companies that rent secure cages to companies to host servers) and more traditional landlords usually have some physical access rights to computer systems, but very limited or no rights to access data (sometimes in the context of disaster recovery or Internet access and troubleshooting arrangements). Legislatures rarely acknowledge exemptions from data privacy laws for data handlers or mere conduits. Customers tend to insist on commitments from their service providers just in case these qualify as data processors, business associates or the like, in order to protect themselves from challenges regarding their own data privacy compliance efforts. 0.35

## The game wardens: data protection authorities, officers

European countries have established independent public authorities responsible for enforcing national data protection laws. Their representatives formed an EU-wide institution that was called "Article 29 Working Party" under Art. 29 of the Data Protection Directive of 1995 and is called "European Data Protection Board" according to Art. 68 of the EU General Data Protection Regulation. This institution has been issuing guidance to companies and legislatures and publicizing views of national data protection authorities. Such guidelines and views are quite relevant to companies, given that the data protection authorities are tasked with enforcing data privacy laws against companies. In many European countries and some non-European countries, companies have to notify the local data protection authority before they start processing personal data. In some countries, companies have to obtain prior approval from the data protection authorities before they engage in certain kinds of data processing activities, *e.g.*, international transfers of personal data outside the EEA. 0.36

0.37 In most European jurisdictions and a few other jurisdictions, companies must (or may, as an alternative to notifying data protection authorities) appoint a data protection officer, either an employee or external service provider, who is tasked with monitoring whether the company complies with applicable data protection laws. Such data protection officers are not government officials, but they are required to cooperate with the local data protection authority and report serious offenses. Similarly, government agencies in Europe and elsewhere (including the NSA since February 2014) have appointed data protection officers whose task is to monitor the particular government agency's own compliance efforts. Whether in government agencies or private sector organizations – the role of the data protection officer is focused inwards to monitor compliance by their own organizations. This distinguishes data protection officers from data protection authorities whose task is to monitor compliance by other organizations.

0.38 In the United States and other countries that have not established data protection authorities, data privacy laws are enforced by consumer protection agencies (*e.g.*, the U.S. Federal Trade Commission) and general law enforcement authorities (including State Attorneys General), but prior notifications or approvals regarding automated data processing is not typically required outside Europe.

# The Field Guide

If you are new at an organization that does not have a formal data privacy compliance program, you could start with Chapter 1, prepare a task list as you go, study or skip Chapter 2 on international data transfers (depending on how domestic or global your business is), and then work through Chapter 3 as you prepare documentation and execute your task list.

If you are tackling an existing program, start with the brief Chapter 4 first and then go through Chapters 1 through 3.

If you just need a quick answer to a substantive question, check the Index at the end of the book and the summaries from A to Z in Chapter 5 for directions and perspective. The Field Guide cannot provide definitive answers to detailed questions, but it is intended to put phenomena into context and give you practical pointers and suggestions on how to solve problems, tackle tasks and find further information.

# 1 Starting a compliance program

When you set out to design and implement a data privacy compliance 1.01 program, you face a number of threshold decisions and preparatory tasks, including the following:

- Putting a person or team in charge of data privacy law compliance

- Preparing a task list by identifying relevant facts, laws and requirements

- Defining priorities based on business objectives, enforcement risk exposure, and ease of compliance

- Executing the task list

- Working with internal stakeholders and outside advisors

## Taking charge

Someone needs to be in charge. If your business is a one-person sole 1.02 proprietorship, then you are in charge. In larger organizations, there are typically a number of individual candidates or departments that could take charge of data privacy compliance, including lawyers, information technology staff, human resources and internal audit personnel. Each of these groups tend to have different approaches, strengths and limitations. Here are some factors to consider as you look for the right person or team:

In-house attorneys in corporate legal departments usually take an 1.03 advisory role and inform others in the organization what applicable laws require, including data privacy laws. Depending on company culture and individual styles, the legal department may advise proactively or upon request. Lawyers are trained to interpret and apply laws, including data privacy laws, but not all lawyers are technology-savvy or good project managers.

1.04 Members of the information technology (IT) department are technology savvy, but may not find it easy to understand and apply laws. IT professionals are trained in deploying and maintaining equipment, software and services that other groups (human resources, sales, marketing, production, etc.) use to process personal data. The IT department supports these other groups and provides technology that aids other departments' business objectives. The IT department usually establishes and implements protocols to protect personal data from unauthorized access (by deploying data security measures), but does not typically decide on access privileges for individuals or legal compliance matters.

1.05 Some companies have separate internal audit functions, which are concerned with monitoring and enforcing compliance with laws and internal policies. Such audit departments are focused on verifying that the rule of law or existing compliance programs is adhered to, but audit personnel do not typically define the rules. You lose an extra pair of eyes if you have the same person create and audit a program. Also, when audit personnel conduct investigations, they are at a particularly high risk of violating data privacy laws. Investigators often want to search email boxes, computers and files, interview third parties about suspicious conduct and occasionally intercept live calls and other communications without prior notice to the data subject. Therefore, some companies feel that they would be letting the fox guard the henhouse if they tasked audit staff with designing a privacy compliance program.

1.06 Another option is to select individuals from data user groups within a company, such as human resources or marketing. Companies that develop or sell information technology products consider data privacy not only a compliance challenge, but also a business opportunity. For example, cloud computing service providers and enterprise software and data storage providers increasingly consider data privacy laws in the product development process to ensure that their customers can effectively use the products in compliance with applicable laws (see 'Privacy by design' in Chapter 5). Whether privacy protections are a relevant differentiator for technology providers depends much on the target audience – larger enterprise customers tend to be very focused on compliance features;

whereas consumers and smaller companies may be concerned about some features (*e.g.*, end-to-end encryption for smartphones and online storage) but choose "free" services or convenience over data privacy considerations in other scenarios.

In most larger businesses, the person in charge of data privacy compli- 1.07 ance usually comes from any of the above departments or areas of specialization. Larger companies with a great exposure or interest relating to privacy laws may decide to create a new department or office. Smaller companies may find it sufficient to put someone in charge on a part-time basis. If a company has a legal department, attorneys are usually involved in data privacy compliance. Often, legal counsel takes the lead regarding data privacy compliance. But, the ideal candidate for project management does not necessarily have to be a lawyer, particularly if a company views data privacy more as a business opportunity than a mere legal obligation.

## Working with internal stakeholders and outside advisors

*Internal stakeholders.* To obtain sufficient resources and support 1.08 from stakeholders within a company, you have to answer the 'Why' question – Why is a data privacy and security program important? For some companies, compliance is a matter of risk management and avoidance of sanctions and liability. Others care additionally about potential reputational risks and opportunities and view privacy compliance as a differentiator. Also, for some companies, data privacy and security compliance is a key condition to selling products and services, for example with data storage or software-as-a-service providers. When you start out implementing a compliance program in a company, it can be very helpful to prepare a brief whitepaper in FAQ format to raise awareness and gain support among key stakeholders within the organization. Additional thoughts regarding the big 'why?'-question can be found in Chapter 5 of this Field Guide, under "Y."

*Outside advisors.* Most companies turn to outside counsel for advice on 1.09 legal requirements beyond their home jurisdiction. Typically, it is too difficult and time-consuming to determine the exact nature and details of formal and substantive compliance obligations in other countries, where laws may be presented in unfamiliar formats and languages. In this Field Guide, you will find some pointers on generally applicable privacy law principles and major jurisdictional differences; however, coverage of country-specific details on formal or substantive compliance obligations is outside the scope of this book.

1.10 Many companies experience one particular challenge when working with outside advisors on compliance matters: every subject matter expert (data security consultant, technology vendor, local lawyer in a particular jurisdiction, etc.) is familiar with the risks and possible sanctions in his or her area of expertise and takes these particularly seriously. But, companies tend to have a limited budget and cannot always address all requirements at once and with the same rigor and effort. Companies generally need to prioritize. If you hire coordinated global teams, they may be able to assist with prioritization between the disciplines they are engaged to cover, but even their abilities are limited and they cannot be expected to take all fundamental considerations into account that can make or break a company, *e.g.*, how to ensure operational continuity, sufficient revenue growth and funding, etc. If you hire individual advisors rather than a coordinated team, such individuals are usually not of much help with respect to prioritization and there is a significant risk that the importance of a particular risk or local law requirement is over- or understated in context. Therefore, it can be helpful to ask outside advisors not only about substantive and formal requirements, but also about practical issues, such as whether particular requirements are observed in practice or only honored in breach, whether challenges by regulatory or private plaintiffs are common and what risks and problems other companies have run into in connection with the particular requirement at issue. Answers to such questions could help put things into perspective and help companies prioritize among tasks.

## Appointing a privacy officer

1.11 Persons who take charge of designing and implementing data privacy compliance programs sometimes hold the title 'Data Protection Officer' or 'Chief Privacy Officer.' The roles associated with these and similar titles can actually be quite different in nature and you should consider carefully whether your company needs one or the other or both.

1.12 One key reason why multinational businesses have a data protection officer is because they have a presence in Germany. Most multinational businesses consider Germany an important market. Under German data protection law, companies have been legally required since the 1970s to formally appoint a data protection officer with a watchdog role to supplement supervision by governmental data protection authorities. Germany was the first country to introduce the concept of a data protection officer in an attempt to force self-regulation via a company-appointed guardian of privacy interests.

Some jurisdictions with early data protection laws, including France, opted instead for government notification and approval requirements. Others such as the Netherlands, Norway, Sweden and Switzerland, adopted a middle ground approach These countries give companies the option to appoint a data protection officer in lieu of submitting more substantive filings to data protection authorities. According to the EU General Data Protection Regulation, companies in all EEA Member States must appoint a data protection officer if they engage in particularly sensitive forms of data processing, including systematic monitoring of data subjects or processing of special categories of personal data on a large scale and as a core activity. Affiliated groups of companies can appoint one person as data protection officer for several or all entities if the person is accessible from all locations.

Some companies model their compliance approach for all jurisdictions 1.13 where they decide to appoint a local data protection officer after the German rules. This should ensure compliance with the EU General Data Protection Regulation and other countries' rules (as the German requirements tend to be the strictest and most comprehensive), but this is not legally required.

Many companies also voluntarily appoint data protection officers or 1.14 privacy compliance liaisons for countries where this is neither required nor incentivized, or even contemplated. In addition, many larger U.S. companies have a Chief Privacy Officer, often as well as compliance officers, internal auditors, specialized legal counsel for data privacy law compliance matters, information security officers and trained privacy professionals. Upon closer review, the purposes, roles and responsibilities of such positions can and often should be quite different. As a reference point in your decision-making process, you could consider the German model for the data protection officer role, or the guidance issued by the Article 29 Working Party around Data Protection Officers and the EU General Data Protection Regulation, and carefully decide which aspects to adopt and not adopt for other specific jurisdictions or a global function.

1.15 *Requirement to appoint a data protection officer under German law.* Under German law, companies typically have to appoint a data protection officer in writing within one month of commencing business. Some exceptions apply, for example, for companies that do not process any sensitive data and have fewer than ten employees.

1.16 • *Qualification requirements.* Candidates must be experienced, knowledgeable or trained regarding data protection legislation, information technology and the company's operations. They must also be reliable and not have conflicts of interests (which typically rules out the appointment of business owners, senior managers and employees with a strong interest in data collection and usage, such as marketing and HR managers). Finally, the company has to enable the data protection officer to perform the statutory obligations; this requires companies to provide information and training and to release internal data protection officers from other work duties (to free up time). Many companies appoint non-managerial employees in their legal, information technology or human resources departments – or contract with external service providers.

1.17 • *External vs. internal candidates.* A company can either appoint an employee or an external service provider. Both options have certain advantages and disadvantages. If a German company appoints an employee, she becomes entitled to even stronger protections against termination than German labor laws afford to all employees. Terminating an external data protection officer tends to be relatively easy by comparison, based on the terms of the applicable services contract. Appointing an employee allows the company to keep all relevant information internal and confidential. Appointing an external candidate means opening the company's systems, processes, security measures and data to someone on the outside. An internal data protection officer tends to be more familiar with actual practices, processes and problems and has better access to information about employee concerns and security weaknesses. External data protection officers may have a better feel for industry standards and more experience and expertise than internal employees who take on the position on a part-time basis. Specialization allows an external data protection officer to focus on the latest developments in data protection law and information technology. Companies also consider the costs and response times: External service providers can be paid on an hourly basis (which can incentivize the data protection officer to be particularly active and responsive to inquiries and make it difficult for the company to control costs) or with a monthly or annual fixed fee (which occasionally results in lengthy response times and thus delays in project implementations where prior consultations with the data protection officer have to be completed). With respect to internal data protection officers, the company has to consider the impact on the candidate's other contributions in light of the time the role as data protection officer will take up.

- A multinational business could appoint as data protection officer 1.18 for a German subsidiary an employee of one of its entities outside of Germany or from a different German subsidiary, if it maintains several entities in Germany. Such person could be qualified as an "external" data protection officer for German law purposes to avoid the implications of German labor laws. Some German data protection authorities are skeptical about the appointment of persons who reside outside of Germany and may argue that such persons are not able to adequately perform their statutory obligations. However, German statutory law does not strictly require the appointment of an employee in Germany and companies with headquarters and data centers outside of Germany have good reasons to appoint someone outside of Germany if the person is closer to the companies' regional or global systems. Multinational companies may prefer to have only one person in the role of data protection officer for any jurisdictions where the appointment is required, so that consultations on multinational projects can be conducted efficiently, quickly and without the risk of conflicting opinions and requests. In jurisdictions where the appointment has to be notified to data protection authorities, companies have to be prepared to answer questions and handle resistance to the appointment of a data protection officer who does not reside in the respective country. But, in most cases it is possible to overcome the authorities' hesitations if the company has good operational reasons. The EU General Data Protection Regulation expressly allows groups of affiliated companies to appoint one single data protection officer provided that the data protection officer is easily accessible in every company and office.

- *Appointment formalities.* Under German law, companies have to 1.19 appoint data protection officers in writing. Under the EU General Data Protection Regulation, companies have to provide the data protection authority and publish contact details for the data protection officer, for example, a dedicated phone number and email address. Companies generally prefer to assign and publish aliases (*e.g.*, dataprotectionofficer@company.com) to avoid a need to update privacy notices whenever a data protection officer is replaced. Companies may impose a time-limit on the appointment, so long as the term is not so short that it interferes with the independence of the position. Two to five years seem reasonable. In German companies that have a works council (collective labor representation), the works council has a co-determination right regarding changes to the employment contract that are involved in appointing an employee as internal data protection officer.

1.20 • *Duties.* A data protection officer is responsible for monitoring the company's compliance with applicable data protection law and ensuring that it documents its data processing activities. Companies have to consult with the data protection officer regarding their data processing activities and any contemplated changes. The data protection officer shall make recommendations and raise awareness and concerns where appropriate, but does not have to formally approve measures. If the company does not act despite being formally notified of concerns, the data protection officer has the right – and in some cases the obligation – to blow the whistle and notify data protection authorities. The data protection officer operates independently, and is not subject to orders or instructions from management. Day-to-day duties can include assistance with documenting data processing procedures in a register; evaluating and further developing data protection and security policies; suggesting, selecting and implementing technical security measures; drafting forms and contracts appropriate for data protection; selecting employees, service providers and others to be involved in the processing of personal data; monitoring data privacy and security measures and the proper use of data processing programs; handling complaints relating to data protection and violations of law or policies; employee training; and preparing, submitting and maintaining notifications to data protection authorities.

1.21 • *Personal liability.* If you pick an employee as a candidate for data protection officer, you can expect a question regarding personal liability. The short answer is that all employees can be held liable for misconduct and violations of laws and third-party rights. Most candidates, however, are probably as much or more at risk with respect to their other job duties than with respect to the role of data protection officer. German data protection legislation does not specifically address the personal liability of a data protection officer. Under generally applicable laws, any individual representative of a company can be held accountable for acts or omission of the company if he or she committed the act at issue or had responsibility to avoid the omission. On this basis, a data protection officer can be held accountable for direct involvement in illegal data processing activities (*e.g.*, recording of phone calls without consent or court order). Theoretically, a data protection officer could also be liable for failure to stop illegal activities that were conducted without his or her direct involvement. But, it is relatively rare that employees are charged because of a failure to act.

*Mandatory or beneficial appointments in other jurisdictions.* If you 1.22 appoint a data protection officer in accordance with German law also for other countries, you typically satisfy the requirements of the EU General Data Protection Regulation and laws of other jurisdictions that define such a role by national statute, such as France, the Netherlands, Norway, Sweden and Switzerland, except that you may have to notify local authorities of the appointment. Companies tend not to formally appoint data protection officers where local law does not offer any meaningful corresponding exemptions from other requirements. For example, French national law provides for rights and duties of a data protection officer, but does not require or significantly reward the appointment by multinationals. Thus, most companies opt against a formal appointment in France. But, companies operating in the Netherlands, Norway, Sweden, Switzerland and other jurisdictions that reward the appointment by dispensing with other filing requirements tend to opt for the appointment of a data protection officer. Some companies appoint the same person for several or all jurisdictions where a formal appointment is required. This is expressly permitted under the EU General Data Protection Regulation and particularly efficient for companies that use global systems and procedures, which can be monitored best by one person.

*Voluntary, informal appointments.* Separate and apart from satisfy- 1.23 ing formal statutory requirements to appoint a data protection officer, larger organizations especially see operational advantages in establishing a network of local liaisons for data privacy compliance and other compliance efforts in order to have specialized local contacts who can help implement and monitor these legal programs. Also, many companies voluntarily appoint a "global privacy officer" or "Chief Privacy Officer" to demonstrate internally and externally that the company takes data privacy compliance seriously. It may also be beneficial to have one point person who takes ownership and responsibility for this topic – which affects many other functions, including IT, HR, physical security, law, finance, and sales.

1.24 For such informal and voluntary appointments and for jurisdictions where the role of data protection officer is not defined by statute (for example, in the United States, except under the federal health data protection law, HIPAA), it is important that the company defines the authority and duties of the privacy officer in a detailed written memo or agreement. In particular, companies need to define expectations as to whether the privacy officer shall advocate primarily for privacy or company interests; provide advice or make decisions; react or be proactive. Similarly, shall the privacy officer coordinate, support, supervise or monitor colleagues in roles with overlapping responsibilities (such as compliance officers, internal auditors, privacy counsel in the legal department and information technology and security staff in the IT, marketing and HR departments)? Companies have to decide and document what the objectives and expectations are: should the Chief Privacy Officer be a coordinator, advocate, advisor and/or guardian of privacy or the company's interests in data and compliance? Each company should find its own way in this respect, and each company should define responsibilities and tasks clearly in writing, so that the appointed individual understands the rights, obligations and expectations of the role. When roles are not clearly defined, a misalignment of expectations could easily result in uncomfortable conflicts. For example, if a global privacy officer at a U.S. company understands her role as independent and public policy-driven as a German data protection officer, she might be quick to notify U.S. authorities of concerns. Or, if a member of the legal department is appointed as 'Chief Privacy Officer' and shifts his approach from acting as legal counsel towards a more executive role, this might undermine attorney-client privilege in certain situations. Companies should consider these and other pros and cons before making voluntary appointments, and then document the role in a detail to increase the chances of achieving the desired benefits and reduce the risk of unwanted consequences and conflicts.

### ▮ ! ▮ Action items

1.25 • Determine where you have to appoint a data protection officer under local law and to satisfy legal requirements (consider internal vs. external, in-country vs. regional or global appointments).

- Determine how your company can best achieve and maintain compliance in jurisdictions where you are not legally required to appoint a data protection officer, and whether your company would benefit from the voluntary appointment of a Chief Privacy Officer and local liaisons; if yes, carefully document the job description, authority and duties, and consider relations to similar or overlapping functions, such as corporate legal counsel, information security, human resources and marketing managers. 1.26

## Preparing a task list

Once you have put someone in charge, it is time to prepare a list of tasks and keep track of implementation status and priorities. Creating and monitoring such lists helps prioritization, planning (budgets, achievements), management of complex situations (*e.g.*, involving several jurisdictions and different types of databases) and transitioning projects from one employee to another. On a task list, you can keep tabs on formal compliance requirements (*e.g.*, notices, filings, appointment of privacy officer, data transfer agreements) and substantive tasks (*e.g.*, implement access controls, deploy encryption technologies, replace vendors, etc.). 1.27

For example, a U.S. company that has incorporated a few foreign subsidiaries may have the following items on its initial task list – perhaps supplemented by columns for status, action items and business owners: 1.28

| Data privacy law compliance task | Purpose |
|---|---|
| 1. Designate role and prepare appointment documentation for global data privacy officer; appoint local data protection officers where required, *e.g.*, for German subsidiary | Manage risks, satisfy compliance obligations |
| 2. Assess where government filings (notifications, application for approvals) are required, prepare and submit | Satisfy local compliance obligations |
| 3. Take inventory of databases and data flows | Compile facts for notices, agreements, filings; satisfy record keeping requirements |
| 4. Prepare and implement intra-group data transfer agreements based on EU Standard Contractual Clauses and/or other measures to legitimize international data transfers (including EU-U.S. Privacy Shield registration, Binding Corporate Rules, Cross-Border Privacy Rules and Codes of Conduct) | Overcome legal instructions on international data transfers |

| Data privacy law compliance task | Purpose |
|---|---|
| 5.  Review, revise and/or translate privacy policies and notices directed at consumers and individual representatives of corporate customers and business partners; determine how best to obtain and document consent | Satisfy notice requirements |
| 6.  Review or prepare notices directed at employees with respect to processing of employee data, including:<br>• Global human resources information system (HRIS)<br>• Monitoring tools *(e.g.,* anti-spam, anti-virus, web surfing protection, data loss prevention, firewalls) and investigations<br>• Whistleblower hotline<br>• Payroll, benefits, stock options | Satisfy notice requirements |
| 7.  Review or prepare standard templates for data sharing/ processing in agreements with business partners such as vendors, customers, intermediaries (resellers, sales reps for advertising services)<br>• Template data transfer contracts (intra-group and third party) and/or intra-group policy(ies)<br>• Review/prepare data processor contracts and policies | Satisfy data security obligations, protect data as an asset, mitigate against risks from unauthorized disclosure/ hacks, etc. |
| 8.  Review or develop internal protocols and processes regarding access to data, data retention, information security, incident response and response to disclosure requests from law enforcement, regulators, private litigants, etc. | Satisfy compliance obligations; protect consumer/employee privacy |
| 9.  Direct Marketing: Implement global or jurisdiction-specific protocols for opt-in/opt-out processes | Satisfy local compliance obligations |
| 10.  Routine training, audits | Manage risks, satisfy compliance obligations |

1.29   To define tasks for your company, you have to determine what data you have, what laws apply, what the laws require and how your company can best satisfy the requirements (where the law gives you options or if resource limitations force prioritization). You could prepare a task list for your company as you read through the remainder of the Field Guide, where typical requirements and tasks are introduced.

1.30   Finding and analyzing all applicable laws and requirements can feel like a Sisyphean task if you work for a large organization or any business with an international scope: by the time you have taken an inventory of existing databases, usage patterns, transfer flows and applicable laws, the company has probably swapped out a few systems, acquired and spun off businesses, entered new jurisdictions, and found new opportunities to commercialize data, while several new data privacy laws have been enacted. Given the rapid pace at which data privacy laws and information technology move, it is usually most effective to design and implement the data privacy compliance program in phases. Focus first on high-risk requirements and low-hanging fruit in both the design and implementation phase. Start with implementation of high priority tasks while you still refine the design of the program. Compile a list of known compliance requirements that your organization and your peers and competitors already try to satisfy, or that are actively enforced. When you identify compliance gaps in high-risk areas, take action immediately. After that, add tasks to the list and turn to prioritization. Companies that start out by trying to develop a complete inventory of applicable legal requirements often find the challenge overwhelming and become paralyzed. 'Perfect' can become the enemy of 'good'.

As you prepare your task list, note the following considerations:  1.31

*Take inventory of your data.* At the outset, consider what personal  1.32 data your business uses. At a minimum, you should prepare a brief summary with basic information on your key databases, including data categories (*i.e.*, data fields populated), primary purposes (*e.g.*, HRIS, CRM, email exchange server), geographical location of servers and who has access (*e.g.*, employees, departments and third party vendors). If you have international operations, you will also need to know names, addresses and headcount of all your legal entities and branches.

If you are working for a small or medium-sized company, it should not take you more than a few hours to prepare such an initial summary: you can go to the IT department, open the various software interfaces for the databases and copy basic information from screen shots; the legal department should have a list of subsidiaries and the human resources department should know headcount. This is enough to get started.

If your company is subject to the EU General Data Protection  1.33 Regulation, you have to maintain more formal and detailed records of data processing activities, including

- names and contact details of your company or companies, their representatives in the EEA and their data protection officer, if any

- purposes of the data processing

- categories of data and data subjects

- categories of recipients to whom you disclose data, including data processors (and customers, if your company acts as a data processor)

- international transfers and specific safeguards

- time limits for erasure

- technical and organizational security measures

1.34 Larger companies sometimes conduct more elaborate assessments and audits of databases and data flows, often with the help – and sometimes at the initiative – of outside advisors. This can be beneficial and even necessary to get a solid grip on the status of data privacy law compliance in complex multinational organizations. However, such exercises can also take a long time, use a lot of resources and produce reports with overwhelming details that do not directly translate into improvements of the organization's compliance status. Consider starting with a high level inventory unless you are fairly sure that your company is past the initial compliance phase and you can stomach a full-blown data flow mapping exercise.

1.35 *Define your objective and priorities.* Companies have different objectives with respect to data privacy compliance per se or specific legal requirements. Some companies view data privacy compliance like any other legal requirement: they want to do only what is legally required (or as much as is commonly done in their industry and market segment). Other companies – particularly companies with information technology products or services – view data privacy as a potential competitive differentiator; consequently, they want to do whatever their customers expect or desire, and perhaps more than the competition. Also, with respect to particular aspects of data processing and compliance, the objectives vary. For example, some companies depend heavily on direct marketing and may want to collect and use personal data to the maximum extent in each jurisdiction, whatever the costs may be, whereas other companies would be content to find and comply with the strictest requirement worldwide and implement a uniform compliance protocol in the interest of uniformity and cost savings. It is important to define and communicate these objectives efficiently to ensure that appropriate priorities are established.

*Find the best approach for your company.* Based on an initial assess-  1.36
ment of applicable requirements and your objectives, you can select an approach that suits your organization and situation:

* Proactive or reactive? It is usually less risky, easier and cheaper to  1.37
take proactive steps to avoid a problem than to cope with a lawsuit, investigation or negative press campaign. At the same time, only a small fraction of potential problems materialize. If cost containment is a key driver and your organization views privacy compliance as just another legal obligation, you may consider a risk-benefit analysis and the 80–20 rule (Pareto Principle). A relatively smaller percentage of potential problems (perhaps 20% in some cases) is responsible for the vast majority of adverse impacts (perhaps 80% in some cases – but the numbers are randomly picked). Conversely, companies can perhaps cover 80% of their problems with 20% of the budget it would take to address all problems. To address the remaining 20% of problems, which may not even be the most serious problems, the company would have to expend 80% of the total potential budget. Based on these insights, companies first try to find and rectify those problems that are most likely to result in major issues or require the least amount of effort and resources to fix.

* Some problems (*e.g.*, outdated website privacy statements) are  1.38
easier and cheaper to fix than other problems (*e.g.*, a lack of budget for encryption technology or replacing a legacy system that does not allow differentiated access controls). Companies on a budget may find it easier to start with 'low-hanging fruit.' Most companies can quickly assess what their main competitors are doing by reviewing their website privacy statements and processing notices, determine whether particular steps are legally required, and then follow suit based on precedents. This approach does by no means guarantee full compliance, but it can help a company catch up to an industry standard relatively quickly and with modest resources.

* If your company is or wants to become an industry leader, you have  1.39
to consider a more comprehensive assessment of legal requirements

and business needs. You can poll stakeholders in various departments (including legal, HR, IT, sales, product management, procurement, etc.) to prepare a list of company-specific priorities, subscribe to legal and trade publications and conferences to obtain a broader picture of the compliance landscape, follow guidance from government authorities, possibly even proactively seek guidance from authorities, and monitor enforcement and litigation cases.

1.40 • In terms of following guidance from government authorities, it is important to determine how much your business is exposed to action from governments. A regulated entity (*e.g.*, a bank or telecommunications service provider) usually has to take its regulator's views seriously whether based on laws or not because it depends on the goodwill of its regulator in many respects. Entities that are neither regulated nor sell primarily to regulated entities, however, are freer to take their own positions and views; such entities will typically ask not only what the views of a particular government entity are, but also if and how such views are enforced. This is particularly important with respect to gauging the relevance of official guidance from government authorities abroad. European data protection authorities, for example, have taken relatively extreme positions on various topics over many years without any enforcement activities that could have resulted in "reality checks" in court. A company that readily follows the official guidance at the expense of missing out on business opportunities may regret doing so if the guidance is not followed in practice or at some point challenged and invalidated in courts of law.

1.41 • Keep in mind that a company may find different approaches appropriate for a particular jurisdiction or part of its business. For example, a company with a large employee population and a hostile works council in Germany would seem well-advised to be particularly proactive with respect to data privacy of German employees, whereas other jurisdictions may present less of a priority. Or, a company with a particularly sensitive information technology product (*e.g.*, a repository of online medical records) may go out of its way to achieve or surpass compliance requirements with respect to its products, but it may decide that following industry standards will suffice with respect to employee privacy. Employee privacy compliance may be even less of a concern for a company that is still managed and operated largely by a group of founders who have a significant financial stake in the company and hence a relatively strong interest in minimizing compliance costs and efforts.

*Identify legal and other requirements.* As you identify legal require-   1.42
ments for purposes of designing and updating a data privacy compliance program, you will find thousands of laws around the
world that address data privacy in one way or another. Even very
large and compliance-oriented companies struggle with keeping
up to date. Smaller organizations have to establish priorities and a
system to ensure that they are capable of complying with key requirements – even if they may not be able to identify each and every law in
detail.

*What are data privacy laws?* Despite different histories and public   1.43
policy motivations, there are common themes that help categorize
and identify laws that are relevant to data privacy compliance programs. Data privacy laws in the narrow sense are typically concerned
with personal data (*i.e.*, data relating to individual human persons as
opposed to legal entities) and place conditions or restrictions on the
collection, use, transfer and retention of personal data. These laws are
of primary concern for the designing and maintaining of data privacy
compliance programs. There are a lot of them, but you can narrow the
realm of relevant laws down by applying subject matter and jurisdictional filters:

*Which laws apply to you? Subject matter limitations.* Some data pro-   1.44
tection laws apply directly only to certain types of entities.

- For example, European data protection laws do not typically   1.45
  apply to data processing by national security agencies or private
  individuals in the course of a purely personal or household activity
  (*e.g.*, what someone posts about friends on Facebook). Healthcare-
  related data privacy laws in the United States (HIPAA) apply only
  to certain 'covered entities' and their 'business associates,' such
  as medical doctors, health insurers and certain service providers.
  Some laws relating to financial or telecommunications data apply
  only to banks or telecommunications providers respectively. Anti-
  spam laws tend to focus on for-profit, commercial enterprises and
  contain exceptions for political and non-profit organizations.

- Also, if your business is – or could be – typically acting as a data   1.46
  processor on behalf of other entities, then your compliance obligations may be much more limited and not extend far beyond following instructions from the data controller and keeping data secure
  from unauthorized access.

1.47   Even if a certain law does not apply to your business, it may nevertheless be relevant if it applies to your business partners or clients. Most businesses, though, are able to remove a significant number of laws from consideration based on subject matter limitations.

1.48   *Which laws apply to you? International applicability.* There are more than 190 countries in the world and within each country, there may be several different jurisdictions (*e.g.*, 50 states in the U.S.). Companies usually take a hard look at which jurisdictions they primarily have to consider.

1.49   • Under customary international law, every sovereign country is free to legislate whatever it is interested in. There is no 'world constitution' or treaty that effectively draws limits on what countries can cover in their national laws.

1.50   • Typically, countries apply their data privacy laws to companies that are incorporated or registered in such country or that deploy employees or equipment on such countries' territory. Some countries go further and also apply their data privacy laws to companies abroad if: such companies collect data remotely via targeted websites (as indicated by country-specific URLs, languages, localized content, local phone numbers, etc.), business partners are located in the jurisdictions concerned, or even just on the basis that the foreign company collects data on residents of the legislating countries. Internet service providers, multinational enterprises and many other companies with more or less direct business connections to other countries find upon closer review that many countries' privacy laws apply to some of their data processing activities. But, there are also many companies with a domestic focus that can rule out most countries' laws (*e.g.*, local banks, hospitals and construction companies).

1.51   • European Union law sets some limitations on the ability of EU member states to apply their national data privacy laws extraterritorially (*i.e.*, outside their own country) to make it easier for EEA-based companies to do business everywhere in the EEA Common Market. An EEA-based data controller has to comply only with the laws of the EEA member state where it maintains a branch or other significant, physical presence, even if it collects data from other EEA member states (over the Internet or otherwise). This privilege is not available to companies outside the EEA. Therefore, a U.S.-based e-commerce company with customers throughout the EEA may have to comply with the laws of numerous different EEA Member States. If it incorporates a subsidiary, however, in, say, Ireland (low corporate income tax rate) or Luxembourg (low value-added tax rate), to become the sole contracting party and data controller for all European customers, then the new subsidiary would have to comply only with the data protection laws of the one jurisdiction where it is incorporated. After the EU General Data Protection Regulation takes effect in May 2018 and further harmonizes data privacy law in the EEA, companies may become less concerned with national laws, but some differences will remain and location planning will still be necessary. Companies in the United States may be able to invoke similar protections under the U.S. Constitution's 'Commerce Clause' against state laws that discriminate against, or unduly burden, interstate commerce. Such jurisdictional privileges provide some companies with a planning opportunity to actively influence which laws apply to them.

- If you apply the above considerations and end up with a shortlist 1.52 of jurisdictions that is still too long, you can prioritize further by identifying the countries where you need to be particularly concerned about enforcement. Concerns tend to be greater regarding countries where you have a subsidiary, employees, key assets, or key customers, or where regulators are particularly active. Aside from business concerns, you should also consider where compliance is particularly easy (*e.g.*, no language hurdles, similar legal system to your home jurisdiction). Based on such practical considerations, most companies can come up with a manageable shortlist of priority jurisdictions.

*Data privacy by region – an overview for orientation purposes.* Before 1.53 you turn to an analysis of national data privacy laws, it may be helpful to take a brief look at different regional legislative approaches for orientation.

- In Europe, data protection laws are worded very broadly and apply 1.54 to most kinds of private and public sector data processing activities. Some jurisdictions (including Austria, Italy and Switzerland) even rope in information relating to legal entities as 'personal data.' The basic premise in most European countries is that the processing of personal data is prohibited, except with valid consent from the data subject or based on another, statutory exception. Such exceptions may be available, for example, if a company needs to process personal data to perform a contract with the data subject, to comply with a statutory duty, to protect vital interests of the data subject, to perform a task carried out in the public interest, or to pursue its legitimate interests, except where such interests are overridden by the privacy interests of the data subject. This last exception, also known as the "legitimate interest exception," requires companies to balance their own interests with those of data subjects. European data protection authorities had taken restrictive views on this exception in the past, but more recently acknowledged the "legitimate interest exception" as a justification of equal standing and not a matter of only "last resort," a development that may foster convergence and interoperability with U.S.-style data privacy law focused on protecting reasonable expectations of privacy. Still, consent and notice requirements are relatively stringent, international transfers of personal data outside the European Economic Area are restricted and many jurisdictions require government notifications, appointment of data protection officers and other formal steps. Due to broad and undifferentiated prohibitions, companies and regulators have taken interpretative liberties in the past. Also, private lawsuits are relatively uncommon. This has resulted in lax enforcement and uncertainties in many countries.

• Things may change in Europe after the EU General Data Protection Regulation takes effect in May 2018. This Regulation constitutes the first significant update of EU data privacy laws since 1995 and it applies directly to companies and individuals (without a need for implementation into national law). Data protection authorities will be able to levy much higher administrative fines of up to the greater of €20m or 4% of annual worldwide sales. Companies face stricter requirements regarding privacy impact assessments, data minimization, deletion and security breach reporting (within 72 hours). The basic default principle under the Regulation remains "verboten": companies must not process personal data unless they can claim an exception from the general prohibition.

1.55 • In the United States, on the other hand, the basic premise is that the processing of personal data is permissible. There are no specific data protection authorities or government filing requirements. Generally applicable privacy laws impose restrictions only where data subjects have a reasonable expectation of privacy (meaning an actual expectation that society considers reasonable). For the most part, companies can destroy such expectations relatively easily by issuing notices informing data subjects of data processing practices. When broad, omnibus data protection laws in Europe were passed in the 1970s, legislatures in the United States decided to take a different approach and legislate only around serious problems. Consequently, legislatures passed laws with specific types of risks and abuses in focus. The United States now has myriad specifically scoped data privacy laws at the federal level and in the 50 states. If and when such laws apply, the restrictions and liabilities for violations can be surprisingly harsh, particularly for European companies entering the U.S. market expecting no significant privacy laws. For example, the California Song-Beverly Credit Card Act of 1971 prohibits retailers from collecting contact and other information from credit card holders, except as necessary to process the credit card transaction. This prohibition applies absolutely, even if cardholders consent in writing to the data collection and subjects merchants to significant liability and exposure to class action lawsuits. Yet the California law places no particular restrictions on information collected from cash-paying customers. As another example of a very strict but narrowly crafted law, the U.S. Congress enacted the Federal Video Privacy Protection Act in 1988 in reaction to publicity around the videotape rental history of a candidate for judicial office to prohibit disclosure of videotape rental information; but, this statute does not apply to book or video game rentals. U.S. federal law on health information privacy (HIPAA) restricts health data collection and usage by 'covered entities' and their 'business associates,' as well as providers of certain 'protected health records,' but not by anyone else; as a result, various online services providers are exempt from the law even though they may collect extremely sensitive health information from consumers over the Internet. Similarly, the Gramm–Leach–Bliley Act (GLB) applies directly only to financial service providers and not to most of the FinTech companies. In addition to U.S. federal privacy laws, companies have to assess state laws and find that California, for example, has enacted many stringent and detailed privacy laws that close perceived gaps in federal privacy laws.

- Consequently, companies have to carefully assess whether their contemplated activities are covered by a sector-specific federal or state law in the United States. If so, companies may find much more rigid restrictions and exposure to liability than under European laws. But, it is also possible that the contemplated activity falls outside the scope of any specific laws (based on the company's original plan or conscious changes in light of the legal situation), and as a result, the company only has to post an appropriate notice and ensure compliance with such notice. As in Europe, violations of U.S. laws can be sanctioned by government authorities (including the Federal Trade Commission and State Attorneys General). On the other hand, in the United States, private lawsuits play a much greater practical role, given the possibility of class action lawsuits, punitive damages, civil jury trials and contingency fees for lawyers (who can pocket attorneys fees and a significant portion of damages awards while plaintiffs do not incur much financial risk if they engage lawyers on a contingency fee basis).

1.56 • Other countries have often modeled their laws more or less after the European templates (*e.g.*, Argentina, Colombia, Israel, Russia and Uruguay) or have pursued a hybrid approach – with some elements of the European legislation but more differentiated or lenient consent and notice requirements and less stringent administrative duties (*e.g.*, Australia, Canada, India, Japan and Mexico).

1.57 *What other laws and requirements need to be considered?* Besides data privacy laws in the narrow sense, companies have to consider a variety of other requirements for purposes of designating data privacy compliance programs, including the following:

• statutory obligations under employment, consumer protection and unfair competition laws, as well as constitutional safeguards, which are applied directly to companies in some jurisdictions,

• contractual obligations (for example, regarding data security standards, breach notifications and incorporation of privacy statements by reference in contract terms),

• promises extended previously to data subjects in privacy policies and notices, and

• customer expectations and other business needs (what data do you need, for how long, for what purposes?).

1.58 *Identify applicable substantive compliance requirements.* Substantive compliance requirements vary significantly in jurisdictions with European-style data protection laws versus the rest of the world. However, there are also a couple of requirements that apply globally.

*Abide by policies, notices, and contracts.* One universal requirement 1.59
is: Do what you say – comply with the limitations you assume in
notices, policies, website privacy statements and contracts. If a
company remains silent on its data processing practices, then this
requirement does not have much significance. But, in more and more
jurisdictions and industries, companies are forced to issue statements
and notices, either as a matter of law, industry practices or technical requirements (*e.g.*, many mobile app stores require developers to
post privacy statements). In the United States, for example, the Federal
Trade Commission urged Internet companies early on based on unfair
competition law theories to publish website privacy statements, and
much of the early enforcement focused on failures to comply with
promises in semi-voluntarily issued privacy statements. If companies
fail to comply with their own notices, policies and statements, they
can be sanctioned in most cases under various legal theories, including
unfair competition laws and tort law (misrepresentation). Therefore,
companies have to focus on keeping their notices, privacy statements,
contracts and other privacy-related communications accurate and up
to date – either by adapting their communications or their practices.

*Data security.* Companies have to maintain reasonable security meas- 1.60
ures to keep confidential data protected against unauthorized access
and dissemination. Security requirements follow also from trade secret
laws and confidentiality agreements and extend beyond personal data,
but the reach of trade secret laws ends once the secret is disseminated.
Data protection laws also require reasonable security measures and
can apply even to personal data that has become public. Therefore,
the typical definitional carve-outs in confidentiality clauses (independently developed information, information in the public domain, compelled disclosures, etc.) may not be used in the data protection law
context. Companies have to confirm compliance with data protection
law requirements separately and in addition to compliance with trade
secret laws and contractual confidentiality obligations.

Companies around the world have been obligated for decades to keep 1.61
personal data secure under statutes and contracts. In the past most
laws and contract clauses simply set forth a general reasonableness
standard and did not prescribe specific safeguards. More recently, after
California enacted the world's first data security breach notification law
in 2002 and companies started reporting security breaches en masse,
more and more jurisdictions have passed data security breach notification laws and lawmakers around the world have started prescribing

very specific technical and organizational measures intended to ensure that companies take more comprehensive steps to prevent security breaches and protect the data and privacy of consumers, employees and other individuals.

1.62 The extent to which companies collect, store, manipulate, transfer, and otherwise process personal data depends on their business needs and legal obligations to collect and retain information. All businesses process some personal data. At a minimum, they handle the contact information of their own employees, customers and business partners. Most businesses also process more sensitive data, such as payroll information, consumer purchase histories, data from credit card transactions, and other financial and medical data. So, as part of implementing a data privacy compliance program, you need to assess the specific requirements on your business regarding data security and develop an information security program that is appropriate for your company, considering specific legal requirements per jurisdiction, your risk profile and tolerance, as well as contractual and practical necessities.

1.63 Successful data security programs typically involve the following parameters:

- methods for keeping track of where data is stored and secured and for what purposes and how long it is needed (records of data processing activities),

- physical and technical protection for premises, networks and devices (including encryption, firewalls, strong authentication, passwords, etc.),

- organizational access controls within the organization ('need to know'-based restrictions),

- employee training,

- secure deletion of data that is no longer needed (*e.g.*, on discarded devices, paper),

- ongoing monitoring plus random audits and investigations into data security,

- prudent vendor selection, management, monitoring and contracting,

* a plan to address data security breaches individually and proactive changes to avoid recurrence, and

* proactive privacy impact and security-by-design assessments before any major changes to data processing activities, including the implementation of new products, processes and data use cases.

As a first step, you should determine whether your company has writ- 1.64 ten policies or unwritten processes addressing these points and representatives in charge of assuring compliance. As a second step, you could prepare a written summary of the existing measures and then assess whether the existing measures meet legal requirements (under laws and contracts) and adequately address risks threatening your company. Next, you could consider validation of your security program by outside advisors to confirm alignment with industry practices. In that regard, it is important to reach a clear understanding and agreement with the outside advisor on objectives and deliverables. Some companies experience frustration because they hire data security consultants who deploy an infinite number of scans and tests but are not willing to advise when enough is enough or issue an opinion regarding the adequacy of the company's security efforts.

*Additional substantive data privacy compliance requirements.* Under 1.65 European data protection laws, companies have to satisfy a number of additional substantive data protection law compliance requirements:

* minimizing data processing and retention,

* maintaining data integrity by updating, correcting or deleting data,

* granting access to data subjects on request, and

* seeking consent or other justifications.

These requirements apply in most European countries, but may not 1.66 apply outside of Europe. Many countries have consciously opted against data minimization requirements because they constitute a particularly severe restraint on innovation, economic liberties and freedom of information.

*Identify applicable formal compliance requirements.* A number of data 1.67 privacy compliance requirements are 'formal' in the sense that you need to generate certain notices, government filings or other paper-work. Such formal compliance obligations do not directly require you to change your data processing activities. But, if you are not substantively in compliance, then you are usually unable to issue appropriate notices, government filings, etc., because you would just be notifying everyone that you are not in compliance. Thus, substantive compliance logically comes first. Practically, however, it is often most efficient to start working on formal compliance tasks because this work will help identify substantive compliance requirements and gaps. Also, most companies find it comparatively easy to achieve formal compliance and see a particularly high risk associated with failing to comply with formal requirements, as such failures are especially easy to prove by government investigators, private plaintiffs and other potential adversaries. The question 'Did you make the required filing or not?' tends to be more black and white than, for example, 'Is a three year data retention time period appropriate for employee records after termination?'

1.68   You have to research applicable details on a country-by-country basis outside the scope of this Field Guide (see the section on Resources at the end of the book). But, for orientation purposes, you can expect that formal requirements typically include the following:

- appointment of a data protection officer,

- preparing records of data processing activities,

- documentation of data security measures,

- concluding appropriate data transfer agreements with affiliates, service providers and other business partners,

- issuing notices to data subjects or obtaining their consent,

- submitting notifications to data protection authorities or seeking their approvals, and

- consulting with works councils, labor unions or other employee representative bodies, if any.

## Executing tasks

Once you have prepared a list of concrete tasks to achieve compliance   1.69
with data protection laws, you should start executing them, perhaps
first on low-hanging fruit and tasks that help mitigate major risks.
Many companies find it helpful to start preparing the required notices
to data subjects because in the process they naturally go over the status
quo and can then best address gaps and other issues. An important
practical point is: don't get overwhelmed. It is better to close some
compliance gaps than none; and even though many tasks are interconnected, it is often possible to complete tasks in some areas without
prejudice to others (*e.g.*, address employee data privacy and security
before or after tackling consumer data privacy, and approach compliance for some priority jurisdictions before turning to others).

# 2 International data transfers – selecting compliance mechanisms

**2.01** If your company does not collect, use or process any personal data from other countries, or transfer data to other countries, you can skip this Chapter or save it for later. But, most companies do, either because they have employees, customers, suppliers or other business partners in other jurisdictions, or because their customers, suppliers or other business partners do. Note that you can cause an international data transfer by simply accessing personal data that resides on a server in another country by calling it up to view on a laptop. Because data itself is not tangible, and because "access" does not feel the same as "using" or "processing" to many, business people often overlook such cross border data transfers and corresponding compliance requirements. If your company receives or transfers data internationally, you will probably have to select and implement specific compliance mechanisms – either because you are required to comply with law, because your foreign business partners demand it or because you are responsible for the compliance status of the foreign entities (*for example, if* they are your company's subsidiaries). Then, the considerations set forth in this Section will need to be taken into account. In practice, companies tend to agonize over this quite a bit, particularly with respect to European data protection law requirements. That is why the topic receives its own Chapter.

**2.02** In general, businesses find international activities challenging because they have to understand and comply with requirements of laws, markets, languages, technology standards, cultures and other factors of multiple countries. The same is true for data privacy law compliance. Few businesses can satisfy themselves that they do not receive, use, host or send personal data across jurisdictional borders. After all, the decentralized data transmission structure of the Internet means that any company using email, Internet, telephony or the World Wide Web routinely sends and receives data through cables, satellites, antennas, routers and other communication equipment on foreign territories. This is true even for companies that have no other foreign interests or nexus, because Internet protocols may route otherwise purely domestic communications across territorial borders. However, most companies do have additional nexus to foreign jurisdictions in today's global economy: companies publish their home pages for visitors anywhere in the world, sell to customers abroad, buy goods or services from suppliers in low cost jurisdictions and use online services hosted in other countries. And even companies that try to keep their business as domestic as possible usually find that their customers and suppliers are exposed to foreign laws and attempt to pass on their resulting requirements contractually.

One legal requirement that companies all over the world are likely to 2.03 be confronted with in one way or another is also one of the most viral legal constructs of all times: the European restrictions on international transfers of personal data. Most companies in the world are more or less affected – either because they or their subsidiaries are directly subject to these laws or because direct or indirect business partners are passing on their own compliance obligations. The question raised is: how do you legally transfer personal data from Europe to other continents?

Companies in the European Economic Area ("EEA") are generally 2.04 prohibited from sending personal data to countries outside the EEA, unless adequate levels of data protection are ensured. This affects multinational groups of companies with headquarters outside Europe directly because their own subsidiaries in the EEA are prohibited from sharing personal data on employees, contractors, customers and other contacts. Indirectly affected are all companies that have customers, suppliers and other business partners in Europe because their European business partners are prohibited from sharing personal data. And, also indirectly affected are companies that provide services to companies with European data. Very few larger companies are completely isolated from the issue given today's tight global connections of businesses.

Some other jurisdictions, including Australia and India, have started 2.05 to include similar concepts into their data privacy legislation and also require companies in their jurisdictions to ensure that recipients abroad are subject to equal or stronger data privacy standards. Companies that are not headquartered in jurisdictions with such laws tend to turn to non-European restrictions on international data transfers after they have addressed the European requirements. They typically find that they can leverage the measures they have taken to comply with European laws for purposes of complying with non-European laws. Therefore, and because the European laws are older, more concrete and more developed, we will take a close look at European laws in this Chapter of the Field Guide.

## Three hurdles

2.06 Companies have to clear three hurdles before they can transfer data from one jurisdiction to another: They must (1) comply with all local requirements relating to the collection and other local processing of the personal data, (2) justify the disclosure to another data controller or contractually limit the recipient company to act as a mere data processor, and (3) ensure that the recipient company affords an adequate level of data protection. These hurdles – and the corresponding requirements to clear these hurdles – are most pronounced and developed in Europe. Therefore, most companies address the European requirements first.

2.07 *Hurdle 1 (local compliance)* requires steps that apply to any data collection and processing. In Europe, this includes various formal tasks (such as notices to data subjects, government filings, appointment of a data protection officer, and preparation of data security documentation) and substantive measures (such as minimizing the scope of processing and data retention time periods, ensuring data integrity and security, offering data access to individuals, etc.). European companies have to comply with these requirements whether or not they subsequently transfer the data abroad. But, any subsequent transfer is relevant in the context of satisfying local compliance requirements because companies have to mention the international transfers in their notices to data subjects and data protection authorities and consult with data protection officers about the international transfer, etc.

2.08 *Hurdle 2 (disclosure restrictions)* requires a justification for the transfer independent of the international dimension. European companies are generally permitted to engage service providers for data processing purposes, *i.e.*, data processors, for example payroll service providers. Transmissions to European data processors are even excluded from the definition of 'transfers' under German data protection laws. More generally, companies do not typically have to make any particular efforts to justify data transfers to service providers under European and other laws. But, European companies are generally prohibited from disclosing personal data to data controllers, even within the EEA, unless they can claim a legally valid justification.

Even if a company is perfectly in compliance with local data protection laws (first hurdle) and it also meets the specific requirements for transfers outside the EEA (third hurdle), it is not a given that such a company may disclose a particular item of personal data to another data controller. Even a wholly-owned, closely-held subsidiary that transfers personal data to its parent company in the same EEA member state has to justify the transfer. Indeed, under German law, even transfers between departments within one legal entity have to be justified. Thus, as a second hurdle to international data transfers, the company in the EEA has to make a case for why a disclosure is permitted despite general prohibitions. This second hurdle is often overlooked by companies focusing on the first and third hurdle. **2.09**

As with any other processing, companies can theoretically justify transfers by obtaining valid consent or demonstrating a necessity to transfer data in order to perform a contract with the data subject or comply with local laws. But, data subjects tend to be reluctant to agree to data disclosures, and contractual necessities are often not clearly present to justify transfers. For example, an employer needs to collect and process certain personal data to pay its employees, monitor and reward their performance, provide benefits coverage and report and withhold taxes, in accordance with contractual and statutory obligations as an employer. But, it is less clear whether the employer may also disclose employee information to its ultimate parent company, which is a common practice in many multinational groups. Many multinationals may be able to refer to legitimate interests in this respect; specifically, a small subsidiary without a HR department may be able to demonstrate legitimate interests or even a contractual necessity for transfers to a 100% parent company that manages payroll and other human resources functions for its smaller subsidiaries. But, for a larger subsidiary with stand-alone administrative functions, the parent company may find it more difficult to justify transfers because some of the functions and data could also be kept locally. Often, management at the ultimate parent company likes to be in control over worldwide operations and achieve cost savings by centralizing data processing and decision-making. Yet, data **2.10** protection authorities, works councils and individual employees do not always accept such objectives as legitimate. In practice, multinational businesses will usually succeed in showing needs for human resources transfers regarding some data categories that the parent company legitimately needs, for example, for cross-border projects and career management, employee stock option grants and secondments (*i.e.*, temporary transfers to an affiliated company in another country). Similarly, companies may have to share certain customer data with suppliers or third-party manufacturers to support expeditious recalls or warranty coverage. However, with respect to data categories that a European company cannot justify to transfer to another controller, the European company should consider engaging its parent company or other affiliate as a mere data processor (for example, under the EU Standard Contractual Clauses for transfers of personal data to processors).

2.11   *Hurdle 3 (restrictions on data transfers outside the EEA)* requires the company to ensure that the recipient country or company provides adequate levels of data protection. By default, companies within the EEA are prohibited from sending data outside the EEA. This third hurdle requires companies to select specific compliance mechanisms for international data transfers.

2.12   The EU Commission has ruled that a number of countries provide adequate safeguards: Andorra, Argentina, Faeroe Islands, Guernsey, Canada, Isle of Man, Israel, Jersey, New Zealand, Uruguay and Switzerland. Companies within the EEA are permitted to transfer data to these countries to these countries. as freely as they may transfer data within the EEA, *i.e.*, subject only to Hurdles 1 and 2 described above; a third hurdle does not apply with respect to countries that the EU Commission, has declared to provide adequate data protection safeguards.

2.13   With respect to the United States, the EU Commission has issued a uniquely limited and conditional adequacy determination in 2016. It finds adequate safeguards only with respect U.S. companies that join the EU-U.S. Privacy Shield Program and commit to compliance with the Privacy Shield Principles. The EU Commission and U.S. Commerce Department developed the Privacy Shield Principles based on EU data protection law to achieve interoperability between the two jurisdictions' very different privacy laws. Most U.S. companies can join the program (only companies that are not subject to the broad jurisdiction of the U.S. Federal Trade Commission are ineligible). Companies that wish to join the program can certify online to the U.S. Commerce

Department that they comply with the Privacy Shield Principles and that they have conducted and documented a self-assessment. They have to agree to cooperate with EU data protection authorities with respect to employee data from the EEA and can set up other dispute resolution options with respect to other data. The Commerce Department reviews the applicants' online submission statement and privacy notice and it can also request information regarding onward transfer agreements. If U.S. companies fail to comply with the Privacy Shield Principles or their own privacy notice, then the powerful U.S. Federal Trade Commission can enforce the requirements, the U.S. Commerce Department can expel them from the program, EU data protection authorities can invoke cooperation duties and private plaintiffs can take complaints to the courts. Thus, the EU-U.S. Privacy Shield Program ensures that legal requirements modeled after EU data protection laws apply and can be enforced against U.S. companies on U.S. territory by U.S. authorities, U.S. courts and EU data protection authorities.

The EU-U.S. Privacy Shield Program replaced the U.S. Safe Harbor 2.14 Program, which the U.S. Commerce Department had operated – and the Federal Trade Commission had enforced – for 15 years, since 2000. On October 6, 2015, the Court of Justice of the European Union invalidated the Commission's adequacy decision regarding the Safe Harbor Program due primarily to concerns regarding U.S. government surveillance. The EU Commission and U.S. Commerce Department had already been working on updates to the Safe Harbor Program and took the court's judgment into account as they finalized their agreement.

At first sight, the Privacy Shield Principles are more elaborate and rigid 2.15 than the Safe Harbor Program: in 2000, the Safe Harbor Principles took up 2.5 pages and the Commission's adequacy decision 40 pages in the Official Journal of the EU; in 2016, the Privacy Shield Principles weigh in at 19 pages and the adequacy decision at 112 pages. This increase in word count parallels the growth of EU data protection legislation from the 19 pages of the 1995 EU Data Protection Directive to the 88 pages on the 2016 EU General Data Protection Regulation.

More substantively, the Privacy Shield arrangement contemplates annual reviews and updating of the Privacy Shield Principles as well as a number of strengthened or new privacy safeguards such as requirements regarding more detailed privacy notices (calling out details on liability, access rights and dispute resolution), more robust onward transfer contracts and access to such contracts by the Commerce

Department, and data minimization, data retention, independent recourse mechanisms at no cost to the individual, as well as publication requirements relating to non-compliance. Companies that voluntarily leave the program must return or delete all previously received personal data or continue to apply the Privacy Shield Principles to such data and recertify compliance on a perpetual, annual basis. If the Commerce Department removes a company from the Privacy Shield Program, the company must delete or return previously collected data.

2.16    Additionally, the U.S. Director of National Intelligence offered concrete and robust commitments to the EU in undertakings accompanying the Privacy Shield Principles. Previously, the U.S. President had already significantly reigned in NSA surveillance and the U.S. Congress had strengthened privacy protections in the Judicial Redress Act and the USA Freedom Act (repealing the infamous USA Patriot Act) as a reaction to domestic and international concerns regarding mass surveillance revealed by Edward Snowden in 2013.

2.17    Immediately after the EU Commission approved the EU-U.S. Privacy Shield Program in July 2016, politicians, activists and data protection authorities in the EU criticized the program and announced plans to challenge it. But, unless and until the EU Commission's adequacy decision of 2016 is invalidated or revoked, companies in the EEA are permitted to transfer personal data to U.S. companies that have joined the EU-U.S. Privacy Shield Program as if such companies were situated in the EEA or one of the countries that the EU Commission has generally declared adequate. Companies in the EEA do not have to clear a third hurdle to legitimize transfers of personal data to companies in the EU-U.S. Privacy Shield Program.

2.18    The third hurdle does apply, however, with respect to international data transfers to U.S. companies that choose not to join the EU-U.S. Privacy Shield Program, and to companies in any of the 150+ other countries that are neither part of the EEA nor generally declared adequate by the EU Commission. In this respect, companies in the EEA have a number of different options regarding exceptions they can rely on, including the following:

+ explicit consent from the data subject;

+ a need to perform a contract with or in the interest of the data subject;

- important reasons of public interest;

- the establishment, exercise or defense of legal claims;

- vital interests of the data subject or of other persons;

- Standard Contractual Clauses promulgated by the EU Commission;

- Binding Corporate Rules; and

- Codes of Conduct approved under the EU General Data Protection Regulation.

## Options to clear hurdle 3 – prohibition of international transfers

Companies in the EEA have to share personal data with companies 2.19 outside the EEA regularly, given the broad definition of what constitutes personal data under EU data protection law. At a minimum, companies have to share names and business contact information of their sales and procurement representatives, for example, when they sell cars to a distributor in Brazil, establish a representative office in China or order computers from Japan; this already constitutes an international transfer of personal data under EU data protection law that must clear all three hurdles. But, most companies must share much more personal data in connection with transactions, parent-subsidiary relations and supply chain arrangements in today's global, interconnected economy. To overcome prohibitions of international data transfers (the third hurdle), companies must and can choose from a number of options that invoke different requirements:

*Data Subject Consent*: Companies can overcome restrictions regarding 2.20 international data transfers and any other data processing activities by obtaining valid consent from the data subjects, *i.e.*, the persons to whom the data relates.

- Valid consent can help overcome each of the three hurdles. However, consent is valid only if it is freely given, specific, informed and in writing, and data subjects can freely revoke their consent at any time.

2.21 • *Necessity under Contracts or Statutes.* Instead of seeking consent, companies can conclude contracts with data subjects. Occasionally, companies are able to legitimize data transfers in reference to statutory obligations. European laws rarely explicitly require a transfer outside the EEA, but this may be possible, for example, in the context of benefits recognition arrangements for cross-border employee secondments, where employers within and outside the EEA have to share personal data with each other and authorities in the respective jurisdictions. More relevant are transfers based on contractual necessities, where a company needs to transfer data internationally to fulfill a contractual obligation, *e.g.*, travel bookings require sharing of personal data with foreign airlines and hotels and shipments of products abroad require sharing of personal data with carriers and customs officials. But, under EU law, the contract has to be with the actual data subject or in the data subject's interest in order to legitimize the transfer.

2.22 *Data Transfer Agreements based on Standard Contractual Clauses.* If a company within the EEA agrees with a company outside the EEA that the latter will comply with certain Standard Contractual Clauses approved by the EU Commission, then "adequate safeguards" are presumed. As a consequence, EEA member states may generally not prohibit data transfers outside the EEA. But, the data protection authorities can require companies to submit signed copies of the agreements and scrutinize the agreements for any derogations from the official text as well as the company-specific details in the required appendices.

2.23 The EU Commission has promulgated Standard Contractual Clauses for transfers between data controllers, one version in 2001 and another version in 2004 in response to industry proposals to modify the standard, without superseding the 2001 version, so both can still be used. These two sets of Standard Contractual Clauses are fairly similar in substance, require both parties to comply with EU data protection law and entitle data subjects to enforce all contractual obligations as a third party beneficiary against either contract party, under local law and in a local court where the data subject lives.

2.24 The EU Commission has also promulgated Standard Contractual Clauses for transfers of personal data from data controllers to data processors, which is binding on EEA member states. The Standard Contractual Clauses for controller-processor transfers impose most obligations on the European data exporter. The data processor outside the EEA is responsible for data security and must 'abide by the advice of' European data protection authorities. If the data processor wants to transfer data to a contractor (subprocessor), then the processor must obtain written consent from the data controller; conclude a data transfer agreement with the subprocessor based on the same clauses, also governed by the laws of the jurisdiction where the data controller is based, assume unlimited liability for any actions and inactions of any subprocessor (even those selected by the data controller or another subprocessor) vis-à-vis the data controller and the data subjects; and keep a list of subprocessing agreements and make the list and copies of the agreements available to data subjects, the data controller and the data controller's data protection supervisory authority. The data subject can sue both or either of the parties in a local court and under local law.

In practice, one of the most significant deterrents to adoption of the  2.25
Standard Contractual Clauses for transfers to processor is that the clauses require the data processor to obtain signatures on the clauses from all subcontractors that have access to European data. This can be nearly impossible in industries where companies have to rely heavily on subcontractors, such as Internet service providers (which would basically have to sign up every company connected to the Internet to comply) and payment service providers (which would have to sign up all banks, credit card companies, clearing houses and other service providers). Yet, after the EU Court of Justice quashed the Safe Harbor option for U.S.-based data processing service providers in October 2015, and before the EU-U.S. Privacy Shield was approved in July 2016, numerous U.S. companies and their subcontractors within the U.S. and other countries started to accept the Standard Contractual Clauses for data transfers to processors. Consequently, these clauses have become somewhat of an international standard.

In order to preserve the benefit of the adequacy finding, companies  2.26
may not modify the Standard Contractual Clauses in any manner that would contradict, directly or indirectly, the clauses or the data protection rights of the data subjects. But, they can conclude separate agreements and supplement the Standard Contractual Clauses (for example, with indemnification agreements), without implicating the EU Commission's binding adequacy finding, as expressly noted in the Standard Contractual Clauses.

Companies that modify the Standard Contractual Clauses or draft their  2.27
own agreements from scratch cannot rely on the EU Commission's

adequacy findings. Such modified or custom-made agreements may be superior from a data protection or business perspective, but they are subject to full scrutiny by every EEA member state and will trigger various requirements to notify or obtain approval from local authorities (which can be time-consuming, costly and difficult to manage). Data processors that sell automated services or platform access to numerous customers and EEA member states cannot be expected to cope with a multitude of differing security standards and data transfer agreements, particularly if these agreements require the data processor to flow all requirements through to any subcontractors verbatim. Therefore, some providers of automated data processing services (*e.g.*, cloud computing) prefer the Standard Contractual Clauses over form agreements promulgated by data protection authorities in individual EEA member states and also over "homemade" agreements proposed by outside legal counsel, industry associations or customers.

2.28    The EU Commission announced plans to revisit its decisions regarding Standard Contractual Clauses and the adequacy of various countries in light of the judgment of the EU Court of Justice relating to the Safe Harbor Program in 2015, because the concerns that the court raised regarding government surveillance and other threats to privacy in the United States apply equally with respect to other jurisdictions and data transfers under other compliance options. Therefore, companies should prepare for changes also to the Standard Contractual Clauses and agree with their business partners to adapt contracts if and when new Standard Contractual Clauses or other precautions become *required.*

2.29    *Binding Corporate Rules:* For intra-group data transfers, multinational groups can also submit to Binding Corporate Rules, *i.e.*, a code or policy statement that reflects and safeguards compliance with European data protection laws throughout a group of companies. Binding Corporate Rules cannot legitimize data transfers to unaffiliated entities, such as customers, suppliers, distributors, service providers, civil litigants, government agencies and other entities. The Article 29 Working Party of national data protection authorities has published guidance on what topics companies need to address in Binding Corporate Rules for transfers of personal data to controllers and processors. But, the EU Commission has not published pre-approved templates as in the case of the Standard Contractual Clauses.

2.30    *EU-U.S. Privacy Shield:* With respect to data transfers from the EEA to the U.S. specifically, companies have another unique option: The U.S.

company can join the EU-U.S. Privacy Shield program and thereby remove the necessity to overcome a third hurdle for companies in the EEA. After the U.S. company joins the program, it is considered to be based within the EEA for purposes of international data transfers under EU data protection law.

## Compliance mechanisms compared

Companies have to consider various advantages and disadvantages 2.31 when they decide how to clear the third hurdle, to international data transfers, including the following pros and cons:

*Substantive compliance obligations:* The Privacy Shield Principles, 2.32 the Standard Contractual Clauses for transfers to processors and the Standard Contractual Clauses for transfers to controllers were created over a span of 12 years with input from different organizations, including the U.S. Commerce Department and the International Chamber of Commerce. Each compliance vehicle contains substantive terms that are intended to commit U.S. companies to core principles of EU data protection laws, but each document uses different verbiage and nuances, which will affect companies differently depending on their business focus and overall situation. For example, the Privacy Shield Principles are specific regarding opt-out rights to onward transfers, dispute resolution process, and data retention. The Standard Contractual Clauses contain more generalized descriptions on these issues, although it is expected that these clauses will be updated with more specificity. The specifics of the substantive compliance obligations companies must assume in Binding Corporate Rules will depend on what they can achieve in their negotiations with authorities for approval. With respect to emerging solutions, such as Codes of Conduct, the specifics of the substantive requirements will depend on private sector proposals and views of data protection authorities in the approval processes. Where companies rely on consent or contractual necessities, they define their substantive compliance obligations in the terms they present to the data subjects in contracts and privacy notice forms, although the sufficiency of such terms may be subject to review and approvals of authorities depending on national rules.

*Flexibility and configurability:* When companies are able to obtain 2.33 consent or contractual agreements with data subjects, they may have the great advantage that they can tailor the scope of the consent or contract to their particular situation and avoid having to adapt to the more regulated frameworks of the Standard Contractual Clauses, Binding Corporate Rules, EU-U.S. Privacy Shield, Codes of Conduct, or certification schemes.

But, consent is valid only if consent is freely given, specific, informed and unambiguous. For international transfers outside the EEA consent additionally has to be explicit. It is not always practical to meet these requirements. Some types of businesses do not have any direct relationship with data subjects, and they therefore cannot approach the data subjects with a request for consent, *e.g.*, cloud, SaaS, or outsourcing service providers and companies that host data or websites to which others submit information that may include personal information on EU residents. Businesses might also have difficulties meeting the "voluntariness" requirement; for example, the data protection authorities in most EEA member states presume that employee consent is coerced, hence involuntary, given the typical imbalance of power in the employment relationship. Additionally, a recital in the EU General Data Protection Regulation states that consent should not provide a valid legal ground where there is a "clear imbalance" between the data subject and the controller, while not providing examples of "clear imbalance." The term might be interpreted to apply regarding employment relationships, where data protection authorities have traditionally found reasons to question the validity of consent based on voluntariness grounds, however, it might also be extended to consumer contracts and other cases. In such cases consent could be an unreliable solution. Most companies also find it challenging to obtain and maintain consent with sufficient specificity, as technology, business practices and purposes change constantly and force companies to update consent forms frequently. Another important consideration is that data subjects can revoke voluntary consent at any time. Therefore, in practice, companies often cannot – or do not wish to – rely on consent to legitimize international data transfers, at least not as the sole compliance measure.

Similarly, contractual obligations vis-à-vis data subjects are not always in place or suited to justify data transfers. Some companies are able to bolster their position regarding data subject consent by creating additional contractual obligations that in turn create a necessity to engage in certain transfers. For example, if a company contractually agrees with a data subject to retain certain third parties in other jurisdictions to provide services or information, or to ship physical items to the data subject, then the company can justify the data transfers to the third parties, as such transfers are necessary to perform under the contract. Some jurisdictions may apply less stringent requirements to online contract formation as they apply to consent under data protection laws, but many European jurisdictions generally empower courts to scrutinize the fairness of clauses in non-negotiated standard contract templates.

*Geographic and topical coverage.* Companies can use consent and 2.34 contracts with data subjects with respect to all **geographies**, so these routes are suited to support uniform approaches across geographies. Uniform **topical coverage** is more difficult because consent and contractual undertakings are often not an option in certain scenarios – for example, in the human resources context (where freedom to contract is limited and consent deemed coerced) or due to a lack of direct contact with data subjects, or a business context that does not induce data subjects to grant consent or conclude contracts. Companies can also use data transfer agreements and data processing agreements incorporating the Standard Contractual Clauses to legitimize transfers of EEA data to any other country. Some companies are concerned regarding the  amount of detail regarding data processing practices and purposes that they are required to include in Appendices to data transfer agreements, which causes some to prepare specific agreements for specific scenarios and accumulate a multitude of limited transfer agreements as opposed to one comprehensive set of rules for all geographies and topics. But, other companies find the incremental effort of preparing detailed Appendices to data transfer agreements acceptable given the fact that they are required to prepare records regarding their data processing activities anyhow under the EU General Data Protection Regulation and some national data protection laws.

Binding Corporate Rules, codes of conduct and certification schemes could theoretically provide a comprehensive set of rules and cover any jurisdiction and all data categories. But, Binding Corporate Rules are  only for intra-group transfers of personal data (*i.e.*, between affiliated companies), and cannot cover transfers of personal data to and from business partners, such as suppliers, customers, distributors, etc., unless, perhaps, if such unaffiliated parties contractually agree to comply with another entity's customized Binding Corporate Rules (which would impose prohibitive administrative burdens on companies in business with multiple entities that have adopted different Binding Corporate Rules). Also, companies may logically be reluctant to implement truly global Binding Corporate Rules, because commitments required with respect to EEA data may not be appropriate or affordable for data from other regions or countries. The EU-U.S. Privacy Shield framework can be used to transfer data of any nature, intra-group and vis-à-vis third parties, but it only addresses data transfers from the EEA to the U.S. (or via the U.S. to third countries). It does not cover transfers from the EEA directly to countries other than the United States.

2.35 *Implementation process and timing.* Consent forms and contractual undertakings are relatively easy to prepare and implement in online click-through scenarios, but offline, negotiation and dealing with concerns or push-back raised by data subjects can take a significant amount of time and effort. Implementing data transfer agreements based on the Standard Contractual Clauses does not typically take companies a lot of time in the intra-group context, because the content of the contracts is largely prescribed and translations in all major European languages are available (courtesy of the EU Commission). But, companies with many subsidiaries or particularly dynamic corporate structures (think: acquisition or spin-off sprees) view the implementation of data transfer agreements as a more significant burden, particularly if local operations are reluctant to execute the agreements. Moreover, getting unaffiliated business partners to sign the forms can be challenging (although, more and more sophisticated companies accept the format and wording of the 'official' Standard Contractual Clauses as a necessity).

The greatest administrative burden has been associated with implementing Binding Corporate Rules. Companies have to decide on the content of the rules "from scratch": although there is guidance from authorities, no official templates are available, and the publicly available precedents do not necessarily suit all companies. Moreover, companies need to obtain approval from data protection authorities and only 21 of the EEA member states have agreed on a mutual recognition procedure. After the EU General Data Protection Regulation takes effect in 2018, approvals will apply across the EEA and it is possible that the approval process may become less burdensome and lengthy over time if more and more companies make the effort to implement Binding Corporate Rules.

By contrast, a registration under the EU-U.S. Privacy Shield framework is relatively easy (online filing only) and most EEA member states did not require companies to seek prior approval with respect to data transfers to Safe Harbor participants, a privilege they may extend to the EU-U.S. Privacy Shield program as it is also based on an "adequacy" decision. U.S. companies will want to take sufficient time before they submit to the EU-U.S. Privacy Shield framework because they should conduct the required self-assessment and prepare the relevant due diligence documentation in order to be prepared to answer any questions from the U.S. Department of Commerce and any enforcement actions by the U.S. Federal Trade Commission. Such a self-assessment should be undertaken and documented in the context of any of the compliance options; in fact, the Standard Contractual Clauses require due diligence efforts as well. Companies will have to consider the dynamics and implications of needing a corporate officer to sign a declaration regarding compliance and self-assessment, a possible review process by third party validators or dispute resolution process providers, as well as the heightened scrutiny from the U.S. Commerce Department and Federal Trade Commission regarding the form and content of privacy notices and onward transfer agreements.

It remains to be seen how soon companies can take advantage of the newly introduced possibility to adduce appropriate safeguards through approved Codes of Conduct or certification bodies' programs. According to the EU General Data Protection Regulation, a data protection authority and the EU Commission must approve such mechanisms.

*Ongoing administration.* The EU-U.S. Privacy Shield program requires   2.36
annual re-certification. Certification schemes per Article 42 of the EU General Data Protection Regulation will be limited to a maximum period of three years and may be renewed. Other compliance options require actions in case of changes (*e.g.*, additional consent, updating contracts or modifying Binding Corporate Rules), but no annual or routine actions in the absence of changes. Approved Codes of Conduct may or may not require ongoing administration, depending on their individual rules.

*Onward transfers.* With each available compliance option, companies   2.37
accept different restrictions and conditions on their ability to share personal data originating from the EEA with onward transferees, such as external service providers, business partners, government agencies (*e.g.*, in case of investigations, litigation or reporting obligations) and other non-EEA affiliates (*e.g.*, subsidiaries in North or South America or Asia).

• *Onward transfer based on consent.* If a U.S. company receives the EEA data based on valid consent or a necessity to perform contractual obligations, the U.S. data importer does not assume any specific obligations, except as the U.S. data importer may commit to in the context of the consent, or otherwise agree contractually with any data exporter in the EEA. In the absence of contractual obligations, the U.S. data importer would not face any direct restrictions under EU data protection law. Of course, particularly in the context of employee data transfers, the U.S. data importer would be indirectly affected by compliance obligations on its EEA-based subsidiaries, the data exporters. The European data exporters should not allow the onward transfers, unless the data subjects have been informed as necessary, and the transfers are covered by the scope of the consent or necessity to perform contractual obligations.

• *Onward transfers based on Standard Contractual Clauses.* U.S. companies that agree to the Standard Contractual Clauses, must pass on their obligations verbatim to onward transferees. This is fairly easy to achieve in the intra-group context, but can be difficult or impossible with respect to some categories of unaffiliated onward transferees, *e.g.*, in the context of litigation pre-trial discovery, if a foreign government demands access to EEA data in the context of investigations, if a foreign regulator or law enforcement authority seeks to compel access, or when dealing with business partners that do not otherwise have to or want to submit to EU data protection laws. But, since many internationally active businesses have become familiar with the workings of EU data protection laws, it seems to become easier and easier to obtain signatures on onward transfer agreements that reference the Standard Contractual Clauses. Under the Standard Contractual Clauses for transfers to controllers, the data importers outside the EEA are not explicitly obligated to implement any particular mechanisms with respect to onward transfers to data processors (only with respect to onward data transfers to controllers). But, for various practical reasons, data importers outside the EEA have to sign onward transfer agreements similar to the Standard Contractual Clauses for processors. Firstly, onward data recipients cannot be qualified as mere data processors unless they are contractually obligated to act only on behalf, in the interest and per the instructions, of a data controller. Secondly, the data importer assumes full responsibility for all actions and omissions of its agents under the Model Controller Contract and therefore, has to pass on compliance obligations and allocate commercial risks contractually to onward transferees.

- *Onward transfers under EU-U.S. Privacy Shield.* If a U.S. company registers with the EU-U.S. Privacy Shield, then such U.S. company would be primarily obligated to ensure that it provides notice and choice to data subjects prior to transferring data to other data controllers. In order to provide data subjects with "choice," the U.S. company would have to obtain affirmative consent regarding special categories of personal data (*i.e.*, data relating to health, race, ethnicity, political opinions, religious or philosophical beliefs, trade union membership or sexual orientation); with respect to other data, an opportunity to opt out would suffice An exception for intra-group transfers does not exist, so companies may also have to offer 'choice' for data transfers to affiliates unless they enter into internal group data processing arrangements.

- *Onward transfers under Binding Corporate Rules.* If a multinational business implements Binding Corporate Rules, it could cause all non-EEA based entities to submit to the rules and thus cover all direct and onward data transfers within the group. But, Binding Corporate Rules do not cover any data transfers outside the group. Thus, groups with Binding Corporate Rules would still have to implement other compliance mechanisms for any direct or onward data transfers to non-affiliated companies. If a group commits in Binding Corporate Rules that it will require onward transferees to adopt the same Binding Corporate Rules or accept them with respect to specific data transfers, such a requirement would be very difficult to satisfy in practice as vendors and other unaffiliated third parties will be hesitant to review, understand and commit to another organization's customized Binding Corporate Rules.

- *Onward transfers under approved Codes of Conduct or approved certification mechanisms.* Approved Codes of Conduct or approved certification mechanisms, require binding and enforceable commitments of the controller or processor in the third country to apply the appropriate safeguards, including as regards data subjects' rights.

*Submission to foreign law and jurisdiction.* The consent and contractual undertaking routes do not present companies with any specific restrictions as to choice of law or jurisdiction (but general public policy   2.38

limitations apply, such as with respect to consumers and employees). The Standard Contractual Clauses, on the other hand, require the data recipients to submit to the data protection laws and the jurisdiction of the courts of the EEA Member State from where the European company transfers the data and data subjects have a third party beneficiary right to enforce the data transfer agreements in a local court. With respect to Binding Corporate Rules, the data protection authorities in each EEA Member State where the Binding Corporate Rules will be implemented may demand similar protections in connection with the approval process. Alternatively or additionally, data subjects could try to enforce the Standard Contractual Clauses and Binding Corporate Rules in U.S. courts.

The EU-U.S. Privacy Shield framework is largely a creation of U.S. law. Enforcement will likely occur primarily in the United States: the U.S. Department of Commerce will scrutinize submissions, handle challenges and possibly request information from organizations that register. Also, the Federal Trade Commission is the primary enforcement authority for Privacy Shield violations, and, at least in principle, the Federal Trade Commission, State Attorneys General and private plaintiffs can bring actions on unfair competition, misrepresentation and breach of contract theories in connection with any compliance vehicles. Courts in the U.S. and the EEA may decide jurisdiction based on traditional rules of civil procedure. Also, with respect to human resources data, U.S. companies have to submit to cooperation with EEA data protection authorities in the context of the EU-U.S. Privacy Shield Program.

2.39 *Enforcement risks.* Regarding Standard Contractual Clauses and Binding Corporate Rules, enforcement actions have so far not yet been publicized. In the relatively few enforcement cases involving data transfers from the EEA to other countries, the European Data Protection Authorities have so far preferred to take action against the data exporter, *i.e.*, the local entity that was fully obligated to comply with local data protection laws anyhow. At the same time, the validity of the Standard Contractual Clauses themselves are currently subject to scrutiny and may be modified by the Commission proactively or invalidated by the Court of Justice of the European Union like the court invalidated the Commission decision regarding Safe Harbor.

With respect to the U.S. Safe Harbor program, on the other hand, the Federal Trade Commission had brought more than two dozen enforcement actions and companies that participated in the program have also been subject to challenges to the program itself in Europe. The U.S. Commerce Department and the Federal Trade Commission have committed to enforcing the Privacy Shield more rigorously than the Safe Harbor Program in the United States and challenges to the program itself are expected in Europe. Therefore, and based on experiences with the Safe Harbor program, some U.S. companies are concerned about potentially greater risks of enforcement actions if they join the Privacy Shield than if they rely on other compliance options.

*Public Relations and Business Benefits.* In the early years of the U.S.    2.40
Safe Harbor Program, U.S. companies advertised their registration on consumer-facing websites, touted their registration status in whitepapers on privacy-compliance, celebrated the program in communications to employees in the EU and benefitted from the ability to "check the box" in responses to requests for proposals . More recently, the U.S. Safe Harbor Program was increasingly criticized in Europe and U.S. companies started to tone down their certification announcements. U.S. companies that are in the business of hosting or processing data for others (*e.g.*, outsourcing service providers, software-as-a-service companies) were expected to register for Safe Harbor and will likely also be expected to register for the EU-U.S. Privacy Shield program, and customers will unlikely see an extraordinary effort or benefit in such a registration (but take it as a given). U.S.-based cloud or processing services providers will also likely not worry much about signing up because the Privacy Shield Principles and EU data protection laws generally do not demand materially more in terms of substantive compliance than what are otherwise required in their services agreements. U.S.-based data processing service providers are also expected to agree to data processing agreements based on the Standard Contractual Clauses. Companies that are not pressured by customers to sign up for the EU-U.S. Privacy Shield and do not want to expose their compliance approach to the public eye might decide not to join the Privacy Shield at this time, and only implement data transfer and data processing agreements.

*Stability.* The EU-U.S. Privacy Shield will be reviewed, and possibly    2.41
renegotiated, annually by the EU Commission and the U.S. Commerce Department. Standard Contractual Clauses are under review and have been challenged in court. Binding Corporate Rules requirements constantly evolve. Requirements for Codes of Conduct and Certifications are still in the process of being developed. Data subjects can revoke

their consent to voluntary data processing at any time. Currently, none of the options offer a great degree of stability.

2.42 *International Interoperability and non-EEA Data.* Most U.S.-based multinationals are not just dealing with personal data and compliance requirements from the EEA. Increasingly, other jurisdictions are enacting or updating data protection laws and introducing additional or different requirements. A company that registers under the EU-U.S. Privacy Shield would not benefit from such a registration with respect to personal data or requirements from other jurisdictions, given that the program applies only to data from the EEA and only to U.S. companies. But, companies that participate in the Privacy Shield program should be able to leverage their self-assessment documentation and privacy notices. Consent, data transfer and processing agreements, and Binding Corporate Rules can also be leveraged for many other jurisdictions and modified versions of SCC-based data transfer agreements or data processing agreements are also useful internationally.

2.43 *Formalities.* The EU-U.S. Privacy Shield requires a formal compliance declaration from an officer of the company in connection with the initial certification and annual recertification. Participating companies are listed on a public website maintained by the Department of Commerce, even if and after they withdraw from the program.

For the execution of contracts based on Standard Contractual Clauses and any amendments, a signature from authorized company representatives is also required, but these do not have to be corporate officers. Many multinational enterprises work with centralized powers of attorney to facilitate the execution of routine contract amendments, *e.g.*, when addresses of entities change. Companies do not have to publicly disclose their contracts.

Signature, publicity and other formal requirements relating to Binding Corporate Rules, Codes of Conducts and Certification vary from country to country. The EU Commission publishes a list of companies that have obtained approvals for Binding Corporate Rules.

2.44 *Summary.* When comparing the various pros and cons of compliance options relating to international data transfers, companies usually find that no one size fits all. Each company (and business unit within decentralized organizations) has to assess its own data flows, business needs and risk sensitivities. This may cause organizations to select different compliance mechanisms for business lines, data categories or other scenarios. Obtaining consent from data subjects is easy and ideal for an Internet-based business model that allows prompting consumers to click-through notice and consent forms, but impractical in the employment context due to risks of push-back from data protection authorities in the filing context as well as individual consent denial or revocation that could bar global database solutions. A financial service provider with thousands of special purpose subsidiaries may find the administrative burden associated with negotiating Binding Corporate Rules less onerous than signing and updating thousands of data transfer agreements based on the Standard Contractual Clauses. Some companies take different approaches for intra-group transfers of human resources data and transfers of customer data. Yet others may opt for an EU-U.S. Privacy Shield registration relating to business lines where customer demand requires this choice, and pursue other approaches for other business lines.

*Compliance Mechanisms for Data Transfers from Europe*                              2.45

| Topic | Consent, Contract with data subjects | Data Transfer Agreements based on SCC | EU-U.S. Privacy Shield Certification | Binding Corporate Rules (Binding Corporate Rules) |
|---|---|---|---|---|
| Binding on national data protection authorities? | No. Authorities can challenge consent and contract terms, formal presentation, acceptance mechanisms, etc. | Yes, but authorities can scrutinize appendices. | Yes. | Binding Corporate Rules are subject to approval by data protection authorities, which some authorities in other EEA Member States currently accept and under EU GDPR will become binding EEA-wide. |
| Geographic scope | Unlimited | Unlimited | Only EEA to U.S. and from U.S. onwards | Unlimited |
| Substantive scope | Unlimited | Unlimited | Unlimited | Only intra-group transfers, not transfers to and from customers, suppliers, etc. |

| Topic | Consent, Contract with data subjects | Data Transfer Agreements based on SCC | EU-U.S. Privacy Shield Certification | Binding Corporate Rules (Binding Corporate Rules) |
|---|---|---|---|---|
| Onward transfers | No restrictions | Onward transferee must also sign SCC | Onward transferee must also certify under Shield, sign qualified onward transfer agreement, or otherwise meet adequacy | Depends on Binding Corporate Rules, as approved by data protection authorities |
| Applicable law, jurisdiction | Not prescribed | Data exporter's local law, courts | U.S. law, courts; Federal Trade Commission jurisdiction; cooperation with EEA data protection authorities for employee data | Depends on Binding Corporate Rules, as approved by data protection authorities |
| Data exporter must comply with . . . | . . . local law where data exporter is based | | | |
| Data importer must comply with the laws where data importer is based and. . . | . . . contract obligations to honor data exporter's promises in privacy notices | . . . local law where data exporter is based | . . . Privacy Shield Principles | . . . Binding Corporate Rules |
| Flexibility | High | None | None | Low – no prescribed clauses, but authorities are restrictive in approval process |
| Implementation time, cost | Minimal (particularly online implementations) | Low (forms are usually adopted unmodified, but Appendices have to be filled out) | Medium (self-assessment, drafting of notices) | High – approval process |

| Topic | Consent, Contract with data subjects | Data Transfer Agreements based on SCC | EU-U.S. Privacy Shield Certification | Binding Corporate Rules (Binding Corporate Rules) |
|---|---|---|---|---|
| Maintenance costs | Often minimal (updated consent in case of changes) | Minimal (updates to appendices as changes are made) | Medium (annual recertification, renewed self-assessment) | Minimal, unless changes and renewed applications for government approvals are necessary |
| Public relations benefit or problem? | Neither | Neither | To be seen – Safe Harbor Program initially provided PR benefits, but recent criticism in Europe re. Safe Harbor and Privacy Shield Program may cause more problems than benefits | Possibly, particularly among experts, if company publicizes its Binding Corporate Rules |
| Helps sales of services B2B? | No. | Yes. | Yes. | Possibly, if customers rely on BCRs. |

## Implementation

Once you have picked your poison, you need to focus on implementa-   2.46
tion. Your tasks will vary depending on the compliance mechanism
you selected. You will find more general guidance on how to prepare
documentation in Chapter 3 while this section provides you with an
overview of what you need to do specifically to implement compliance vehicles for international transfers of personal data from the
EEA to countries that the EU Commission has not generally declared
adequate.

*Consent.* Under European laws, consent is valid only if it is freely given,   2.47
informed, specific and in writing. In most scenarios, companies can
satisfy the written form requirement with electronic mail and click-
through processes, which tend to be easier to manage. In order to meet
the requirements for specificity and informedness, companies have to
provide detailed notices and connect the consent to a clearly defined

data processing proposal (as opposed to a general 'privacy policy' that is subject to changes from time to time).

2.48 *Statutory, contractual transfer obligations.* If you decide to justify data transfers with a necessity arising under a contract with the data subject or applicable law, you only have to confirm that the applicable statute or contract actually supports the necessity. Companies can influence the creation of contractual obligations in support of data transfers. For example, they can promise in click-through and other form contracts that they will transfer a customer's data to a business partner in a certain jurisdiction for fulfillment or shipping purposes, or that they will pass on contact information to affiliates for purposes of having the affiliates provide valuable information about products or services (which may contain content similar to marketing emails). Companies have to be mindful of various jurisdictions' laws on unfair contract terms or adhesion contracts that may invalidate surprising or unfair clauses in consumer contracts.

2.49 *Data transfers based on Standard Contractual Clauses.* If you decide to legitimize international data transfers based on Standard Contractual Clauses, you will be working with templates that should not be altered but need to be supplemented with specific information on the companies and data involved. You could take the following implementation steps:

2.50 • Map your data flows: prepare a brief outline of what categories of data are sent from the EEA, where they are sent and what the purposes of the transfer are. Identify data recipients outside the EEA as data controllers or data processors and as affiliated companies and third parties.

2.51 • Retrieve the form agreements (search the web for 'EU data protection law standard contractual clauses'; in September 2017, you could find them at http://ec.europa.eu/justice/data-protection/international-transfers/index_en.htm).

2.52 • For recipients outside the EEA that a data controller engages as a data processor, use the Standard Contractual Clauses for data transfers to processors.

   • Prepare a list of data controllers in the EEA, data processors outside the EEA, and subcontractors of data processors. The

Standard Contractual Clauses contemplate that each data controller signs a bilateral agreement with each data processor, and the subprocessor joins this agreement somehow by declaration. But, it should also be acceptable to create framework agreements for several data controllers that transfer to one or more processor (by defining all controllers collectively as 'exporter' and all processors collectively as 'importer').

♦ Before signing the Standard Contractual Clauses as 'importer' or sub-processor, the non-EEA parties need to confirm that they can get all of their contractors and sub-processors with access to the data to also to agree to the Standard Contractual Clauses.

♦ Complete the blanks (in the preamble, above the signature lines, etc.) and remove the footnotes. Do not modify the operative text of the Standard Contractual Clauses, otherwise, you may trigger additional scrutiny and discretionary decision powers of national authorities.

♦ Complete the appendices. A reference to an existing information security policy, attached as a separate document, should suffice but needs to be reviewed for compliance with applicable data protection law requirements.

• For transfers to data controllers outside the EEA use the data Standard Contractual Clauses for data transfers to controllers. 2.53

• When unaffiliated entities sign data transfer agreements based on the Standard Contractual Clauses, they also usually sign commercial agreements to address other aspects of their relationship. Such commercial agreements should cross-reference the data transfer agreements and acknowledge that the data transfer agreements shall prevail over any conflicting terms as far as rights and remedies of data subjects are concerned. With respect to commercial terms, including allocation of duties, risks and liability, companies may agree that between themselves their commercial agreements shall trump the Standard Contractual Clauses, as long as they do not affect the rights of data subjects. 2.54

• Once data transfer agreements have been signed, the parties must update them whenever changes occur, and must implement 2.55

additional agreements when the need arises. Multinationals that maintain dozens or hundreds of such agreements may find it practical and convenient to grant powers of attorney to contract administrators who can then either update individual pages (without resigning) or sign revised versions of the agreement. To keep track of most recent versions, maintain binders and electronic folders with a list of the agreements, updates and copies of the actual agreements.

2.56 *EU-U.S. Privacy Shield Certification.* If you decide on the Privacy Shield-route, you can find practical guidance at www.privacyshield.gov and take the following steps:

2.57 • Conduct and document a self-assessment on how the U.S. company complies with the Privacy Shield Principles, for example by preparing an inventory of database descriptions, contracts relating to transfers or sharing of personal data, data security checklists, and a dossier that summarizes the company's practices with respect to each of the Principles. You can also include other privacy principles in this process, *e.g.*, the Safe Harbor Principles (if your company collected personal data from the EEA under the Safe Harbor Program), principles under the General Data Protection Regulation (to satisfy record-keeping obligations with respect to data processing activities), and other laws and regulations.

2.58 • Confirm adequacy of – or update – supplier contracts and other agreements relating to transfers or processing of personal data ; if data processing service providers have previously executed the Standard Contractual Clauses for transfers to processors that should also meet or exceed requirements regarding onward transfers to processors under the Privacy Shield Principles.

2.59 • Prepare notices to the European data subjects concerned, ideally closely mirroring the organizing headers of the "Notice Principle" in the adequacy decision of the EU Commission regarding the EU-U.S. Privacy Shield Program:

2.60    • Employees can receive their privacy notices from the U.S. company in conjunction with the notices that the European employer entity provides. Some multinationals try to issue one combined, uniform notice to all employees worldwide, which allows for simplification. It seems preferable, however, to keep the U.S. notice required under the EU-U.S. Privacy

Shield Program and the local employer notice required under local data protection laws separate. This helps emphasize the separate nature of the legal entities and their data processing purposes and practices. Such separation also helps address the fact that legal requirements and company practices vary from country to country. It also helps to reinforce the corporate shield that serves various unrelated tax, commercial and liability mitigation objectives. And last but not least, separate notices are easier to update as legal requirements change.

- All other data subjects can be reached with a EU-U.S. Privacy   2.61
Shield Notice' that companies can post on their home pages (for example, next to, or linked within their website privacy statement) and that should also follow the organization and headers of the "Notice Principle" in the EU Commission's adequacy decision regarding the EU-U.S. Privacy Shield Program.

- Select a method for dispute resolution (where data subjects can   2.62
launch complaints if they do not receive or accept the company's own response, before they turn to the Federal Trade Commission). With respect to HR data, cooperation with EU data protection authorities is required, and many companies select this method for other data categories because  no additional steps are required. Alternatives include various arbitration and consumer protection associations, or commercial certification providers. Some companies believe that the names or logos of third party certification providers can help increase consumer trust and they value input from a company that specializes in reviewing consumer privacy statements, given that privacy statements and updates thereto are increasingly monitored by consumer protection organizations and regulators. Other companies shy away from additional reviews due to concerns about costs and hassles associated with having every change to website privacy statements scrutinized by yet another body (possibly in addition to internal and external legal counsel, marketing, internal audit, etc.).

- Have a corporate officer sign a declaration confirming the comple-   2.63
tion of the required self assessment. Often, a Chief Privacy Officer, Chief Information Officer or Chief Technology Officer signs such declaration, but it may not be necessary to present a C-level officer, and many companies authorize other representatives to sign the declaration and manage the Privacy Shield Certification.

2.64 • Submit the application on the Department of Commerce's website and pay the applicable certification or recertification fees. It is also possible to apply via email or regular mail, but this may be more complex and force various decisions as to what information should or should not be provided, whereas the online certification process is fairly easy to manage.

2.65 • Confirm the self-assessment and recertify once every twelve months. After you submitted the initial application, you should calendar a reminder for re-certification (perhaps in nine or ten months) and prepare a folder or binder with all relevant information and documentation that you or your successor can review and confirm for currency/accuracy at the time of renewal.

2.66 *Binding Corporate Rules.* If you select this compliance method, you are still somewhat of a pioneer, as few organizations have managed to obtain government approvals for Binding Corporate Rules as a method of transferring data internationally. Relevant steps include:

2.67 • Mapping of data flows and databases; listing data controllers and processors in the company group (Binding Corporate Rules do not help with data transfers to unaffiliated companies).

2.68 • Preparing of an initial draft of Binding Corporate Rules, either based on one of the few versions that have been approved by data protection authorities, or the terms of the EU Commission's Standard Contractual Clauses (because the data protection authorities can be expected to demand a similar level of protection and obligations).

2.69 • Completing an application for approval.

2.70 • Deciding whether to cover only personal data from European residents, or any and all personal data which would allow a globally uniform policy but could create unnecessary exposure or conflicts under laws of other jurisdictions that do not require or appreciate the effort.

## Data transfers from other jurisdictions

2.71 Once you have selected and implemented one or more compliance mechanisms for transfers of personal data from the EEA to other jurisdictions, you can usually leverage your information gathering, decision making and documentation for other jurisdictions. Switzerland and other countries that the EU Commission has generally declared to provide adequate data protection safeguards largely accept the same international transfer compliance vehicles as the EU itself, except for the EU-U.S. Privacy Shield Program, which covers only data transfer to the United States (Switzerland has approved a similar program as it did while the Safe Harbor Program was operational). The United States and many other countries outside of Europe do not differentiate in their data privacy laws between domestic and international data transfers, so you can work with notices or consent for all transfers of data within or from such jurisdictions. A few other countries, including Australia and India, have enacted laws that require companies to apply additional safeguards in the context of international data transfers, but without offering or requiring specific mechanisms or templates to comply. For these and all countries that do not apply any specific restrictions on international data transfers, companies should consider contractual, notice and consent solutions. As you are preparing documentation for these less regulated jurisdictions, you could start with notice and consent forms that you prepared for Europe, given that the information you want to convey tends to be similar for all jurisdictions (although the level of detail may vary). But, most companies would decide against using the EU Standard Contractual Clauses as a starting point when they draft data transfer agreements for other jurisdictions, given that the EU Standard Contractual Clauses place significant risks, liabilities and obligations on companies that are neither required nor rewarded in countries outside the EEA and the small circle of countries that obtained 'adequacy' blessings from the EU.

In 2004, the 21 member states of the Asia-Pacific Economic   2.72
Cooperation (APEC) agreed on a privacy framework and cross-border privacy rules (CBPR). Only four countries (Canada, Mexico, Japan and the United States, have implemented the rules so far) and only a few multinational businesses have certified. Whether it will gain traction remains to be seen. Multinational businesses are interested in, and tend to be supportive of, increased convergence and interoperability of national data privacy law regimes around the world. Companies will consider certifications if this helps meet regulatory requirements. Unlike the member states of the European Economic Area (EEA), however, the APEC member states have not yet imposed strict prohibitions on international data transfers that require formal government approvals. Thus, companies feel far less pressure to seek certification

under the cross-border privacy rules of the APEC System than to clear the hurdles established by the EEA data protection law regime.

2.73   Companies have to be careful about representing support for the program if they do not actually meet all of its requirements. In 2016, the United States Federal Trade Commission charged a company with falsely representing that it participated in the APEC CBPR system even though the company had not obtained a certification from an APEC-recognized accountability agent.

# 3 Drafting documentation

Before you set out to create documentation relating to privacy law compliance and you put pen to paper, consider two threshold questions:

* Why are you creating the document?

* Who is your audience?

After answering these two threshold questions, you can proceed to preparing an outline and consider the next two questions:

* What requirements and considerations apply regarding content, form and organization?

* What traps and pitfalls should you avoid?

In this Chapter, you will find suggestions on how to answer these threshold questions, suggestions regarding documentation that companies tend to need and not need, as well as guidance and considerations regarding the drafting of documents.

## Why are you creating the document?

As a general matter, businesses prefer to create less rather than more 3.01 documentation for a number of reasons: it takes resources to prepare, review, follow and maintain documentation. Published documentation can limit what a company may do with personal data. Plaintiffs and regulators may exploit any failures to comply with promises and representations in written documentation.

Companies create data privacy-related documentation primarily for 3.02 three reasons: laws, market demands and organizational necessities. More specifically:

◆  To satisfy legal requirements or enjoy benefits that are legally conditioned on having certain documentation,

◆  To respond to market demands (for example, from customers, suppliers, or employees), and

◆  To communicate and memorialize rules, instructions and restrictions internally within the organization.

Sometimes, it can be possible and most effective to pursue more than one of these three objectives within the same document. But, usually it is best to create separate documents for each purpose and it is always important to determine and focus on your particular objective(s):

3.03  *Legal purposes.* If you are trying to satisfy a particular legal requirement, you should first carefully analyze the source, applicability and elements of the legal requirement. For example, California law requires that a company post a website privacy statement before the company collects any data online from consumers in California. The California law specifies how this statement has to be posted and which topics it has to address. Similarly, the U.S. Federal Trade Commission has encouraged companies to disclose in website privacy statements how the company processes consumer data. But, companies that sell to enterprise customers and do not deal with consumers online are not subject to the same requirements. If such companies decide to post website privacy statements anyhow, they should be cognizant of the fact that they are not legally required to do so and focus on their alternate purposes (*e.g.*, to satisfy market expectations).

Similarly, you should consult the legislative text whenever you are creating documentation to ensure you benefit from the advantages that are conditioned on such documentation. For example, a law may require you to seek affirmative consent from consumers residing in a particular country before you send marketing emails. If you are trying to satisfy such a law, you should re-read the legislative text to assess whether your emails at issue qualify as marketing emails, when and how you need to obtain and document the consent, what information you have to provide to the consumer and what you can or should do if the consumer denies or revokes consent. Then you can assess whether the burden and disadvantages of compliance (*e.g.*, seeking consent) might frustrate or outweigh the benefits of the planned activity (*e.g.*, email campaign). Sometimes the available benefits may not be worth the hassle.

Companies are not typically required under privacy laws to extend an express promise in a privacy policy to never share customer data. Some companies expect that more consumers will grant consent in consideration for voluntary promises. Other companies believe that most consumers do not read or appreciate privacy notices at all. If a company extends a promise not to share data, this can severely limit the value of their databases with respect to potential future business models as well as in merger and acquisition situations or bankruptcy.

With respect to the sources of notice and consent requirements, companies should not merely consider statutory law, but also contractual obligations that they may have assumed in dealing with business partners or the data subjects themselves.

*Business purposes.* When you are trying to address business needs, you  3.04
should clearly formulate (or ask other stakeholders in the company to formulate) the exact objectives, the expected negative consequences from satisfying versus not satisfying the demands, and how the company will benefit. Even if you do not have much time and resources to dig in deep, you should insist on a minimum rudimentary assessment of the perceived benefits and burdens. Too often, companies seem to copy language from competitors or perceived industry trendsetters without closely analyzing why other companies choose the particular language and without assessing the pros and cons of adopting templates for their own business. In lieu of thoughtful analysis, the term "best practices" tends to be (ab)used to justify following examples of other companies that may be in a completely different situation. For example, consumer businesses face different expectations depending on whether they offer free services or paid subscriptions. Also, consumers may not be particularly sensitive regarding the security of music files but may care deeply about their credit card information or family photos. Suppliers of business offerings experience varying levels of scrutiny depending on whether they target private start-up companies, large public enterprises or regulated industries. All companies tend to be affected to some degree by their competitors and any industry-wide practices. You have to gather some information about these parameters before you can effectively tailor documents to pursue a market-driven agenda.

You should be conscious of the minimum requirements you have or want to satisfy and whether going above and beyond is rewarded in any respect. Your company could be harmed if you include representations without a particular need or justification, for example, 'marketing fluff' about having extraordinary respect for consumer privacy or deploying state-of-the art security technologies. This is typically neither required by law nor readily substantiated, but easily challenged by plaintiffs.

3.05 *Organizational purposes.* If you are creating documentation to communicate instructions within the organization for operational reasons, carefully consider and define the addressees of your instructions. Many companies implement lengthy privacy and security policies, addressed to anyone and no one, covering a whole array of topics from management of employee files to installation of software updates. Individual employees are unlikely to read or remember such unwieldy documents. Employees can be better reached with short, pointed protocols addressed to particular departments or groups of employees, ideally presented in places and at times as close as possible to the moment when the employee should follow the particular instruction. Warnings regarding network security should pop up when system users connect private devices or access the network remotely. Reminders on locking away physical employee files are best presented on folders and file cabinets. When you create protocols, consider also which kinds of rules can realistically be expected to be followed. Companies that disseminate protocols that they ultimately do not follow can subject themselves to claims from employees and others who assert that they relied on the safeguards contemplated in the protocols. To reduce such risks, you can add disclaimers to protocols according to which the document should not be relied on, is not intended to create third party beneficiary rights or privacy expectations and contains only internal instructions. But, it is better to create only protocols that can and will be followed.

## Who is your audience?

3.06 After you answer the big 'why' question, you should identify your audience. With a particular audience in mind, you can pick appropriate language and style, assess which details have to be explained or are presumed to be known, and decide which points have to be highlighted.

3.07 For example, if you are addressing regulators or attorneys, you want to be precise and follow statutory terminology as much as possible. You should have the text of the particular statute or other source of law right in front of you when you draft your document, to identify the minimum requirements as to content, form and delivery. You can presume that your reader knows, or can access and understand, the law and you should focus on facts and circumstances relevant to your particular situation. On the other hand, if you are writing to consumers or employees outside the legal department, you may have to lead in with some basic explanations and use every day language to get your message across. In an enterprise business process outsourcing agreement, you may refer to "Customer" and "Supplier" as defined terms, but in website terms of use, you may prefer to write about "you" and "us."

If you are drafting documentation to meet marketing demands or communicate instructions to employees regarding data processing and privacy-related matters, you should tailor the content, form and delivery of your notice to the particular needs at hand. You should start with points that are particularly important and least likely to be already known to your particular audience, use terminology that the audience is familiar with and present your document at a place and time when it is most likely to have its intended effect. For example, if you want to induce prospective customers to choose your products or services because of superior data privacy or security features, you should tout such features in advertisements, product descriptions and other text that prospects read when they make their purchase decision. Privacy statements or services terms are less suited for advertising purposes. Most prospective and actual customers do not truly read privacy statements or terms of service. Plaintiff's counsel and regulators do, however, and they tend to use any promotional touting against the company. Also, if you want employees to follow company rules about personal phone calls and Internet use, you should consider pop-up screens on computers rather than burying notices in wordy policy statements, standard contract terms or thick employee handbooks. Those can perhaps be used to support disciplinary actions, but tend to do little to prevent offenses in the first place. So, think about where, when and how best to get your intended message across to your audience, and consider all options that old and new media offer, including real-time pop-up screens, video and audio prompts, interactive quizzes, etc. **3.08**

To serve the document's purpose efficiently, it can be helpful to clarify already in the title to whom the document is addressed. If you find a 'privacy policy' in your company that is not addressed to a particular audience, ask whether its purpose is to notify data subjects, **3.09** regulators or other audiences (and consider renaming the document 'Privacy Notice for All Employees' if that is the intended audience). If you cannot determine the purpose or audience from reading the document, chances are that you do not need it.

## Categories and examples of documentation

Most companies use the following categories of documentation:

3.10 • **Notices**, *i.e.*, documents in which companies disclose information about their data processing practices, for example in employee or patient privacy notices and website privacy statements; notices primarily serve legal purposes and their audiences are data subjects.

3.11 • **Consent forms**, *i.e.*, documents in which companies seek permission to process personal data in a certain manner, for example, to send marketing emails. Consent forms primarily serve legal purposes and their audiences are data subjects.

3.12 • **Agreements**, *i.e.*, documents with promises and permissions regarding data processing, for example, service agreements with data subjects or suppliers. Some agreements exclusively serve legal compliance purposes (*e.g.*, business associate agreements under HIPAA, data transfer agreements under European laws); others also serve business purposes (*e.g.*, protection of valuable data shared with service providers). The agreement's audience can be data subjects (*e.g.*, consumer agreements), business partners (*e.g.*, suppliers, customers) or employees (*e.g.*, data security undertaking, appointment of privacy officer).

3.13 • **Protocols**, *i.e.*, instructions on how to process and protect data. Protocols usually serve organizational needs and their audience are usually employees or contractors.

3.14 • **Data submission forms**, *i.e.*, documents in which companies allow or solicit the submission of information, for example, consumer feedback, surveys, job candidate questionnaires, registration pages, and web forms to specify communication preferences or launch complaints regarding infringements. Such forms can serve legal, marketing and organizational purposes and their audience varies accordingly.

- **Descriptions** of internal policies, data security measures, compli-   3.15
  ance self-assessments, security-by-design analyses, privacy impact
  assessments, and due diligence efforts. Descriptive forms can serve
  legal purposes (*e.g.*, satisfying record requirements under the EU
  General Data Protection Regulation or self-assessment documentation obligations under the EU-U.S. Privacy Shield Program), marketing purposes (*e.g.*, answering customer requests for information
  on security measures) and organizational purposes (*e.g.*, policy
  statements to memorialize decisions on approaches, internal audit
  reports) and their audience varies accordingly.

- **Government notifications** and other filings with data protection   3.16
  authorities serve legal purposes and their audiences are primarily
  government representatives, but may be posted on government-
  run websites.

*Other labels, e.g., policies.* Companies, legislatures and regulators use   3.17
different terminology for documentation. Specifically, you can find the
term "policy" used in reference to notices (*e.g.*, website privacy policy),
protocols (*e.g.*, describing a process on how to conduct investigations)
and policy statements (*e.g.*, memorializing an approach to compliance
the organization decided to take for various reasons). If you are not sure
what to call a particular document, consider whether a law, industry
practice or audience expectation favors one label over another. In the
absence of other compelling considerations, it is probably best to use
the term prescribed in a law you are trying to comply with. For example, California law requires a 'website privacy policy' and the EU-U.S.
Privacy Shield Program requires a "notice," each for purposes of informing data subjects what you do with their data. Whatever label you end
up using, you should make sure that titles or labels do not obscure
the purpose or audience for the document. Particularly with respect to
policies, it sometimes seems that drafters are confused about purpose
and audience. You find a mix of aspirational marketing fluff, internal
instructions and external notifications in documents labeled "policies."
This usually means that neither audience nor purpose are effectively
served. Companies are typically not required by law to maintain any
general company-wide data privacy policy. Yet, many organizations
create broad and abstract policy documents that contain statements
as to satisfaction of customer needs, compliance with 'all domestic and
international laws and industry standards,' implementation of 'state-
of-the-art' data security measures and practices regarding data collection, use, sharing and retention. Aside from not being legally required,

such documents are typically too lengthy and abstract to drive specific employee behavior or inform data subjects. But, such policy documents can be cited against the company by plaintiffs and regulators.

*Examples.* Every company has different needs for documentation. You may not need all of the documents in the following table, or you may need additional documents. But, if you are just getting started, it may be helpful to ask yourself whether your company has or needs some or all of the following documents.

| Category | Title | Addressees | Primary Purpose |
| --- | --- | --- | --- |
| Notices | Website Privacy Statement | Website visitors | Satisfying legal notice requirements |
| | Customer Privacy Notice | Consumer customers | Satisfying legal notice requirements |
| | Call Monitoring Warnings | Callers | Satisfying legal notice requirements |
| | Employee Privacy Notices regarding employee files, computer monitoring, whistleblower hotlines | Employees | Satisfying legal notice requirements (*e.g.*, in Europe) or negating privacy expectations (*e.g.*, U.S.) |
| | Candidate Privacy Notice | Job candidates | Expanding rights to process, retain resume data |
| | Data Security Breach Notification | Customers, employees, regulators | Satisfying legal notice requirements, damages mitigation |
| | EU-U.S. Privacy Shield Notice | Employees, others | Satisfying legal notice requirements |
| Consent forms | Direct Marketing | Customers, prospects | Allowing email marketing, newsletters |
| | Employee Consent | Employees | Satisfying legal requirements or expanding employer rights |
| Agreements | Confidentiality / Data Security Agreements | Individual independent contractors, employees | Keeping personal data secure; prohibiting violations by third parties; keeping proprietary rights to data; satisfying compliance obligations |

| Category | Title | Addressees | Primary Purpose |
|---|---|---|---|
| | Data transfer and processing agreements based on Standard Contractual Clauses, HIPAA, PCI | Data processors | Keeping personal data secure; compliance with restrictions on international data transfers from the EEA |
| | Appointment of Data Privacy officer | DPO | Satisfying legal requirements; defining term, role, rights, duties and limitations |
| Protocols | Computer Use Policy | All employees | Satisfying organizational requirements, *e.g.*, prohibit excessive personal use and enumerated abuses, guide on security, preclude/limit expectation of privacy |
| | Information Security Policy | IT department | Defining security measures, technologies, processes; meeting statutory obligations |
| | Data Access Policy | IT department and user groups, *e.g.*, HR department for HRIS, sales department for CRM | Defining technology requirements for access restrictions and process for assigning access privileges |
| | Data Retention Policy | IT department and user groups | Prohibiting document destruction during litigation hold; requiring minimum/maximum data retention |
| | Direct Marketing Policy | Sales and marketing department | Limiting promotional mailings as required by anti-spam or other electronic marketing laws or corporate policy |
| Data submission forms | Content Complaints | Third party rightsholders | Secure immunities available to website hosts who offer take-down processes |
| | Online Registration Form | Consumers, Employees | Data collection |

| Category | Title | Addressees | Primary Purpose |
|---|---|---|---|
| Descriptions | EU-U.S. Privacy Shield Self-Assessment Documentation | Regulators | Satisfying legal requirements under EU-U.S. Privacy Shield Principles |
| | Information Security Statement | Customers | Satisfying market demands, particularly on service providers |
| | Brief outline of compliance program; list and location of key documents and decision makers; summary on the scope of previous compliance assessments (*e.g.*, jurisdictions, vendors and services covered) | Colleagues and successors; auditors; third parties who conduct due diligence (*e.g.*, in M&A) | Efficient management of compliance program, transitions, audits, due diligence investigations |
| Government filings | Notification, Application for Authorization, etc. | Data protection authorities, other government entities | Satisfying legal requirements |

## Notices

3.18   When you start preparing or reviewing documentation for a data privacy compliance program, notices are typically a good starting point for a number of reasons:

- You will find notice requirements as a minimum standard in most privacy laws around the world. You need notices everywhere.

- If you do not issue notices as required, data subjects and regulators detect omissions and deficiencies relatively quickly and complain.

- Notice requirements tend to cover most data processing and business activities of a company, including human resources, sales and supply arrangements. Thus, when you prepare notices you get a full picture of what the company does and this is helpful as a basis for all other tasks.

- Notices are conditions and building blocks for other documents. For example, you need to issue a notice before you can obtain informed consent. In connection with some government filings, you have to attach the notices you have issued.

What exactly you have to disclose in a privacy notice depends on the particular legal requirement you are trying to satisfy. The following examples and summaries regarding typical legal requirements are not intended as a short cut or alternative to consulting the official source text of the applicable law or regulation. But, the following paragraphs are intended to help find, understand and navigate relevant legal requirements more easily and quickly.

*To whom do you have to issue notices?* Under European-style data pro-   3.19
tection laws, the EU-U.S. Privacy Shield Program, U.S.-style sectoral laws (*e.g.*, HIPAA, GLB), labor and employment laws and consumer protection laws, companies have to inform data subjects about how their personal data is processed. Most companies have to issue notices to three or four groups of individuals:

- Their own employees (*e.g.*, regarding intra-group data sharing in an HRIS or otherwise, computer monitoring, whistleblower hotlines, sharing with external service providers, etc.).

- Website visitors (*e.g.*, regarding online tracking).

- Individual representatives of corporate customers, resellers, suppliers and other business partners (most companies collect only business contact information in this context without notice and assume this is commonly known, but occasionally, sales staff may record information on entertainment preferences, educational history and private circumstances that can be more sensitive).

- Individual customers, if any, *e.g.*, regarding billing, order and other customer relationship data, as well as data that may be collected in the context of performing healthcare, telecommunication or other services.

*Who should issue notices – service provider or customer? Occasionally,*   3.20
companies also describe in their website privacy statements particulars of data processing services that they sell to corporate customers. For example, companies that offer enterprise cloud computing solutions or business software-as-a-service (*e.g.*, consumer support portals or employee benefits applications) may describe in their website privacy

statement not only how they collect data from website visitors, but also how their service works, is secured, etc. This is usually not required and often not appropriate. With respect to the cloud computing or software-as-a-service solution, the provider is a mere data processing agent (*a.k.a.* data processor) of its customer (*a.k.a.* data controller). It is up to the customer to notify the individual data subjects (*e.g.*, the customer's employees or customers). If a service provider nevertheless addresses notices directly to the customer's employees, customers or other data subjects, the provider accrues no benefits and can suffer a number of adverse consequences, including that the service provider may:

•   create the impression that the provider is responsible as data controller (*e.g.*, for data access and correction purposes – which the provider cannot possibly live up to without violating its customer contracts)

•   expose itself to direct liability vis-à-vis data subjects

•   contradict the customer's own notices (which could result in confusion and corresponding liability)

•   lock itself into particular limitations, which can prevent the provider from accommodating customer requests regarding customization.

Data controllers should not leave it to their service providers (data processors) to issue notices. The data controller should be the one to issue appropriate notices and include information about data processing activities performed by vendors. Vendors can help prepare such notices, but the customer and data controller need to ensure via contracts and audits that vendor activities comply with the customer's representations in privacy notices. In general, companies should be careful to inform data subjects in privacy notices about all data processing activities that the company controls (whether conducted internally or by vendors).

3.21   *Which topics do you typically have to address in privacy notices?* In notices to data subjects, you typically have to address the following points:

3.22   *Who is issuing the notice?* Generally, you are required to spell out the correct entity name. Under some laws, you are also required to provide a physical address. Even where such information is not strictly required by law, you should consider providing sufficient information to identify a particular legal entity within a multinational group of companies rather than vaguely referring to a brand name. It is rarely in a company's best interest to subject several or all group entities to the restrictions described in one particular notice. Laws and data subject expectations vary from country to country. Companies that use one notice for all legal entities will have to satisfy consent or notice requirements for all markets in case of changes (as opposed to having to change only one country- and entity-specific notice when a change occurs in the particular jurisdiction or market). Often, notices have to be translated into local language to be effective. For tax reasons, one entity may not be authorized to legally represent the others and extend promises on the other entities' behalf. Under some data protection laws, the various entities may not be allowed to freely share the data amongst each other. Some relevant disclosures apply only to one entity in the group (*e.g.*, only U.S. companies can participate in the EU-U.S. Privacy Shield Program). However, multiple privacy notices must be carefully tracked internally, including how they are presented (*e.g.*, paper, email, exact URL address), when they were last updated and what changes were made.

*What is the scope of the notice and who is the notice addressed to?* In 3.23 order to inform the data subjects concerned, and only them, you have to clarify what types of activities you cover in your notice. If you are vague about scope and addressees in your website privacy statement, for example, your employees and others may be able to invoke your promises in scenarios that are unrelated to your online presence. If you do not expressly limit representations in notices required under the EU-U.S. Privacy Shield Program to data subjects in Europe, then customers and employees in the United States and Asia may be able to sue based on misrepresentation and unfair competition laws.

*What categories of data do you collect?* Generally, you are required to 3.24 provide a comprehensive list with sufficient detail. You should strive to provide particularly high levels of detail where you collect data without active participation or perception by the data subject, *e.g.*, via Internet cookies, online tracking, covert video surveillance, phone call recording, RFID tags and various forms of technical employee and user monitoring. You can provide less detail with respect to information that data subjects actively submit themselves to (*e.g.*, list a few high-level categories and just remind the data subjects that they will know what they submit because they will be actively typing the data into a form). Obviously, you cannot provide any specifics with respect to data that data subjects choose to submit on their own initiative (*e.g.*, in free text fields, via email, on social networking pages or in storage solutions).

3.25 *For what purposes do you collect data and what do you do with it?* If you only use data as necessary to perform under a contract with the data subject or comply with applicable law, you could just write that. But, you need to provide additional information if you want to use data for marketing purposes, to improve or develop services and offerings, to monitor the conduct of data subjects (*e.g.*, to detect and sanction violations of company rules by employees and service users), etc. If purposes vary with respect to particular data categories, you could explain your agenda in real time where you collect data, *e.g.*, on a website questionnaire with a link 'Why we collect this information' next to each data field. Abstract and vague references to "legitimate business purposes" or "as required or permitted by law" are not suited to inform data subjects and do not typically belong in legally required notices, except, perhaps, where regulators themselves use, propose or accept such generalities. Understandably, companies are concerned that they may not be able to anticipate all future needs or opportunities relating to data that they collect over the years. Therefore, you may feel an urge to qualify statements and hedge your bets. But, catch-all clauses or open-ended language intended to reserve future flexibility will typically not suffice or help satisfy notice requirements with respect to the purposes of the future. They tend to signal that you are either not adequately disclosing current purposes now or that you may be planning to add purposes in the future without giving detailed notices at that time.

3.26 *Who do you share data with?* If your company wants to share data with other data controllers that will use such data for their own marketing or other purposes, you may need to obtain consent from the data subjects. In order to render such consent informed, you need to provide details about the identity of the data recipients as well as data processing practices and purposes. Vague references to "trusted business partners" or weblinks to broad policy statements by ad networks may be sufficient under the laws of some jurisdictions in the sense that they signal to the data subject that the notice issuer shares personal data relatively broadly. But, such vague references would not satisfy information requirements under European laws. Also, data sharing within a group of affiliated companies is not typically privileged under applicable laws. In other words, you also have to provide detailed information about the identities and practices of your affiliates. It may be easier from a practical perspective to satisfy information requirements with respect to affiliates, because you may be able to state that they follow similar rules as set forth in the particular notice. If your company shares data with service providers, it should disclose this fact and consider naming key (categories of) service providers if this is relevant to the data subjects (*e.g.*, because the data subjects will directly interact with the service providers). Often it will not affect the data subjects much how a company organizes itself and whether it uses statutory employees, individual independent contractors or individual representatives of corporate contractors to process data. Individuals in each of these categories can be more or less reliable, competent and careful. Therefore, companies do not typically have to provide much detailed information on the involvement of service providers in data processing. Similarly, it is not particularly helpful to let data subjects know in notices that the company will disclose their data 'as required by law.' It goes without saying that companies have to comply with laws and privacy notices are not the place to teach what legal requirements exist. If and when a company makes a disclosure to law enforcement, it should assess whether an individual notice about the particular disclosure is allowed and required. But, a general acknowledgement about the possibility of compelled disclosures in a privacy notice does not help inform data subjects. Companies should, however, inform data subjects in notices if companies routinely or proactively share personal data with domestic or foreign law enforcement officials without being compelled to do so or if they will only share data with governments when they are compelled to do so; this can affect data subjects significantly and the basic principles of the company's practices in this respect should be disclosed.

In some jurisdictions, additional details may have to be disclosed, including the following:

*Where is data located?* European data protection authorities tend to take the position that companies are required to disclose whether data is transferred outside the EEA. European data protection statutes do not usually prescribe such a requirement expressly but merely state that data subjects have to be informed about all relevant details regarding the processing of their data. Companies should form their own opinion on whether it is particularly relevant for data subjects to know where their data is stored and transferred, within or outside the    3.27

EEA. For example, Internet users can be expected to know that data transmitted over the Internet can pass through any country worldwide due to the Internet's architecture. Also, if consumers access websites hosted by U.S. companies at a .com URL, it would not seem necessary for the U.S. company to expressly disclose that it will process data in the United States. On the other hand, if a German hospital collects sensitive health information offline from German patients, it may find it appropriate to disclose to the patients if the hospital uses data processing service providers and equipment in other countries, whether within or outside the EEA.

3.28 *How long is data stored?* In some cases, data subjects are reasonably concerned about data retention times, because the date on which certain data on them will be deleted can be very relevant. For example, a job applicant may be able to re-apply to a prospective employer after the employer deletes records about the prior application or after information on public criminal or driving records is purged. Also, online services users can only access and use data – or have data used against them – until the service provider deletes such data, for example, back-up copies of deleted emails or SMS messages, blog postings, location data, etc. Thus, data retention times can be relevant enough that companies have to disclose them. Yet, few companies currently disclose more than relatively vague references to "as long as needed for legitimate business purposes" or "... as permitted by applicable law." Such statements do not provide much useful information but are quite common, probably because few companies have been able so far to implement robust record retention and deletion programs. If companies provide more detailed information about storage and deletion times, they need to carefully word their statements to avoid misleading statements regarding system architectures that de-identify, disconnect or block rather than actually delete data.

3.29 *How can data subjects access, correct or delete data concerning them?* European and some other data privacy laws require data controllers to allow and enable data subjects to access data concerning them and to request correction and deletion. Companies are typically free to determine implementation details, *e.g.*, how they allow, invite or channel such requests. Most jurisdictions allow companies to charge reasonable fees , although the EU General Data Protection Regulation does not generally allow any charges. Only a few jurisdictions expressly require companies to notify data subjects regarding their statutory rights. If you want to minimize the number of data access requests, you could decide to expressly address this topic only for those jurisdictions where your company is legally required to notify data subjects regarding their rights. But, if you do not offer specific communication channels, rules and contact information for such requests, you may receive unstructured demands that are difficult to process and actually increase the administrative burden on your organization. Therefore, many companies specifically address data access requests in privacy notices even where they are not legally required to. They commonly mention the possibility of charges and prescribe online or offline forms and ask sufficient information from data subjects to allow an efficient processing of the request.

Under the EU General Data Protection Regulation, companies must 3.30 address various other details in privacy notices, including the identity a foreign data controller's representative in the EEA; contact details of the data protection officer; the legal basis for the data processing (which could be interpreted to require cross-references of sections and subsections of statutes); a description of the legitimate interests claimed to justify data processing; any intent to transfer personal data outside the EEA and information on the existence or absence of an adequacy decision by the EU Commission regarding each of the destination countries; information on safeguards taken for international data transfers and the means by which to obtain a copy of them or where they have been made available; information on the right to data erasure, data correction, data portability, withdrawal of consent at any time, file complaints with a data protection authority; whether the provision of personal data is a statutory or contractual requirement, or a requirement necessary to enter into a contract, as well as whether the data subject is obliged to provide the personal data and of the possible consequences of failing to provide such data; and information about the existence of automated decision-making, including profiling and "meaningful information about the logic involved, as well as the significance and the envisaged consequences of such processing for the data subject." At the same time, companies are required under the EU General Data Protection Regulation to issue privacy notices in "concise, transparent, intelligible and easily accessible form, using clear and plain language." Companies cannot realistically meet the requirements regarding easily intelligibility if they also address all mandatory details listed in the EU General Data Protection Regulation (except perhaps in privacy notices specifically addressed to data protection officers or privacy law professors). In practice, many companies will likely err on the side of being over-inclusive at the expense of easily intelligibility, because in an audit or enforcement case, it will be difficult to defend against charges that they failed to address a certain mandatory information topic. If, on the other hand, an authority or individual in the EEA complains that a privacy notice is too long, unwieldy and unintelligible, the company can defend itself by pointing out that it was required to address all the topics listed in the EU General Data Protection Regulation. Under the Regulation, companies have to provide information on highly technical details such as "the existence or absence of an adequacy decision by the Commission" with respect to each jurisdiction to which personal data is transferred, a topic that will easily take up a page or two in a printed privacy notice.

3.31    Data subjects outside the EEA will find many of the details and explanations required by the EU Data Protection Regulation irrelevant or of little interest. If companies include such information in global notices, they may run afoul of any plain language requirements. Therefore, companies should consider issuing separate privacy notices to data subjects in the EEA on global web or mobile sites, *e.g.*, hyperlinked within or at the end of a truly intelligible privacy notice addressed to all data subjects worldwide. Data subjects can also be presented with country-specific information within a layered privacy notice that begins with a concise and easy-to-understand set of important disclosures and offers additional information on particular topics or for different jurisdictions under inlinks that one can click on to review at one's discretion.

3.32    Multinational businesses dread the proliferation of country-specific privacy notices, which require additional resources and discipline to ensure that an ever-increasing number of privacy notices remains accurate and up-to-date. It is worth noting, however, that diverging notice and form requirements only require different notices, not actually different data processing practices. Most companies can operate relatively uniform data processing practices on a global basis independent of how they have to describe such processes in jurisdiction-specific privacy notices.

3.33    Frequently, companies include information in privacy notices that is not required and should normally not be included, for example:

• *Marketing fluff and declarations of good intentions,* such as "We take privacy seriously," "Your privacy is important to us" or "We deploy state-of-the-art data security measures." Such statements do not provide the data subject with meaningful information and merely provide additional ammunition to plaintiff's attorneys and regulators that believe the company did not in fact sufficiently respect privacy interests or comply with laws.

• *Restatements of legal obligations*, such as elaborate acknowledgements that privacy laws apply and what they prescribe. Companies are required only in a few jurisdictions to educate their customers about what laws and regulations apply, and then usually only about consumer rights (*e.g.*, right to request erasure, correction, data portability and information on how to file complaints). Where such notices are not legally required, the inclusion of statutory text into privacy notices increases their length and makes it difficult for the data subject to capture the relevant disclosures that apply to the particular situation.

*Form and delivery requirements:* Many laws state that companies have    3.34
to deliver notices in writing. This can mean on paper but usually also via email or on a website if the data subject can easily download and save the notice. Exemptions from written form requirements tend to apply for situations where companies cannot practically deliver notices, for example, in connection with call recording for call center quality control. Companies are not typically required to obtain affirmative acknowledgements of receipt from the data subjects. But, some companies obtain acknowledgements nonetheless, to retain evidence in case a data subject or regulator asserts in a dispute that notice has not been given. This practice should also be considered in situations where companies are not strictly required to, but gain benefits by providing notice, for example in the United States, where companies can negate 'reasonable expectations of privacy' by, issuing notices to employees or consumers. Alternatively, companies may be able to structure data collection processes in a manner that allows them to prove that the data subject must have received notice because all data subjects are prompted with notices, *e.g.*, during an online registration process, before calls are recorded or at reception desks where visitors or employees have to sign in before they enter premises that are subject to video surveillance.

## Consent

3.35 Some laws prescribe absolutely that companies have to obtain consent from data subjects before they engage in certain types of data processing activities. For example, under U.S. federal law (namely the HIPAA privacy rule), hospitals have to obtain certain qualified authorizations from patients if they want to use personal health information outside the scope of statutory permissions. Under European data protection laws, companies have to seek prior consent before they send promotional emails or place cookies on consumers' computers, unless certain exceptions apply. Colombia and Russia also postulate general consent requirements with few exceptions. In situations where such absolute laws apply, companies have only two options: obtain consent or refrain from the restricted data processing activity.

A few laws are even more restrictive and prohibit certain forms of data processing regardless of whether the data subject consents. For example, under a 1991 law in California (the Song-Beverly Credit Card Act), retailers may not store personal data of credit card holders unless certain narrow exceptions apply – regardless of whether the credit card holder consents or not. Where such laws apply, companies must refrain from the restricted data processing activity and consent is not even an option.

But, besides situations where consent is absolutely required or absolutely insufficient, companies frequently find they have to decide whether they could and should obtain consent. For example, under European laws, companies have the option to obtain consent from data subjects to overcome the general prohibition of automated data processing. As an alternative to seeking consent, companies can also conclude contracts with data subjects that require the processing or determine whether they can rely on a "legitimate interest exception." In practice, it can be unclear whether such alternative justifications are truly applicable. The balancing of interests involves a fair amount of discretion and one can also argue whether certain processing arrangements are truly 'necessary' under a contract. Therefore, companies often consider whether they should perhaps seek consent 'just in case.' Also, under the laws of many countries that have not (yet) enacted specific data privacy or data protection laws, local attorneys often recommend seeking consent from data subjects to protect against the risk of challenges mounted on general tort statutes or vague constitutional principles.

Before you decide to seek consent 'just in case,' you should answer the following questions:

- Do any laws restrict the validity, effect or scope of consent, or establish burdensome formal or substantive conditions? If you are dealing with children, for example, you must seek parental consent separately. 3.36

- How easy is it to obtain and keep track of consent? In the context of online registrations and purchases, for example, companies and adult consumers have to expend a relatively low amount of effort on click-through consent. If consent can only be obtained on paper, the process becomes more burdensome. If it is too difficult to obtain valid consent, you may be better off not asking, unless you absolutely and clearly need consent. 3.37

- Are any government authorities, works councils or other institutions opposed to your seeking consent? For example, data protection authorities and collective employee representatives in Europe tend to be skeptical of employers that seek employee consent to data processing because they suspect that employees are coerced. This is a legitimate concern in situations where the employer needs all employees to consent in order for a project to be successful (*e.g.*, deployment of network security tools, implementation of global human resources information systems or outsourcing of payroll administration). But, in situations where employers can truly customize systems or optional benefits to employees' choice, it would seem perfectly legitimate for employers to seek employee consent, (*e.g.*, in the context of stock option grants by U.S. parent companies to their European subsidiaries' employees where the employees can simply reject the optional benefit and avoid data transfers). Nevertheless, some European data protection authorities presume employee consent to be invalid and companies need to take other compliance approaches to avoid confrontation with the authorities. 3.38

- Is there a risk of disrupting an existing business relationship by seeking consent? Often, if you ask something of an employee or business partner, they expect something in return. If you are offering a benefit and your request for consent is legitimately related to such benefit, you will usually be able to secure consent easily (*e.g.*, if you offer additional travel insurance to employees that requires data sharing with an insurance company). But, obtaining consent 3.39

may be more difficult when you are seeking consent to a data processing activity that does not benefit the data subject and perhaps even affects the data subject adversely (*e.g.*, computer monitoring or certain forms of direct marketing). Thus, consider what you can offer to induce data subjects to grant consent voluntarily.

3.40 • What can and will you do if data subjects deny their consent? If you have to proceed with the data processing proposal anyhow, then seeking consent may not be an appropriate option, unless you are able and content to do business only with consenting data subjects.

3.41 • What can and will you do if data subjects grant their consent and later revoke it? If this is not an acceptable option, you may have to look for compliance approaches that do not require you to obtain consent in the first place. Under most European data protection laws, data subjects remain free to revoke consent. It is often questionable whether companies can protect themselves by contractually holding data subjects responsible to pay for any business disruption, losses and costs resulting from consent revocation.

3.42 • Are you prepared to go back to the data subjects and seek consent to changes when you need to expand or modify the processing or use of the data? If you seek consent in situations where you do not have to, you are creating actual expectations and perhaps even contractual entitlements to come back and ask for consent before you make any changes.

• Are you invoking additional legal regimes, scrutiny and jurisdiction by seeking agreement? German consumer protection watchdogs take action against unfair contract terms under German national law, including privacy statements that are referenced in consent declarations.

## How to obtain valid consent

3.43 If a company decides to obtain consent from a data subject, it has to determine the legal requirements that it needs to satisfy with respect to such consent. For example, under European data protection laws, consent is valid only if it constitutes a "freely given, specific and informed indication of his wishes by which the data subject signifies his agreement to personal data relating to him being processed." If 'special categories of personal data' (*i.e.* 'sensitive personal data') are concerned, the consent must also be "explicit." If international transfers outside the EEA are contemplated, consent must additionally be "unambiguous"; consent relating to cookies is valid only if declared after the company provides "clear and comprehensive information ... about the purposes of the processing."

When you determine the applicable requirements, look for the following attributes in the applicable statute or contracts:

- *Prior*: consent laws usually imply that companies have to obtain consent before they do whatever it is that requires consent, but some laws expressly call out that 'prior consent' is needed;    3.44

- *Informed*: typically, the data subject has to receive sufficient information to allow an informed decision; similar considerations as with respect to notices apply;    3.45

- *In writing*: some laws require handwritten or qualified digital signatures or even witnesses and notarization; in the absence of specific form requirements, however, consent can be obtained verbally or electronically – the latter usually being preferable for evidentiary reasons;    3.46

- *Voluntary*: some laws specifically state that consent is valid only if the data subject agrees voluntarily; even where voluntariness is not specifically called out as a condition in the applicable law, most laws would not recognize coerced declarations as valid; a key question, then is what negative consequences will the data subject suffer if she denies or revokes consent and whether the resulting pressure renders the consent invalid; for example, patients in a hospital or employees during their probationary period tend to be under more significant pressures than online gaming fans; to mitigate against the risk that consent is found involuntary (and hence invalid), companies should clearly inform the data subject of the consequences of denying or revoking consent, and make a judgment call as to whether such consequences are unnecessary harsh and could be mitigated (*e.g.*, by offering alternative business models, services or prices for non-consenting data subjects);    3.47

- *Express, explicit, affirmative, unambiguous and similar attributes*: these criteria establish requirements relating to the actions required of the data subject when consent is obtained. For    3.48

example, a data subject might be deemed to consent impliedly by proceeding with a registration without unchecking pre-checked boxes or by failing to respond to a prompt. Yet, such inaction will not usually satisfy requirements that consent be express, explicit, affirmative, or unambiguous. To satisfy such extra requirements, companies may have to require data subjects to sign a declaration, click on a button, check an uncheck box, or otherwise take more active steps towards declaring consent;

3.49 • *Specific and similar attributes*: these requirements can relate to the scope of the consent (which can be limited to particularly identified data controllers, subjects, categories and processing purposes, or be broad and unspecific) or the focus of the document with which a company obtains consent (which can be limited to data processing or also cover various contract terms, program benefits, technology features, use recommendations, etc.);

3.50 • *Separate or distinguishable*: some laws (including HIPAA and the FCRA in the United States) require that companies obtain consent on separate documents, not combined in other declarations; according to the EU Data Protection Regulation, companies must present requests for consent in a clearly distinguishable, intelligible and easily accessible form, using clear and plain language.

## Opt-in, out and in between

3.51 Consumers, employees and most other data subjects rarely formulate or otherwise shape the scope or terms of consent themselves. Usually, companies and governments prepare standard consent declarations and prompt data subjects to declare consent in a prescribed form and process to allow uniform data processing practices and easy confirmation of whether consent has been granted. If you do not obtain consent through preformulated forms, but rather via telephone calls or in-person conversations, you will inevitably face challenges regarding the interpretation and documentation of consent.

3.52 *Examples of consent mechanisms.* Before you settle for a particular approach, you should consider applicable legal requirements and the many different practical ways in which data subjects can declare consent, including the following options arranged roughly in descending order of explicitness:

(a) By signing their name on a paper form specifically relating to data processing;

(b) By checking two unchecked boxes on an online form specifically relating to data processing, one where the data subjects declare that they have understood the scope of the consent, and another one where the data subjects declare that they wish to consent (*a.k.a.* the 'French double-click process');

(c) By responding to an email that is automatically sent after an online registration and consent process to expressly confirm that the data subjects have read and understood the request and want to consent (*a.k.a.* the 'German double opt-in process');

(d) By checking an unchecked box on an online form specifically relating to data processing;

(e) By saying 'yes' after being asked about call monitoring or recording during a phone conversation;

(f) By signing their name or checking an unchecked box to agree to a set of contract terms that include a pre-formulated consent declaration (for example, in an online banking services agreement, car rental agreement, terms of use regarding a charge-free website, etc.); implementations vary in many ways, such as:

  (i) The consent declaration regarding data privacy can be presented with a separate heading in CAPS and bold print within a larger document, at the top or end of the larger document, or it can be included somewhere in the middle without any special formatting that would catch the data subject's eyes;

  (ii) The document containing the consent declaration can be presented

    1. In a separate window that website visitors have to scroll through before they can proceed;

    2. On the same page – beneath or above an 'agree' or 'consent' button;

3.  On a separate web page, which the data subject can access by clicking on a hyperlink that is placed above or beneath a consent button; or

4.  On a separate web page that is linked on the bottom of the page via a general text link 'data privacy' or just 'legal,' unrelated to the website portions with which visitors interact to declare consent;

(g) By proceeding with an online registration or other process without unchecking a pre-checked box presented on a web page;

(h) By proceeding with an online registration or other process after having received a notice (*e.g.*, a link to a privacy statement) according to which the data subject can opt out of certain data processing activities *such as* sharing or email marketing (*e.g.*, by re-configuring 'communication preference' settings in an online account or sending an unsubscribe request);

(i) By proceeding with a phone call after receiving notice from an individual caller, call center representative, or in a pre-recorded statement that it is possible to request that the call not be 'recorded or monitored for quality control or training', without making such request; or

(j) By not taking any action after receiving a notice that the data subject is able to opt out of certain data processing activities (*e.g.*, marketing emails).

3.53 An important additional alternative applicable to all previous scenarios is whether a company prompts the data subject with a consent request before entering into a relationship (*e.g.*, in the context of enrollment in a new online service or as a condition to accepting online job applications) or after concluding a contract (*e.g.*, a prompt for consent declaration pops up during the installation of software that the data subjects previously purchased in a store).

3.54 *Minimum requirements.* In all of these scenarios, the data subject arguably declares consent. Thus, any of these deployment alternatives may be sufficient if a law simply requires consent without specifying any additional attributes.

*Selecting implementation options.* For data collection and processing   3.55
activities that most data subjects would not expect or that could affect
them adversely, companies should consider implementing more conspicuous consent mechanisms (*i.e.,* those higher on the above list).
Even if this is not strictly required, there is a higher risk of challenges.
Conversely, companies should limit themselves to less conspicuous
mechanisms for data processing activities that have little impact on
data subjects or that are generally expected (*e.g.,* website cookie placement to support site functionality). An indiscriminate use of 'middle of
the road' consent mechanisms for all types of data processing activities
would inevitably lead to consumer dissatisfaction and an adverse business impact, or the "numbing" of consumers, who will stop reading
privacy notices and indiscriminately click 'accept' on consent prompts
if most prompts are irrelevant (which in turn would undermine the
validity of consent that is actually required).

*Silence as consent.* Many legal systems generally follow the principle   3.56
that silence and inactivity do not typically imply consent. Therefore,
scenario (j) above will often not be sufficient to constitute consent.
Particularly, silence or inaction is not likely to be considered consent
in a scenario where the data subject has already agreed to certain terms
and a subsequent notice constitutes a change to those terms, unilater-
ally presented by the data controller. In such a scenario, silence could
only be considered consent if the company originally expressly and
validly reserved the right to communicate unilateral changes to data
processing practices by way of such a notice. Many companies reserve
the right to change data processing practices in their terms of use, particularly relating to charge-free services, but in some countries, a broad
reservation of rights can be invalid under consumer protection laws.

*Affirmative, express consent.* Many regulators, commentators and   3.57
attorneys claim without much discussion that companies have to present unchecked boxes to obtain valid consent if the applicable legislation requires 'affirmative' or 'express' consent. But, this issue has not
really been decided in courts much and you should carefully consider
the literal wording of the applicable statute and the pros and cons
of all available implementation options before you accept such guidance. In everyday language, the terms 'affirm' and 'consent' can be used
synonymously and both mean 'agree,' 'answer positively,' or 'say yes.'
When the term 'affirmative' is used in combination with 'consent,' the
term 'affirmative' must mean something more than just 'consent' and
requires a positive action on the data subject's part directed towards

the declaration of consent. Similarly, the attribute 'express' means that the data subject positively and intentionally acts to communicate consent as opposed to taking actions that could be interpreted to just imply consent. In all scenarios other than (j), the data subject is taking a positive action and expresses consent. Thus, arguably, the data subject consents affirmatively and expressly in scenarios (a) through (i) so long as the data subject is confronted with the request for consent in a sufficiently conspicuous manner and the fact that the consumer proceeds with a registration or purchase can constitute an answer also to the consent request.

3.58   Regulators and courts may take issue with the fact that in scenarios (f) through (i) the data subject expresses consent regarding data processing and other aspects of a transaction or relationship at the same time. Technically, however, consenting to several combined points with one single action does not render the consent less 'express' or 'affirmative.' If a data subject is presented with a large, conspicuous warning page during a registration process with language such as 'do you really want to consent to our processing of your personal data – think twice and click "next page" only if you are really sure,' the data subject's declaration of consent would appear to be more 'express' and 'affirmative' than in an implementation where the data subject is prompted to check a box with barely readable small print next to it. Nevertheless, if you select one of scenarios (a) through (e) and you require a separate, targeted consent declaration from the data subject specifically relating to the processing of data, you avoid the risk that regulators or courts might insist on such a separate declaration where statutes require 'affirmative' and 'express' consent.

## Above and beyond opt-in consent

3.59   Above and beyond obtaining affirmative, opt-in consent, companies can take additional steps to verify and confirm that the data subject really understands the situation and really wants to grant consent. Companies are not typically required to go the extra mile and verify that the data subject really meant it when he or she granted affirmative opt-in consent in the first place. Also, approaching the data subject with additional requests to confirm consent over and over again can confuse and irritate. Yet, in some scenarios, companies find it in their best interest to go above and beyond, particularly in the context of novel and complex technologies and services with features or aspects that are not expected by lay persons and that could easily be misunderstood. If such misunderstandings result in harm, you can expect regulatory scrutiny or litigation. For example, highly publicized scandals in using new social media platforms might have been preventable if the platform operator had presented the data subjects with real time notices (*e.g.*, 'Do you really mean to send this photo to all your followers or only to the sender of the message you are responding to?'). Likewise, a "flashlight" app for smart phones was challenged with regard to collection of location data that seemed unnecessary and surprising to consumers given the purpose and functionality of the app. The newer and more complex an application is, the less likely it is that users read and understand all implications for their data privacy, even if the company provides detailed disclosures upfront and requires affirmative opt-in consent.

If the company additionally provides brief, pointed 'just in time' follow-up notices as the data subject uses particular features of the application, the user is much more likely to grasp the situation and make an informed decision whether to continue using the application or to quit. Similar to how Microsoft, for example, embeds an "office assistant" feature in new versions of its software that reminds users of certain options and implications, online service providers can build in notices and reminders into their process flows. To avoid annoying users, each notice or consent prompt could contain an option to unsubscribe from future warnings. Another approach is to require or reward users who are willing to go through a brief quiz or summary tutorial on privacy features to improve and confirm their understanding of the data processing they are consenting to. For example, the social gaming company Zynga offers a game ('Privacyville') to educate users and offers users free credits for completing a quiz on the privacy features of the platform. Another option to reach users who do not read detailed notices is an audio and/or video tutorial. If transmission quality can be assured, then this could also be effective in the mobile space where small screen sizes often undermine the effectiveness of written notices because users cannot reasonably be expected to read longer texts on a small mobile screen.

In the context of platforms, *e.g.*, mobile apps for smartphones and tablets, it is additionally very helpful if platform operators create standardized permission categories that consumers can understand and relate to more quickly because they apply across the board for all apps and can be viewed not only in the individual app's privacy notice, but 3.60

also in the device's system settings. After pressure from the California government, major platform providers agreed to standardize permission settings and set a good example of privacy by design.

## Other considerations for consent drafting

3.61 *Incorporation of notices into consent declarations.* Notice and consent forms often look fairly similar because before companies can obtain informed consent from a data subject, they have to provide sufficient notice regarding the details of the proposed data processing. Therefore, when you prepare a consent form, you usually also have to prepare a notice form – or incorporate an existing notice form by way of reference. Often companies link to their website privacy statements to supply the 'boilerplate' elements of privacy notices. But, this is not always appropriate. The circumstances and rules for website visitors and other data subjects often differ. Companies should therefore first verify that anything in the notice they want to incorporate by reference actually applies to the situation at hand. If only some elements of the referenced privacy notice apply to the particular data processing activity and requested consent, then these elements should be highlighted in the text that incorporates the broader privacy notice. If you include or reference too many superfluous or inapplicable details into a notice, you can expect courts and regulators to question whether the notice is effective and creates a sufficient basis for valid consent.

3.62 *Expressing focused consent.* When you draft consent declarations, you have to determine whether you must or want to obtain specific and express consent for a particular activity or more general consent to all your data processing practices. If you want to obtain specific and express consent, be sure to cover the key aspects of what you plan to do with the data.

For example, if you want to obtain consent from consumers to send them marketing emails, you could present an unchecked box on a website or paper form with the words:

[ ]Yes, please email me news about your products and services, in accordance with your Website Privacy Statement [hyperlink to the statement].

3.63 If you merely obtain consent to the general website privacy statement where, in turn some disclosures regarding general marketing practices are buried, you may not be able to meet the requirements of 'express' or 'specific' consent. Also, by soliciting agreement to privacy practices, companies may invoke additional legal requirements, remedies and jurisdiction, for example, of German consumer protection watchdogs, which enforce national law on unfair contract terms even where they would otherwise have to respect another EEA member state's data protection law. Nevertheless, more general consent declarations may be appropriate in some jurisdictions where you are required to obtain consent but not necessarily 'express' or 'specific, consent'. Your implementation could then look like the following:

[ ]Yes, I have read, understood and agreed with your Website Privacy Statement. [hyperlink to the statement]

*Placement of consent mechanism and declaration.* In any event, any 3.64 pre-formulated consent declaration should appear close to the check box, 'click accept' button or signature line, so that it is clear that the consumer's mouse click or signature infers the consumer's agreement. This is usually not the case if the consent declaration language appears under an "accept" – or "submit"– button. But, it is usually sufficient if you place the consent declaration just above or right next to a check box or signature line.

*Who should obtain consent – data controller or processor?* Only the 3.65 data controller must – and usually can – obtain consent because only the data controller has a direct relationship with the data subjects and, therefore, opportunities to request consent. Usually, the processor is not required to obtain consent because data protection laws tend to impose this obligation on the data controllers. Even where vendors are technically liable (*e.g.*, because they process data that should not have been collected in the first place), the data controller tends to be more at fault and an easier target for legal actions. Nonetheless, the service provider has a vested interest that privacy laws are complied with. If violations occur, result in legal action or are publicized, the service provider has to deal with unhappy customers and revenue impact if the incident gives its technology, service or business practices a bad reputation. Therefore, it is not uncommon that specialized service providers (who are more familiar with consent requirements than their customers, the data controllers) develop and share appropriate notices and consent forms. For example, a high tech company providing web analytics or behavioral tracking services to a low tech company for its home page may raise the consent requirement as an issue and present consent form templates to its customer. Some service providers even contractually require the data controller to obtain consent. Other service providers do not like to raise such issues and rather defer to the data controllers, or assist with consent language only upon request from their customers or if their customers try to contractually shift responsibility for data privacy law compliance onto the service provider.

## Agreements

3.66 *Agreements with data subjects vs. consent from data subjects.* Agreements involve consent from two parties. Where a company obtains consent from a data subject outside the scope of an agreement, the declaration of assent goes one way – from the data subject to the data controller. In agreements, parties exchange promises. Thus, one conceptual difference between seeking consent and concluding agreements is that agreements bind both sides. A consequence of going the contract route is that the company not only has to consider data protection or privacy laws, but also contract law, including consumer protection laws relating to contracts. From a practical perspective, companies tend to focus consent forms on data processing only whereas agreements often address additional topics and usually contain various terms to define aspects of the contractual relationship, such as duration, termination, notices, choice of law and forum, etc. Companies occasionally form or modify contracts with data subjects as an alternative to obtaining consent from data subjects.

3.67 *Asking for an express acceptance of website privacy statements or general privacy notices.* When companies deliver notices or seek consent specifically relating to data processing, they often prompt the data subject to also accept the company's website privacy statement or other general notices regarding data processing practices. This approach is common but it brings a number of disadvantages, but few advantages to the company:

- By asking for acceptance, the company implicitly concedes that it needs consent from the data subject; this expands the company's obligations (because the company is then responsible to ensure that consent is and remains valid) and narrows the company's options going forward (the company then has to seek consent for any future changes to its privacy practices or statements and cannot simply proceed with changes after posting a revised privacy statement).

- It is possible that the data subject does not declare acceptance, or, the company cannot prove later that the data subject accepted (*e.g.*, because acceptance is not documented in a manner that satisfies evidentiary requirements or the company cannot prove that it was the data subject who clicked on an 'accept button' or similar mechanism).

- Even if the data subject accepts, it is possible that acceptance is considered invalid due to formal deficiencies (*e.g.*, because the notice or acceptance mechanism was not sufficiently conspicuous, translation requirements were overlooked or the data subject is a minor).

- If a company obtains the data subject's express acceptance to the contents of a privacy notice, it typically creates a contractual agreement to the effect that the company will process data only in the manner described in the privacy notice; this may have the consequence that if the company wants to change its practices in the future, it will have to seek express acceptance again, and, the data subject may be entitled to terminate or cancel the agreement with reasonable notice, *i.e.*, withdraw acceptance, with the effect that the company can no longer process personal data as contemplated in the notice.

- By seeking consent to the contents of a privacy notice, companies may attract additional scrutiny and jurisdiction. For example, German consumer protection watchdogs apply national laws on unfair contract terms to privacy notices that are presented in the form or context of an agreement even if they otherwise have to defer to the laws and jurisdiction of other EEA member states with respect to data processing practices of companies that are established in another EEA member state.

- Under U.S.-style laws, companies need to notify data subjects in order to overcome restrictions based on 'reasonable expectations of privacy', but companies can accomplish this best by issuing unilateral notices rather than asking for express acceptance. Also, under European-style laws, companies cannot obtain the "specific" consent required by prompting data subjects to consent to a comprehensive description of a company's data processing practices in a website privacy policy or similarly general notice.

♦   On the plus side, if a data subject receives a conspicuous notice and then expressly and voluntarily declares acceptance, the data subject may be less likely to challenge the data processing practices described in the notice; also, in jurisdictions without specific data privacy laws, it may appear safer to proceed with express acceptance to protect against claims and challenges under vague constitutional or tort theories.

3.68   *Agreements instead of consent.* Companies should always consider one important alternative to seeking consent or acceptance from data subjects to data processing practices in a privacy statement. Instead of asking for consent, permission or acceptance, companies can undertake obligations to process personal data in commercial agreements with data subjects. The contractual obligation will then require and at the same time allow the company to process the data. Under European data protection laws, contractual obligations are listed as an alternative means of justification. While consent has to be specific, voluntary, informed and in writing, data protection laws do not set forth criteria for contract formation and companies often have more flexibility in connection with contractual approaches. For example, a company that offers online information services could seek consent from website visitors to send marketing emails about new services and renewals, or it could include a clause into its online services agreement according to which the company shall be obligated to provide updated information about new services or upcoming renewals. In connection with the first approach (seeking consent), the company needs to obtain specific, express, voluntary, informed and written consent; in connection with the second approach (contractual agreement), the company simply needs to facilitate contract formation, which can be achieved via implied acceptance and does not typically require written form under most jurisdictions' laws. Similarly, a company that offers an advertising-financed social networking platform, email service or informational website can seek consent from users for behavioral tracking, inviting friends, data sharing and other processing practices, or contractually promise the delivery of targeted ads, the option to invite friends, forwarding of data and other actions that require processing of personal data.

3.69   *Commercial agreements between companies.* From a data protection law perspective, companies can conclude three fundamentally different types of agreements with other companies: (1) data processing services agreements, (2) data sub-processing services agreements, and (3) controller-controller agreements.

- Under a data processing services agreement, one company processes data as a service provider (*a.k.a.* 'processor') for another company (*a.k.a.* 'controller'). The data controller is in charge of and responsible for compliance with most obligations under data protection laws. The data processor follows instructions and directions from the data controller and processes the data only in the interest and on behalf of the data controller. The data processor must not use any data for its own purposes or retain any data after the arrangement ends. The data controller does not typically need consent from data subjects or to provide particularly detailed notices regarding the data sharing because the data controller remains fully responsible and in control of the data processing.

- Under a sub-processing agreement, a data processor engages a subcontractor and passes on obligations under the data processing agreement between the data controller and the data processor.

- Under a controller-controller agreement, one data controller shares data with another company, also a data controller, for the other company's own interests, for example in connection with joint marketing initiatives, email list renting or selling and human resources data transfers within a group of affiliated companies. In such scenarios, both data controllers have an interest in the data and assume compliance obligations. Usually, the first data controller needs consent from the data subject or a contractual obligation towards the data subject to legitimize the sharing of personal data with the second data controller.

- Mixed agreements (with characteristics of data processing services agreements and controller-controller agreements) are possible. A data controller could hire a service provider that also pursues its own interests in connection with the data processing. For example, a company hires a brokerage to administer the company's employee stock option program and the brokerage also wants to sell other investment-related services to the company's employees. In such situations, the first data controller typically has to comply with the stricter rules applicable to controller-controller agreements and either obtain consent from the data subjects or limit the data sharing to what is necessary to perform contractual obligations with the data subject.

3.70 *Terms for data processing services agreements.* Companies should address the following points in a data processing services agreement:

+ Data processor shall only process data in the interest and on behalf of data controller.

+ Data processor shall follow instructions and directions from data controller (subject to change order management and possibly extra charges).

+ Data processor shall not change key aspects of data processing parameters without obtaining data controller's instructions, for example regarding data processing locations and subcontractors (subject to change order management and possibly charges, termination and/or early termination fees if data processor has to modify standard services offerings and data controller does not wish to instruct data processor accordingly).

+ Data processor shall keep data secure. Ideally, the parties agree on specific technical, organizational and administrative data security measures, for example, the data processor's or controller's information security policy.

+ Where data controller's responsibility for data security ends and where data processor's responsibility begins. Ideally, companies define clear lines in order to ensure that data is ultimately kept secure and other parties are clear on their respective responsibilities.

+ Notification, cooperation and indemnification obligations in the context of data security breaches, data access or correction requests, audits, and government investigations. Under what circumstances the provider shall notify the customer, how the parties will cooperate on investigating and remedying the situation, how much input the service provider will have on the wording of the notification to data subjects and who pays for costs and damages resulting from an actual or suspected breach.

3.71 *Terms for data sub-processing agreements*

+ Data processor needs to pass on to the sub-processor some or all obligations that data processor assumed in the data processing services agreement.

• Whether instructions will be communicated directly from data controller or from data processor.

• All of the issues that the original data processing services agreement must address should also be addressed in the sub-processing agreement.

*Terms for agreements between data controllers.* In agreements between 3.72 data controllers, companies should consider the following points:

• Should either data controller assume contractual restrictions vis-à-vis the other controller regarding the use and processing of personal data?

• Which controller is responsible for ensuring that the data transfer is legal – the sender, recipient or both parties? Often, this obligation falls naturally on the sender, but occasionally, the recipient is in an equal or better position to obtain consent from the data subject, for example, when two companies have direct relationships with the data subject, as realtors, banks and title companies have in the context of real estate sales.

• Indemnification and cooperation obligations in case the transfer or one controller's actions or omissions result in claims against one or both controllers.

• Are data flows bi-directional so that rights and obligations should be drafted to apply mutually?

*Terms dictated by laws and compliance agendas.* Companies have 3.73 to agree on some standard clauses and form contracts because laws require them. For example, in order to comply with European laws on international data transfers of personal data, companies can implement Standard Contractual Clauses promulgated by the EU Commission. Also, under U.S. federal healthcare privacy laws (namely the HIPAA privacy rule), covered entities and certain service providers have to conclude business associate agreements. When you are confronted with these kinds of agreements, you have to change your mindset and appreciate the fundamental difference in purpose compared to ordinary commercial contracting: these kinds of agreements are not typically enforced by one party against the other, but implemented by both parties to satisfy legal requirements. Any enforcement will likely come from regulators, data subjects and other third parties. Therefore, at the negotiation stage, the interests of the parties tend to be far more aligned than with respect to commercial contracts and you can usually implement such types of agreements more efficiently if you get on the same page with your contracting partner that you are both dealing with a compliance challenge.

## Protocols

3.74   Companies are usually not strictly required by applicable law to prepare protocols. On the other hand, larger organizations face a practical necessity to define and communicate policies regarding data collection, usage, disclosure, access, protection, and other processing aspects. As an organization, the company must comply with numerous requirements under data privacy laws (*e.g.*, keep data correct and secure, and in some instances encrypted; grant notices, access and correction rights to data subjects; etc.). In order to satisfy these substantive compliance requirements, companies have to ensure that each employee, independent contractor and third-party service provider acts in accordance with applicable laws and contractual undertakings. Companies can achieve this objective with a number of different courses of action, including training, technical and organizational measures, as well as protocols and contractual obligations on staff and contractors. Such protocols are best drafted with a focus on a particular position to keep the protocol short and targeted. Lengthier, all-encompassing policy statements tend to be discarded as "red tape" by employees who do not take the time to understand which aspects of the document apply to their particular jobs.

3.75   How many protocols a company needs with respect to data privacy law compliance depends on the company's practices, how many employees it has and how specialized and sophisticated the employees are. A large, multinational enterprise with highly sensitive consumer data probably needs a whole host of protocols around its data usage. A small startup company that sells to enterprises, on the other hand, may need only some basic rules on keeping employee files and the customer list locked up. When you prepare protocols, consider who you are addressing, what the department knows and how you can best get your points across. Each protocol should ideally only contain rules that are relevant for each person addressed by the protocol.

## Questionnaires and data submission forms

When companies collect data via questionnaires, web forms or other   3.76
means, they should consider the following points:

- With a form, companies can influence the categories of informa-   3.77
tion they will receive. The more specific the questions and the more
narrow the options for answers are, the less likely it is that the
respondents submit data that the company prefers not to receive
or that may lead to liability. For example, companies that host user-
generated content can offer relatively narrow and detailed web
forms to third-party rights holders to launch copyright infringement complaints in order to reduce the risk of receiving vague
allegations that trigger a need to investigate the situation further
(which can be expected if the company simply publishes an email
address for complaints). On the other hand, the more specific the
information a company asks for, the more responsibility the company assumes for the type of answers the inquiry generates. For
example, a company that allows landlords to post advertisements
for their properties may not be able to escape contributory liability for user-generated online content if it induces those landlords
through specific questions to express discriminatory preferences
(whereas the same company would not normally be held responsible for discriminatory comments that website visitors post via
free text uploading options). Similarly, an employer who posts
questionnaires for job candidates can decrease the risk of receiving
too much or too sensitive information (which could later be cited
in anti-discrimination lawsuits) by posting narrowly crafted questions or present pre-formulated answers or pull-down menus that
restrict what candidates can include in their responses.

- If a company sends a questionnaire via email with the intent to   3.78
obtain consumer feedback but also to advertise its products, the
questionnaire may qualify as advertising and anti-spam laws may
apply as a result (requiring, for example, prior opt-in consent, valid
opt-out mechanisms, etc.).

- A company that is already seeking express consent from data sub-   3.79
jects regarding certain types of data processing activities should use
the opportunity to let the data subject also confirm, update or supplement the data at stake. This helps the company comply with data
integrity requirements, discharge notice requirements and alleviate

concerns that the data subject may otherwise have regarding the type of data that is at issue. For example, in the employment context, employees tend to be more willing to grant consent to processing of their personal data in a human resource information system by a foreign parent company if they are provided with a print-out of their specific data on file that they can update, correct or simply confirm.

## Documenting decisions and compliance efforts

3.80 Companies are required to prepare records of their data processing activities under the EU General Data Protection Regulation and also under the EU-U.S. Privacy Shield Program. Companies also prepare such documentation in response to customer inquiries, due diligence information request lists in mergers and acquisition transactions, and to defend against possible future charges of negligence in litigation. Such descriptions are more helpful in conducting a legal review of existing or planned practices (*e.g.*, under foreign laws in connection with international expansion or new product launches) than a mere review of privacy notices, which may not describe all relevant facts and circumstances.

3.81 To prepare such documentation, you could identify and expressly list the requirements that you are addressing and then describe next to each requirement what your company is actually doing. For example, you could copy and paste each of the EU-U.S. Privacy Shield Principles, applicable requirements under the EU General Data Protection Regulation and key obligations under other privacy laws into a blank word.docx document, divided by page breaks, and then add company-specific information on how the company addresses each requirement. Before you finalize or share the documentation, make sure that the efforts described are accurate and sufficient (or change your practices) and that they are consistent with your representations to data subjects (in notices), government authorities (in filings), business partners (in contracts) and others.

3.82 Even smaller organizations usually benefit from creating a compliance binder to collect and monitor all the various compliance tasks and measures (such as filings, appointment of data protection officers, execution and maintenance of data transfer agreements, policies, vendor agreements, etc.). This will also help ensure that the information communicated to various local authorities is consistent to the extent global systems, processes and policies are concerned.

## Government notifications, approvals

Most EEA member states and a few other countries, including 3.83
Argentina, Israel, Morocco, Russia, Switzerland and Uruguay currently require companies to notify data protection authorities of some or all processing of personal data or databases. In some cases, companies have to obtain prior approval from the authorities. A recital to the EU General Data Protection Regulation notes that existing notification obligations produced administrative and financial burdens, did not contribute enough to improving data protection and should therefore be abolished. The EU Member States could not agree on an actual abolishment and some or all national notification obligations may remain in place even after the regulation takes effect in May 2018.

The requirements for notification and approval vary significantly 3.84
depending on:

+ The circumstances that trigger filing requirements (*e.g.*, all automated processing, processing by more than a certain number of employees, processing of certain types of data, processing for certain purposes, international transfers, controller vs. processor activities, whistleblower hotlines, etc.);

+ The degree to which the authorities provide guidance on the information that should be provided. Some jurisdictions, including Belgium, France, Spain and the UK, offer online registration with restricted text fields or multiple choice questions; other jurisdictions require paper forms or allow free form notifications with respect to some or all required reports (*e.g.*, updates);

+ The amount and kinds of information to be provided;

+ The extent to which companies have to notify and disclose information regarding onward transfers of data by the initial recipients;

+ The extent to which exemptions from notification requirements apply to different approaches for justifying international data transfer to outside of Europe (*e.g.*, EU Standard Contractual Clauses, EU-U.S. Privacy Shield certification, consent, etc.) or in case the company appoints a data protection officer;

- Whether data transfer agreements or other supporting documentation must be submitted along with notification forms. Authorities in some jurisdictions routinely require submission of data transfer agreements where international data transfers are concerned, while authorities in most other jurisdictions reserve the right to request supporting documentation at any point;

- Whether controllers must specify the data processors to which personal data is provided and to what extent;

- Whether the filings must be translated into the local language. Typically jurisdictions require filings to be in the local language(s), although there are exceptions (*e.g.*, in the Netherlands, data controllers may submit requests for data transfer permits to the Ministry of Justice in English);

- Whether mere notification or prior approval is required regarding some or all aspects of data processing.

3.85   In most cases, companies have to submit notifications and applications for approvals on official forms in local language. However, companies should prepare and keep drafts of all filings in their preferred language. Before submitting the filings, you could have the drafts reviewed and revised as necessary from a local law and local language perspective and conformed to the official required format.

3.86   Whenever companies are faced with any changes to the previously notified information, they are generally required by statute to update their notices to data subjects and government authorities. For example, companies may have to notify the authorities about office relocations, transitions of authorized contact persons, replacement of data protection officers or changes regarding key vendors.

3.87   The format for updating governmental filings varies from country to country. Some EEA member states have enacted materiality thresholds and specific timelines regarding changes. For example the Netherlands requires companies to notify the government of changes regarding the name or address of the Dutch data controller within one week; other changes have to be reported annually and only if they are significant, including material changes to the purposes of the data processing, the categories of data subjects and data categories, recipients of data, planned security measures and transfers of data to countries outside the EEA. Many national laws however are ambiguous on exactly which changes require notification and do not specify any exemptions for trivial modifications or permissible delays regarding the notification of changes to data protection authorities.

Keeping up with the various, ever-changing local requirements can be a significant burden, especially for companies with a large number of foreign subsidiaries and data uses. Companies should consider implementing a process that ensures that relevant changes are reported to a central person in charge (*e.g.*, the Chief Privacy Officer, Corporate Counsel or a foreign corporate compliance administrator), who can then update filings either instantly in case of particularly relevant changes, or over certain intervals (*e.g.*, at the time of an annual EU-U.S. Privacy Shield re-certification).   3.88

# 4 Maintaining and auditing compliance programs

4.01 *The maintenance challenge.* Once you implement a data privacy compliance program, the work does not end. The maintenance phase begins. Some laws and programs require periodic actions. The EU-U.S. Privacy Shield Program requires companies to re-certify annually. Lawmakers around the world issue and revise laws constantly. Organizations transform in various ways, through mergers and acquisitions, spinoffs, reorganizations, relocations, international expansion, increased headcount and technology acquisitions. Employees in charge of privacy compliance may come and go. All of these changes have compliance implications.

4.02 *Documentation.* In order to assure efficient maintenance and continuity, you should consider preparing a brief outline of your program, list the location of key documents and decision makers and compile information on the scope of previous compliance assessments (*e.g.*, jurisdictions, vendors and services covered). Based on such documentation, you can answer questions about the program, assess quickly whether organizational changes trigger a need to update or expand the program, document periodical re-assessments, guide audits, and train colleagues or successors with respect to the data privacy compliance program.

4.03 *Taking over or auditing an existing compliance program.* When you take over an existing compliance program (for example, in a new job) or when you audit a program (*e.g.*, in the context of M&A due diligence), you could go through the same tasks as if you are implementing a new program and then ask for documentation or other confirmation that the requirements have been satisfied. Or you could ask more open-ended questions about what the company has done to date in order to achieve compliance and then follow up with more specific requests for information. For example, you could ask initially for the following information:

- Name, address, employee headcount and works council or other collective employee representation body of each company and branch in scope.

- Name and contact information of data protection officers and any other representatives in charge of privacy law compliance.

- Inventory of databases and data flows (with summary of data categories, types of data subjects, purposes of data processing and details on processing operations).

- Copies of external privacy notices, statements and consent forms as well as internal policies and protocols relating to data privacy and security compliance.

- Copies of notifications, approvals and other relevant correspondence with data protection authorities.

- List of key service providers with access to data and copies of services agreements.

- International data transfer compliance mechanisms chosen and copies of relevant documentation.

- Information on any data security breaches, data privacy-related complaints, disputes or problems. Specifically with respect to direct marketing programs, it is instructive to hear how the company manages opt-out requests, how many such requests it has received and if the company has received complaints about failures to honor opt-out requests.

Any transition or audit process typically involves interaction and phased approaches (question, answer, follow-up question, etc.), even if the company has its compliance program in excellent order. Yet, having key information and materials readily available can save time and inefficient, duplicate and recurring efforts. 4.04

*Due diligence in M&A scenarios.* When one company buys another business, the buyer usually conducts a due diligence investigation into the compliance status of the target company. How thoroughly such due diligence focuses on privacy compliance depends on how crucial personal data and data privacy is regarding the transferred business. 4.05

For example, if the buyer is interested in acquiring consumer customer relationships, then it will investigate carefully whether the seller and target are permitted to transfer the customer data, and whether there are concerns about looming compliance deficits that the buyer would inherit and become liable for. On the other hand, if the buyer is interested only in the target's intellectual property to make products for other businesses, then data privacy compliance should be just one of many compliance topics and might be addressed primarily in contractual warranties (if the buyer retains sufficient recourse in case of warranty breaches). Depending on the relative importance of personal data and compliance for the transaction, the buyer could approach the transaction due diligence similarly to the take-over of an existing privacy program (which would follow the closing of the transaction in any event) and add the questions and requests listed in the preceding paragraph to the due diligence information request list.

4.06   Alternatively or additionally, the buyer can include desirable answers to said questions into the warranty and representation section of the purchase agreements. This can prompt the seller, however, to confess compliance deficits in the disclosure schedule of the purchase agreement. Such confessions can in turn haunt the buyer if the transaction closes and the buyer becomes liable for the target's violations of law, if they are well documented and shared without attorney client-privilege. This is not a privacy-specific issue, but applies to many compliance-related topics in M&A situations.

4.07   Another point to consider in the context of M&A due diligence is how buyer and seller can assure compliance with data privacy and security laws in the context of the transaction. Often, buyers ask for information on the seller's employees and consumer customers that the seller cannot legally provide without violating applicable privacy laws. While such violations are initially only the seller's or target's problem, they can ultimately become the buyer's problem if the transaction closes. Therefore, both sides should cooperate to redact/de-identify personal information as much as practical and secure the data room (where the seller uploads information and documents in response to buyer's information requests) via strict access limitations on a 'need to know' basis. The parties and their counsel should also consider, for example, whether information and documents in the data room or email correspondence will be encrypted, who on either side shall be permitted to view the information, whether downloads or copying of documents shall be permitted at all, and if and how information must be deleted or returned if negotiations end.

With respect to employee information, it is increasingly common that    4.08
targets produce only redacted information. For rank-and-file employees of large organizations, it may be sufficient if you remove names and employee identification numbers from spreadsheets. With respect to smaller organizations, small subsidiaries in a large group and key employees, the buyer can often still guess which individual information relates to, even if you delete names from spreadsheets. But, partially effective measures may be legally acceptable in situations where the data controllers have an otherwise legitimate and strong interest to share the data and the data subjects are not adversely affected by the disclosures.

*Due diligence on service providers and vendors.* When you vet a service    4.09
provider or other vendor, you will typically not have to conduct a complete audit but merely focus on compliance aspects that matter to your company as a customer. Typically, customers care only whether the service provider keeps data secure, follows the customer's directions regarding privacy compliance and returns or deletes data after the relationship terminates. Customers would typically be less interested in the vendor's compliance with the vendor's own government filing requirements, privacy notices to the vendor's own employees, etc., because a data controller would not be liable for its vendors' unrelated data compliance issues.

Where service providers are based in other jurisdictions, the customer    4.10
should also assess the vendor's compliance approach with respect to international data transfers. For example, a company should not share personal data from Europe with services providers or subcontractors outside the EEA or allow such sharing between the vendor and its subcontractors before the data controller has confirmed that appropriate data transfer agreements or other compliance mechanisms are in place and up to date. Such additional investigations and confirmations should be made in addition to all other vendor due diligence, not in lieu thereof.

# 5    Data privacy A to Z

In this Chapter, you can find introductions and key considerations regarding hot topics and fundamental substantive privacy compliance obligations. A Field Guide cannot supply comprehensive commentary, but this Chapter is intended to provide context and to supplement the previous, task-oriented Chapters. Topics are presented by common buzz words, in alphabetical order. Feel free to fast forward to topics of particular interest and skip topics that do not apply to you. If you cannot find a particular buzz word listed as a header, please consult the Index for keywords.

# Advertising

Collection and use of personal data for advertising purposes is valuable, common and increasingly controversial.

*Direct marketing* involves consumers receiving phone calls, email, text   5.01
messages, postal mail or other marketing communications that are
directly addressed to individuals. Advertisers and their service providers need to ensure that they:

• Obtain the consumer's contact information legally. If sourced from
address trading businesses, the legality of collection and transfer
should be scrutinized.

• Are permitted to use the data for marketing purposes. Specifically,
the consumer must have received prior notice or granted consent,
if and where legally required, and no contrary commitments can
have been made in the past, *e.g.*, promises in website privacy statements or service agreements that data will be used only to provide
services.

• Employ a method of communication and include content that is
allowed under applicable anti-spam laws (see U – Unsolicited
Communications).

*Behavioral or targeted advertising* involves companies building con-   5.02
sumer profiles with extensive details on the interests and activities
of individuals, which may include name and contact information
(*e.g.*, loyalty programs) or not (*e.g.*, browser tracking profiles, see T
– Tracking). Collection of the relevant data (*e.g.*, through web tracking) requires the consumer's prior, informed, express consent under
laws in Europe, although in practice, a notice and opt-out system has
evolved.

*Sweepstakes* often involve companies asking for contact informa-   5.03
tion and other personal data, which is not problematic so long as
they need and use such data only to administer the contest (*e.g.*,
determine and notify winners, enforce exclusion rules regarding employees and their relatives, etc.). But if companies want to
use such data for other purposes (*e.g.*, to create a mailing list), the
data may become viewed as a wager and turn an otherwise legal
sweepstake into an illegal lottery, unless participants are offered an

alternative means of entry whereby they do not have to provide the data or consent to marketing and participants are notified that providing the data is voluntary and does not increase the chances of winning.

# Brexit, GDPR, ePrivacy and Privacy Shield

After more than 20 years of sleepy stability in EU data protection laws    5.04
from 1995 to 2016, companies are facing a number of rapid, significant changes: The EU enacted a General Data Protection Regulation
(GDPR) in May 2016 to replace the EU Data Privacy Directive effective May 2018. The new requirements and penalties are considered
and addressed throughout this Field Guide and summarized in paragraph 0.20 (Key Concepts – the Territory). Some EU Member States
are updating their national laws to exercise their numerous rights to
exceed, limit, modify or further clarify new principles established in
the GDPR.

Also planned for May 2018 is a new EU Regulation on Privacy and
Electronic Communications to replace a Directive that was first
enacted in 2002 (lowering existing general consent requirements to
an opt-out regime for web cookies, among other things) and updated
once in 2009 (to raise the consent requirements for web cookies to an
opt-in regime, among other changes).

In July 2016, the EU Commission declared the EU-U.S. Privacy Shield
program an adequate basis for international transfers of personal data
from the EEA. By September 9, 2017, 2475 U.S. companies registered
voluntarily for the new program. The EU-U.S. Privacy Shield program
succeeds the U.S. Safe Harbor Program, which the EU Commission
had declared adequate in 2000 in a decision that the Court of Justice
for the European Union declared invalid in October 2015. Between
October 2015 and July 2016, the data protection authorities in the EU
had compelled companies in the EU to stop relying on U.S. Safe Harbor
registrations and instead conclude EU Standard Contractual Clauses
(SCC), a globally available alternative to legitimizing international
data transfers. These SCC are expected to also change in due course,
either due to pending court proceedings or at the EU Commission's
own initiative. Details, advantages and disadvantages of SCC, Privacy
Shield and other international transfer mechanisms are summarized in
Chapter 2 of this Field Guide.

Last but not least among dramatic changes in the EU is the fact that
in March 2017, the United Kingdom formally triggered the process
to withdraw from the EU within two years (by March 2019). If and
when the United Kingdom leaves the European Union, the EU General

Data Protection Regulation will cease to apply to UK companies and companies in the EEA will be prohibited from transferring personal data to the UK. National UK data protection laws will remain in effect in the UK and should suffice to justify an adequacy decision by the EU Commission. Also, the UK Parliament could implement the rules of the EU General Data Protection Regulation into national law like an EU Directive. Companies may expect generally turbulent transition times due to Brexit but specifically with respect to data privacy some leniency.

# Cloud computing

Companies that host data in several remote and perhaps dynamically- 5.05
used storage facilities often refer to their computing arrangements
with buzz words such as 'cloud computing,' 'software as a service
(SaaS),' 'platform as a service' or 'application service providing (ASP).'
In line with current nomenclature, this Section of the Field Guide will
use 'cloud computing' collectively for all hosted solutions that allow
users to obtain additional functionality, storage or processing capacity
without having to buy additional devices or software copies. Everyone
should, however, carefully consider whether the use of the term 'cloud'
is really helpful in a particular situation, given the negative connotations in European countries plagued by constant rain and possible
associations with reduced visibility and clouded minds.

From a data protection perspective, data controllers and consumers 5.06
experience many advantages: quick access, easy back-up, fewer software interoperability issues, and typically improved data security.
Customers (*i.e.*, the data controllers) and providers (*i.e.*, the data processors) have to face one significant challenge, namely the need to keep
the customer in control of data that is stored somewhere in the cloud. If
the customer loses control over the data, the service provider becomes
a co-controller, which triggers various compliance obligations, possibly including a need for the customer to seek consent from data
subjects (which typically is not practically available, *e.g.*, if an Internet
Service Provider wants to outsource email scanning for anti-spam
or anti-virus protection). Therefore, providers have to contractually
commit to processing data only on behalf of and subject to instructions
from their customers, meeting relevant security standards, and keeping customers reasonably appraised of key characteristics of the data
processing (which would typically include the countries where servers
are located, categories of subcontractors and possibly the identities of
key contractors that have access to the data, and an overview of data
security and retention standards).

Depending on the data and solutions at stake, customers may also seek 5.07
qualified data transfer agreements from their providers, including EU
Standard Contractual Clauses, onward transfer agreements under the
EU-U.S. Privacy Shield Framework, HIPAA business associate agreements, PCI Standard commitments, etc., and companies who specialize
as service providers are well-advised to secure corresponding commitments from their subcontractors (as required under 'viral' clauses

in many data transfer agreement templates and laws and to ensure back-to-back protection). Finally, companies should exercise due diligence and review the approach to data security measures by potential providers because data controllers are fully liable for their data processors and should consider them part of the extended enterprise.

5.08   While users increasingly embrace cloud computing, data privacy advocates, regulators and lawyers are less enthusiastic. Critics increasingly raise concerns about the cloud's risks to the privacy and security of personal data. To them, cloud computing means primarily that users transfer data to far away systems that they do not understand, own, control or even know about. As is often the case with respect to legally and technologically complex topics, the issues can be overly simplified and (ab)used to pursue various policy and competitive agendas, including keeping jobs within the country, protecting local industries and shielding established business models from disruptive alternatives.

Before you decide to offer or buy cloud computing solutions, consider the common myths that tend to obstruct the decision-making process:

5.09   *Myth 1: Cloud computing presents fundamentally new and unique challenges for data privacy and security compliance.* Fact is that consumers and companies have been entrusting specialized service providers with personal data for a long time, including telecommunications companies, payment processors, accountants and various outsourcing service providers (*e.g.*, payroll, call centers and IT support). For nearly two decades, we have made the Internet an integral part of our information society and economy, and the Internet is founded on the principle of decentralized transfer of data across geographies, devices and connections. The very services and models that are currently hyped as 'cloud computing' have been promoted for more than 25 years by a maturing industry that initially referred to itself as 'application service providers.' Transferring data to service providers and remotely hosted solutions certainly creates challenges – but they are neither new nor unique.

5.10   *Myth 2: Cloud computing involves more data sharing and that is inherently bad for privacy.* Fact is that transferring data to data processing agents (who process data only on behalf and in the interest of the customer) is very different from transferring data to data controllers (who use data in their own interest and possibly impair the data subject's privacy). Transferring data to processing agents is so different from transferring to data controllers that many data protection laws specifically exclude engagements of data processing service providers from restrictions on data transfers.

Data sharing with data processing agents is not inherently bad or good 5.11 for privacy – it is neutral. Companies always need people to do things and people need to share data to work together. Companies are a legal fiction. When companies use and process personal data, they have to act through humans, and such humans can be statutory employees, individual independent contractors or employees or contractors of corporate contractors. In each of these scenarios, it is important that the individual person who processes the data acts on behalf and under the control of the company that is responsible for the data, *i.e.*, the data controller. And it is important that the data controller in turn complies with applicable data protection laws. It is not important, per se, for privacy compliance purposes how the data controller engages and compensates the individuals who conduct the processing – as employees or independent contractors. It is important that each of the individuals involved follows the law and the data controller's instructions.

For most companies, the switch from internally maintained human 5.12 resources databases to an external cloud-based solution does not result in more sharing or transmission to additional geographies. Most data these days is transferred across geographical borders because it is needed in various locations. Traditionally, data has been shared over the Internet via myriad devices, connections and persons with access. Switching from paper files, spreadsheets and email that uses legacy systems with varying degrees of data protection to a centralized cloud computing solution with access controls will not add to the privacy risks associated with data sharing. Usually, it just means more orderly, organized and secure sharing.

*Myth 3: Cloud computing is bad for data security.* Fact is that employee 5.13 malice and negligence (*e.g.*, lost laptop) cause many data security breaches. Hacks by cybercriminals are also on the rise. Whether personal data is safer on a system secured by the data controller 'in-house' or an external vendor depends on the security measures deployed by each particular organization. Moving data to the cloud can be a bad thing for data security if the vendor is weak on security and careless. It can be a good thing if the vendor brings better technologies to the table and helps the data controller manage access, data retention and data integrity. And it can be neutral if the vendor's cloud system is more secure, but the way the customer uses the system keeps exposing the data (*e.g.*, because the customer does not configure security settings to properly restrict data access to the appropriate users, the customer uses unsecured connections or the customer downloads data from the cloud to unsecured local devices). Some organizations are also concerned that a large multi-tenant cloud facility could be a more attractive target for hackers; they may prefer a dedicated, 'private cloud' arrangement. Other companies see additional protection in the relative anonymity or obscurity offered by a facility used by many other organizations. Each company needs to ask itself whether its own information technology capabilities and security policies are superior to the measures deployed by a specialized vendor that can leverage economies of scale and is highly motivated by the risk of reputational harm to keep its customers secure.

5.14   *Myth 4: Cloud computing causes additional problems under privacy law because data is transmitted internationally.* Fact is most companies are already transmitting data internationally, because they use the Internet internally across jurisdictions (for example, to email spreadsheets to various office locations), or because they have subsidiaries, customers, suppliers or channel partners in other jurisdictions. In most cases, data transfers occur because data is needed in different jurisdictions, not because of where the data is stored. With respect to employee data in a global human resources system, for example, companies need to transfer personal data across borders to populate the system, whether they host it themselves or engage a cloud computing service provider.

5.15   *Myth 5: Data in the U.S. is endangered by the USA Patriot Act and the NSA.* Fact is that following the terror attacks of September 11, 2001, the United States enacted the Uniting and Strengthening America by Providing Appropriate Tools Required to Intercept and Obstruct Terrorism Act ("USA Patriot Act") to fight terrorism and money laundering activities by providing additional investigative powers to law enforcement and intelligence agencies, including the National Security Agency. These powers were reigned in again by court and executive decisions and when the USA Freedom Act canceled and superseded the USA Patriot Act in 2015. Even before then, it has been worth considering that:

- U.S. authorities seem to have little difficulty accessing data stored in other countries, via the Internet or with the cooperation of intelligence and law enforcement agencies in other jurisdictions, as the revelations about programs of the NSA have demonstrated,

- law enforcement and intelligence agency surveillance are not relevant for many types of data in cloud computing arrangements,

- the U.S. government is much more likely to obtain the data directly from the data controllers (*i.e.*, users of cloud computing services) than from service providers, which are typically not known to the government at the outset,

- if data controllers and data subjects are not based in the United States and have no strong nexus with the United States, chances are the U.S. government is not interested in the data, regardless of whether the data is hosted in the United States,

- if the U.S. government is interested, it can usually obtain access to the data through foreign governments via judicial assistance and cooperation treaties, regardless of where the data is hosted,

- similar powers and less safeguards exist in many other countries,

- data is typically much more at risk of being accessed by governments at the place where the data controller or data subject are based, and

- the NSA and U.S. government surveillance issues are often raised abroad to support unrelated agendas, which has created overblown fears of the Act's actual reach.

The information that the U.S. government seeks to fight terrorism and money laundering is not what most companies store or process in the cloud. As an example, take a global human resources information system (HRIS) hosted in the cloud. It is quite unlikely that the U.S. government would be interested in the kind of data that resides in a HRIS system. Even if the U.S. government were interested, it would likely turn to the employer first to obtain the data because the employer is more closely connected to the data subjects, may have additional information and the government would not know initially what cloud services the employer uses. If the employer is located in another country, the U.S. government can typically exercise pressure to obtain disclosure anyway (even Swiss and other foreign banks, for example, had to turn over banking details to the U.S. government due to pressure on their market presence and activities in the United States).

The U.S. government can obtain information through cooperation with foreign governments and has entered into mutual legal assistance treaties with over 50 countries as well as a mutual legal assistance agreement with the EU. The cooperation under mutual legal assistance arrangements can involve substantial sharing of electronic information between law enforcement authorities. Also, the publicity around NSA programs since 2013 has shed quite a bit of light on similar intelligence and cybersurveillance programs operated by other governments (for a detailed global overview and country-by-country comparison and heat maps, see http://globalitc.bakermckenzie.com/surveillance/).

All countries allow their own law enforcement and intelligence agencies access to personal and confidential information under certain circumstances. Many countries have updated their data privacy laws since September 11, 2001 to provide for additional law enforcement powers and minimum data retention and residency requirements. In some cases, the fact that data is physically located in another jurisdiction will make a difference for a data subject's privacy protections, but this can work both ways. For example, in one case, a U.S. bankruptcy court refused to hand over emails to and from a German resident to the German government. In this case, the German resident's privacy was better protected due to the fact that his emails were stored in the United States. The German government would have easily gotten access to his email if he had used a German Internet Service Provider.

In one of the first cases that raised concerns regarding the USA Patriot Act in the context of international outsourcing, a Canadian trade union sued the British Columbia Ministry of Health Services. The union tried to prevent the British Columbian government from contracting out the administration of the province's public health insurance program to a U.S.-based service provider. The union argued that the proposed outsourcing would contravene British Columbia's public sector privacy law ("FOIPPA") by making the personal health information of British Columbians accessible to U.S. authorities pursuant to the provisions of the USA Patriot Act. The court dismissed the case and the trade union initiative has since been cited as an example of privacy concerns being raised as an excuse for other agendas, such as local job or industry protectionism.

5.16 *Myth 6: Record keeping laws require data to stay local.* Fact is that some tax, bookkeeping and corporate laws in some jurisdictions historically

required certain records to stay inside the country. But, such requirements apply only to certain kinds of records and they do not prohibit
the transfer of data into the cloud so long as originals or backup copies
are kept locally. If and to the extent such laws apply to employment
records, for example, the global employer can still upload copies of
the records into a global cloud computing system, whether self-hosted
or hosted by a cloud computing service provider. Very few countries
have enacted broad data residency requirements, including so far only
China, Kazakhstan, Indonesia and Russia.

*Myth 7: The EU-U.S. Privacy Shield Program does not apply to ser-* 5.17
*vice provider arrangements.* Fact is that data processors are eligible to
participate and achieve adequacy through certification. Data protection authorities in all EEA member states must consider U.S. companies as being situated in an 'adequate' jurisdiction if they join the
EU-U.S. Privacy Shield Program, whether they act as data controllers
or processors.

Of course, users of cloud solutions need to verify that each particular
service provider can be trusted with personal data, but this requirement applies equally with respect to providers in the EEA. When
comparing the relative strengths and weaknesses of data protection
technologies and laws across geographies, it is worth noting that some
EEA member states have a far less impressive information technologies, infrastructure or data protection law than the United States.

*Myth 8: Contractual clauses are unnecessary if the service provider is* 5.18
*Privacy Shield-certified.* Fact is that the EU-U.S. Privacy Shield certification only qualifies a service provider outside the EEA to be as
adequate as a service provider within the EEA is presumed to be.
Additionally, European laws require particular contractual clauses for
data transfers to any service provider – whether the provider is in the
EEA or outside.

A company has to pass three hurdles before it may transfer European
personal data internationally (into the cloud or otherwise). First, the
collection and use has to be permitted (based on consent, contractual
duties, statute, etc.). Second, the transfer has to be justified. Third,
the recipient has to achieve adequacy if it is not based in the EEA or
a country that has been declared adequate by the EU Commission.
By certifying under the EU-U.S. Privacy Shield Program, a U.S.-based
service provider helps its customers over the third hurdle (adequacy),

but the Certification does not justify the transfer as such. Whether a recipient is in the U.S. or in the EEA, the customer has to justify any transfer. In the context of data transfers to other data controllers (*i.e.*, recipients that want to use the data in their own interest), data controllers typically have to obtain consent from data subjects or rely on statutory data transfer obligations. But, when a company transmits data to a service provider, it does not have to obtain consent so long as it retains control over the data via an adequate contractual arrangement. This is where the need for certain particular contractual clauses comes into play.

One option is to sign the Standard Contractual Clauses promulgated by the EU Commission for data transfers to data processors. Alternatively, companies can implement agreements that satisfy national law requirements for agreements with service providers. The templates promulgated, blessed or prescribed by the various data protection authorities in the EEA member states vary quite a bit and it is less clear how binding such clauses are and whether they will be accepted without questions and scrutiny in data protection authority approval processes. Consequently, any customer or service provider opting for "self made" or "national government templates" should be prepared for time- and cost-consuming legal analyses, lengthy negotiations and ultimately a multitude of agreements. By comparison, the EU Commission's Standard Contractual Clauses may be more attractive because all EEA member states are supposed to accept this form as assuring 'adequacy.' Therefore, it is in both parties' best interest not to negotiate or modify the EU Standard Contractual Clauses to preserve the preemptive blessing of the EU Commission regarding 'adequacy' and because one form agreement can be used for the entire EEA.

5.19 *Myth 9: Data privacy and security law compliance is the provider's responsibility.* Fact is that data privacy and security laws primarily hold the data controller responsible for compliance – *i.e.*, the customer in a services context. Customers should take the initiative to identify the various compliance obligations that apply to a particular type of data processing activity and then consider which of these obligations can or should efficiently be handled by service providers and which are better discharged by the data controller itself. In the end, the various compliance obligations on the data controller depend on where the data controller is located. If the data processor is based in another jurisdiction, the data controller will need to educate and instruct the data processor about the compliance requirements that need to be satisfied.

*Myth 10: Cloud service providers cannot cede control to their custom-* 5.20
*ers.* Fact is that many organizations find it difficult to stay in control
over modern IT systems whether they hire service providers to provide
hosted IT infrastructure as a service or whether they host the systems
themselves. Even with respect to self-operated systems, most companies usually have to work with support service providers who have to
be granted access to the systems and data to perform maintenance.
Most companies find it prohibitively expensive to customize systems
(whether self-hosted or hosted by a service provider) beyond the configuration options provided by the vendor as part of the standard offering. Consequently, there are significant limits to the degree of control
that users can and want to exercise over their systems.

Yet, from a legal perspective, it is imperative that the service provider
remains in the role of a data processor and the customer in the role
of the data controller. If the service provider obtains or retains too
much discretion about aspects or details of the processing, the service
provider could become a co-controller, which is not acceptable for
either party; the service provider would suddenly assume all kinds of
compliance obligations. A cloud computing service provider cannot
discharge these data controller obligations because it does not know
the data subjects or what data is uploaded into its systems. If the service provider did in fact qualify as data controller, then the customer
would typically violate statutory prohibitions and privacy policy promises regarding data sharing. Therefore, both provider and customer
have to work towards an arrangement that keeps the provider limited
to the role of a data processor.

In the context of self-hosted systems, it tends to be easier to prove that
the provider retains little or no control over the system after delivery.
In the cloud computing scenario on the other hand, the data resides
on servers on physical premises that the provider controls. But, it is
important to note that 'control' from a data protection law perspective refers to 'control' of the data – not 'control' of the premises where
data resides. Landlords, for example, are not viewed as data controllers merely because they own a building where data is stored and
have access and repossession rights under contract and statutory law
regarding the building and tenant property.

The focus of control regarding cloud computing is to ensure that the
customer decides what data to upload, download, access, transfer,
delete and otherwise process. This is the case with respect to most

cloud computing offerings because the service providers tend to offer a platform or software functionality as a service, without any interest, knowledge or influence regarding data types and processing purposes. For example, with respect to a hosted HRIS, the service provider does not have any need to view or use the data that the customer uploads and processes, but the customer may need the provider to access data in order to provide technical support. If the parties contractually and technologically assure that the vendor's personnel will access data on the system only to provide the service and address technical issues, then the customer is nearly as much in control as the customer can be with respect to self-hosted systems. In order to more closely mimic the control of self-hosted systems where the customer can monitor and safeguard physical safety and access limits, the cloud computing service provider has to provide key information about storage locations, processing practices and subcontractors (although some service providers withhold such information based on trade secret protection objectives). Additionally, any contractual clauses to safeguard control and data protection need to be passed on to subcontractors.

In connection with cost-efficient, standardized cloud computing solutions, it can be very difficult and expensive for providers to accommodate customization requests by individual customers. But, a customer can also remain in control over data processing if the customer retains a right to receive prior notice regarding all relevant details of the data processing and changes thereto so that the customer can withdraw data or change the use of a cloud solution in case changes are not acceptable. Or, the customer could agree or instruct the provider to update service and technology from time to time, as the provider deems appropriate, on the condition that the provider will not lessen the data security measures set forth in the agreement. Whether customers and providers also agree on contract termination rights and early termination fees is a commercial point and not prescribed from a data protection compliance perspective.

5.21 *Myth 11: The vendor has and should accept unlimited liability for data security breaches.* Fact is that service providers may not always be able to limit their liability vis-à-vis the data subjects in scenarios where they contract with corporate customers and not the data subjects themselves. If hackers gain unlawful access to employee information residing in a global HRIS, the service provider may theoretically be liable directly vis-à-vis the employees under negligence theories.

However, data protection laws do not prescribe the allocation of commercial liabilities between the parties. Sophisticated companies usually slice and dice exposure in various ways in indemnification, limitation of liability and warranty clauses. It is quite common to differentiate in risk allocation clauses based on: whether customer and/or service provider contributed primarily to a breach or resulting harm; whether the service provider was in compliance with its contractual obligations, its information security policies and applicable law; and whether a risk materialized that could not reasonably have been prevented by any company, including the customer (*e.g.*, a widespread cyber attack or software security weakness, like the 'heartbleed bug' in 2014).

Also, cloud service providers are increasingly mindful that they can be held liable for violations of laws by their customers or their customers' customers, for example in the context of uploaded viruses, illegally copied files and pornographic materials. Similar concerns could theoretically also arise if a customer uploads data that was collected in violation of data privacy laws, because the provider would then be processing personal data that may not be processed under data privacy laws. Any such risks can be shifted contractually from the provider to the customer.

*Myth 12: Customers need to have the right to access the provider's data centers and systems for audit purposes.* Fact is that customers need to reserve a right to audit the cloud service provider's compliance measures because the provider is part of the customer's extended enterprise and the customer needs to remain in control of the data that it stores in the cloud system. But, it is also a fact that the service provider may not let customers into multi-tenant data centers because that would impair the security of other customers' data. Instead, cloud service providers can arrange for routine, comprehensive audits of their systems by a generally accepted, neutral audit firm and make the results available to all customers. If customers demand additional topics on the audit list, providers can expand the scope of the next scheduled audit if the customers are willing to pay for the additional effort and the controls are within the scope of the service. By comparison, individual audits would be unnecessarily disruptive and costly and often not more meaningful to an average customer. 5.22

*Practical Steps for Outsourcing Data Processing Activities (to Clouds or Elsewhere).* Companies that want to engage cloud computing service providers or any other services providers that would be granted access to personal data should take the following steps: 5.23

**！ Action items**

- Conduct due diligence investigation into the service provider's and any subcontractors' technical and organizational measures to keep the data secure from unauthorized access;
- Conclude a contract with the service provider that obligates the provider to: (1) process the customer's data only in the interest and on behalf of, and subject to instructions from, the customer; (2) maintain technical and organizational data security measures that are sufficiently defined in the contract; (3) assume compliance obligations that the customer cannot satisfy alone due to the data processing arrangement; (4) notify the customer of any relevant changes that could affect data security as well as data security breaches; (5) indemnify the customer from any costs and damages resulting from the provider's failure to comply with its contractual obligations (and assure that the provider is sufficiently strong to stand behind such indemnification obligations); (6) provide reasonable audit reports, and (7) return or delete all customer data on request (subject to reasonable transition and compensation arrangements);
- Take technical and organizational measures to ensure that its own employees use the cloud computing system in a manner that safeguards the data, such as by implementing access controls and policies regarding secure transfers of data to and from the cloud system.

Service providers that want to offer attractive cloud computing solutions to customers should take the following steps:

- Educate themselves about their prospective customers' compliance needs and offer standard contracts, certifications, audit reports and disclosures that the target customer group needs to remain in compliance with legal obligations. For example, providers should consider SSAE 16/SOC audits and detailed information security policy disclosures and certifications under applicable industry standards, such as the standards of the Payment Card Industry ('PCI'). Providers in the United States should additionally consider joining the EU-U.S. Privacy Shield Program, signing the EU Standard Contractual Clauses for data transfers from controllers to processors, and HIPAA business associate agreements where personal health information is concerned;
- Conclude adequate contracts with (sub)contractors to back up the provider with respect to compliance obligations vis-à-vis the customer (for example, the provider cannot offer signing the EU Standard Contractual Clauses for data transfers from controllers to processors unless the provider first assures that all contractors with access to customer data will also sign up);

- Implement effective technical and organizational measures to safeguard data security at an appropriate level for the type of data (high security would be warranted for tax return information, for example);
- Protect themselves contractually from liabilities caused by customer actions or omissions (such as uploading illegal data or malicious code) or more appropriately borne by customers from a commercial perspective (such as the costs of responses to investigations or data access requests, early termination, special audit requests, and special data access or deletion requirements).

# Data retention and residency requirements

5.24 Data privacy, data retention and data residency (also known as "data localization" or "data sovereignty") are concepts that are often confused. Russia enacted the world's first broad data residency law effective September 1, 2015 in the form of an amendment to its general data privacy law. Kazakhstan followed suit with a similar amendment to its similar general data privacy law, effective January 1, 2016. China, Germany and Indonesia also added data residency requirements to their data privacy laws. But, data privacy and data residency requirements have actually very different and quite opposite purposes and effects: data residency and data retention requirements are intended to ensure that government officials, courts, auditors and others are able to gain access to data when they need it. Data privacy laws, on the other hand, are intended to restrict availability and access to personal data. Data transfer restrictions, for example, limit companies' ability to transfer personal data from one jurisdiction to another. European countries have been restricting international data transfers for decades in the interest of privacy protection. But, true data privacy laws do not include any requirements to keep data for a minimum period of time (data retention) or in a particular location (data residency), because such requirements are detrimental to privacy interests. Data privacy laws are about protecting personal data from access and use by governments and companies. Data retention and data residency laws secure access to personal data. They are anti-privacy laws.

Companies are caught in the cross-fire of data privacy, data retention and data residency laws, which impose contrary and often conflicting requirements.

European-style data protection laws require companies to delete data that they no longer legitimately need, so companies have to observe maximum data retention periods. Other laws can specify minimum data retention periods, during which companies must retain data and make it available on request, for example to tax authorities and law enforcement officials. Also, accounting standards, contracts and business needs require companies to keep data for a certain minimum data retention period, such as to keep user account information available for users, retain proof to support or defend against potential claims and track employee performance for career management purposes. Thus, for every category of data, companies have to consider three types of data retention periods – a minimum required by law, a period desired by the company for business reasons and a maximum required by law. To make things more complicated, these requirements vary per jurisdiction and do not only apply on a per-record basis, but per category of data and purpose of processing. If a particular document serves more than one purpose or jurisdiction, it may theoretically be required to be partially retained and partially deleted. On top of this, under U.S. law, companies have to preserve evidence that could be relevant for litigation under certain circumstances (litigation hold), which will override regular data retention policies.

Many companies have capitulated before the overwhelming complexity of creating a legally compliant record retention program and simply store data indefinitely. Given the magnitude of risk arising under laws that require minimum retention periods, companies choose a violation of the maximum retention period requirements under data protection laws as a lesser evil. This has resulted in a continuous increase of stored data and made companies increasingly vulnerable to data security breaches in addition to increasing costs of document protection duties in litigation.

Some companies have approached the issue methodically and prepared record retention schedules, listing certain categories of records, min/max/desired retention periods per jurisdiction and summarizing retention protocols. Depending of the size of the business, companies deal with thousands of different record types and have to create voluminous tables, for example in the following format (just to illustrate the format and some of the considerations to address):

In order to define the desired, minimum and maximum retention period and formal aspects of the retention protocol, companies have to reach out to various stakeholders and subject matter experts (data privacy counsel is not typically familiar with retention requirements and statutes of limitation under tax, corporate, customs or employment laws). The effort and resources expended for one jurisdiction is then multiplied by the number of jurisdictions where a company maintains presences, subsidiaries, customers, etc. Also, laws and business needs change frequently, so by the time a country-specific schedule is prepared, the first updates are probably already due.

In light of the prohibitive costs associated with 'getting it right' and the unacceptable risks resulting from making no effort at all, some companies try to strike a balance and start preparing retention

Table 6.1  Data records

| Type of record | Business desired period | Min. period, source/law | Max. period, source/law | Retention protocol |
|---|---|---|---|---|
| Consumer invoices | 4 years, statute of limitation | 3 years, sales tax laws, accounting standards | 'until no longer needed' – data privacy laws | 3 years original paper invoice; 5 years electronic copy; to be deleted, unless flagged for hold |
| Job candidate application forms | Indefinitely | 1 year, anti-discrimination laws, evidence retention | 'until no longer needed' – data privacy laws | If candidate is hired: employment tenure plus 5 years; if not, 1 year original form and 5 years electronic copy, unless flagged for hold |
| Emails | Depends on content; 180 days (unless individual employee selects email for longer storage, then as individually selected) | Depends on content | 'until no longer needed' – data privacy laws | Server copies and back-up for 180 days, then deletion of back-up copy. Employees can save copies to personal folders and retain as they choose. After employees leave, personal folders will be kept for 4 years |
| Whistleblower hotline reports | Indefinitely, for future reference | Until risk of litigation is resolved | 3 months after decision not to pursue investigation | Archive after 3 months if no investigation is launched, otherwise keep until investigation is completed and action taken |

126

schedules and protocols for key records. Instead of determining the exact minimum and maximum requirements, companies can pick a number of years that should satisfy most minimum requirements (*e.g.*, 10 years) and that is not too close to 'indefinite' as a default, and then apply shorter retention periods to record types whose retention is particularly costly or risky, for example, email, credit card numbers, system logs and certain paper records. Alternatively, companies can start on a department-by-department basis and tackle 'low-hanging fruit' first – for example human resources and accounting departments which often have systems in place and industry standards to guide them.

Data subjects can be entitled to demand that companies delete data 5.25 about them, for example if the data is false or if the company was not permitted to collect the data in the first place (*e.g.*, if consent was required by not obtained). But, data subjects do not have property rights or a general right to deletion regarding personal data about them. The Court of Justice of the European Union, the EU Data Protection Regulation and national laws of Russia and a few other countries have created "rights to be forgotten," which entitle individuals demand to erasure of inconvenient information about them that may be accurate but no longer relevant. Such laws protect privacy and at the same time raise serious concerns regarding freedom of information and speech, as "rights to be forgotten" are often misused to silence criticism and cover up past scandals. Under California law, online service providers are required since 2014 to enable minors to remove their own posts, but are not obligated to censor online search results or third party re-publications.

# Employee data and monitoring

Employers collect data on employment candidates, employees and former employees in various systems and for different purposes. In this context, employers have to observe restrictions not only in data privacy laws, but also labor and employment laws that are intended to protect workers' rights and vary significantly from country to country including within the European Union.

5.26   *Recruitment and background checks.* Employers should carefully prepare a list of questions that they should and can ask of candidates (*e.g.*, on job application web pages and in interviews) and of background check providers. Background checks are common in some jurisdictions, but practically meaningless in other jurisdictions (due to a lack of data), or even illegal. Employers are well-advised to carefully confer with background check service providers about the sources and legality of their inquiries. Some U.S. states restrict inquiries into credit and driving history, even with employee consent. In some jurisdictions, resumes have to be kept for a certain period of time, while in other jurisdictions it is common or even legally required to return the application materials to candidates who are not hired.

*Employee files.* Many countries regulate what must and may be in employee files (minimum and maximum content) and give employees a right to access the information and demand correction and removal of incorrect or outdated information. Also, information pertaining to criminal actions and sanctions can either not be included or have to be removed after certain time periods. Within the parameters set by labor and employment laws, employers can and must process employee data. Employers do not typically face significant issues from a data privacy law perspective because employers are legally required to collect and process the data (under the employment contracts and various tax, social security and labor laws). But, if employers want to process data beyond the scope of legal requirements, data privacy laws have to be considered, particularly with respect to global human resource information systems within multinational groups, whistleblower hotlines, employee monitoring and investigations.

5.27   *Consent from employees.* Employers should carefully consider the implications of seeking consent from employees. By asking for consent, employers set an expectation or possibly create a contractual entitlement that consent is required for any future changes. In most of the

EEA member states, employee consent is deemed coerced and therefore invalid, except where consent relates to truly optional, ancillary programs (*e.g.*, employee stock options from a U.S. parent company, registering of airline meal preferences in connection with corporate travel arrangements, relationship to emergency contact person, etc.). Even where employee consent is not deemed coerced, employees may be entitled to deny or revoke consent, which would put employers in a difficult position with respect to programs that require participation from all employees. Therefore, most employers seek consent only where it is required and easily available, or with respect to programs that employees can truly accept or reject on a voluntary basis.

*Global HRIS.* Human resource information systems (HRIS), also 5.28 known as 'global employee databases,' are commonly implemented by multinationals for purposes of global planning with respect to human resources needs, career advancement, and to support cross-border interaction. In the interest of economic efficiency, data integrity and security, multinational groups of companies often use global employee databases instead of local systems in each country. Implementing HRIS involves significant data collection, sharing of personal data with other legal entities within the affiliated group and transfers of personal data across borders. Employers in a multinational group of companies that contribute to a HRIS have to clear three hurdles:

+ *Hurdle 1.* The legal entity that acts as employer has to justify the collection of the data for the HRIS. An entity that acts as employer can usually clear this hurdle with relative ease because the employer may or must collect much of the required data categories already for purposes of administering the employment relationship (*e.g.*, payroll, tax withholding, benefits, evaluations, etc.). Where the ultimate group parent company is based in a different country, it is possible that it may ask for data fields to be populated that cannot be legally collected in other countries. For example, U.S. companies routinely collect data on ethnicity and German companies have to withhold church taxes as part of payroll compliance, but data on race and religion cannot typically be collected in other countries. Therefore, companies should assess which data categories can legally be collected in each jurisdiction before populating the HRIS.

+ *Hurdle 2.* The employer has to justify the sharing of data with other group companies that will also access the HRIS. In many countries, the employer entity can obtain employee consent for such data transfers without practical issues. But, in most of the EEA member states, employee consent is deemed coerced and therefore invalid. Many multinational employers therefore shy away from seeking employee consent where it is not possible or absolutely required and instead try to justify the data transfers based on organizational necessities. and a "legitimate interest exception." For example, multinationals find international data sharing necessary based on a number of considerations:

* All group companies need basic information on employees' names, job titles, qualifications and contact information to facilitate global cooperation, communication and team work within the global group.

* The ultimate parent company of the group and, on a 'need to know' basis, supervisors in other affiliated companies, need performance and salary information for purposes of planning and managing human resources on a worldwide basis, including but not limited to ensuring appropriate staffing and evaluating employee fitness for a particular job, promotions, secondments, accounting and cross-charging for salary expenses among group companies.

* If and to the extent the ultimate parent company provides services or benefits directly to employees of subsidiaries (*e.g.*, employee stock options), the parent company needs additional data to offer and manage the respective plans and programs.

* The ultimate parent company is responsible for, and legitimately interested in, legal compliance matters concerning its subsidiaries, *e.g.*, compliance with international embargoes, anti-corruption laws, customs requirements, anti-trust matters, etc.

Companies carefully need to evaluate which data categories are legitimately needed for such purposes – probably not all that the employer can or must collect. To the extent that certain data categories do not need to be used by other group companies, it may nevertheless be possible to store such data in a global HRIS that is hosted by one company, acting as a data processing service provider for the other entities, so long as only the employer entity can access certain data fields for its own purposes.

- *Hurdle 3.* In order to overcome restrictions on cross border data transfers, companies have to select and implement specific compliance mechanisms to comply with laws in Europe and a number of other jurisdictions (see Chapter 2). Most jurisdictions do not restrict international data transfers specifically or allow employers to address the international dimension of the data transfer by obtaining employee consent.

*Monitoring technologies.* Employers are required to make reasonable 5.29 efforts to ensure that their employees follow the law, perform their job duties and protect the company's interests, intellectual property, and data. As part of these efforts, many companies deploy technologies to protect network security and to detect and prevent theft of company intellectual property, excessive personal computer use and illegal or inappropriate behavior by their employees. Companies may also use these technologies to comply with statutory, regulatory or industry requirements, for example mandates for the prevention of harassment in the workplace, stock exchange rules requiring retention of correspondence with the public, and data security requirements arising under data privacy laws.

State-of-the-art network security tools offer the capability to monitor a variety of aspects of an individual's use of company computers, smartphones, networks and systems. Such tools can log addresses of websites visited and also the actual content of data sent and received, including form data submitted by the user to websites and the full text of e-mails and chat sessions between the user and third parties. Some employers also deploy security cameras (in office space or laptop devices), track keystrokes and monitor employee locations via RFID tags in vehicles and devices.

Such monitoring technologies can be very effective and thus be required to support compliance with data privacy and security laws. But, such technologies can also intrude into the privacy of employees and people outside the company with whom employees communicate. Therefore, companies have to observe a number of restrictions and limitations regarding the use of monitoring technologies.

In the United States, most privacy laws restrict monitoring only where the monitored have a reasonable expectation of privacy, *i.e.*, an actual expectation of privacy that courts find reasonable under the circumstances. Employers can destroy their employees' actual expectation of privacy via conspicuous, detailed and broadly worded notices. It can be more difficult for employers to destroy the actual privacy expectations and rights of those with whom employees communicate (customers, suppliers, personal contacts), but employers can add notices to outbound email, websites, contracts and call center scripts. Also, employers can contractually obligate their employees to notify their contacts. It is important that employers keep the notices up to date with actual technologies deployed because courts may otherwise find limited, reasonable expectations of privacy in employees and others. Additionally, U.S. employers should carefully review state law requirements with respect to particularly intrusive forms of monitoring, such as cameras in locker rooms (which is prohibited in California, for example), location tracking via RFID tags and similar tracking technologies (also prohibited in California, and a consent exception exists only for certain forms of vehicle tracking), and the interception of live communications, such as plain old phone calls, text messages, instant messages and probably email correspondence (which requires consent from all parties in a number of U.S. states). Whether email filtering for anti-spam and anti-virus protection constitutes interception, requiring all-party consent, has not been completely decided by U.S. courts yet; and most companies do not seem concerned as such filtering technologies are commonly used by companies and governments around the world. Some companies decide, however, to leave it to the discretion of individual employees to turn anti-spam filters on or off to eliminate concerns regarding interception. Intended recipients tend to be free to filter or discard communications in their own discretion under most laws, although restrictions apply to recording of voice communications without the consent of all parties.

In Europe and some countries outside of Europe, employees and other data subjects are protected against monitoring and other privacy intrusions regardless of whether a reasonable expectation of privacy exists. Most labor laws outside the United States require employers to reach an express agreement with employees about changes in employment conditions, including the introduction of monitoring technologies. Non-consenting employees can be sanctioned or laid off in some jurisdictions, but typically not in Europe. Additionally, employee consent is presumed coerced and ineffective in most European countries. Companies in Europe can justify email searches in cases of substantiated suspicions of wrongdoing, but the deployment of continuous monitoring technologies is difficult to justify and may require agreements with collective employee representatives (such as works councils or unions) and prior approval from data protection authorities, labor courts and other government authorities. Therefore, many companies do not subject European employees to continuous monitoring save in cases of suspicions generated by other circumstances (*e.g.*, specific complaints or supervisors' observations).

With respect to global systems, it can be challenging to disable monitoring features for a specific country or region. Some companies try to use contractual approaches and obligate their technical staff to refrain from activating or actively using certain monitoring features on European employees. Theoretically, employers could also overcome some restrictions by categorically prohibiting employees from using company equipment and communication networks for any personal or private purposes, as access to purely business information tends to be far less regulated. But, most employers do not find such prohibitions practical and a selectively enforced policy to this effect would be disregarded by courts (for example, if an employer states a policy prohibition but in practice tolerates personal use by employees).

Some companies condition the permission to make personal use of company systems on the employees' grant of express consent to monitoring. Employees who grant such consent are permitted to use systems for personal and private purposes, subject to monitoring. Similarly, employees who want to use their own smartphones and other devices at work, or for work-related purposes, are allowed to do so under voluntary 'bring your own device' (BYOD) programs on the condition that they agree to submit their own devices to the same monitoring and security measures that the employer deploys to protect company-owned systems. This means, for example, that the employer may remotely delete all data (including personal pictures) if a device is lost or stolen and that the employer may search a personal device or apply a litigation hold. Employees who do not grant such consent are also subjected to monitoring regarding company-owned devices. Such monitoring should not unreasonably affect their personal privacy, because they would not be using the company-owned devices for personal matters. Such a policy would seem to ensure employee awareness and strike a compromise between employee privacy interests and legitimate data security and compliance interests of the employer. But, it is not clear whether courts and government authorities will accept this approach in all circumstances.

If companies do not observe these legal requirements, they risk violating labor, privacy, wiretap and other laws, many of which carry severe criminal penalties. In one high profile case in France, an employer searched an employee's emails on company systems and discovered evidence that the employee operated an illegal, competing business during work hours and by using employer resources; but, because the email search was found illegal, the employer had to reinstate the disloyal employee and pay damages. Also, companies may end up with evidence that they are required to act on under the laws of one jurisdiction while being prohibited from having or using such information under the laws of other jurisdictions.

In conclusion, employers should:

 **Action items**

- Keep track of what technologies they buy and deploy that record data relating to their employees, including technologies whose primary goal is monitoring (such as security cameras, key stroke logging, web logs, call recording, automated email storage and location tracking devices) and technologies that have other purposes but also store data without affirmative, intentional actions by employees (such as email filtering, network security tools and location tracking to retrieve stolen devices);
- Assess whether deployment of any of these technologies is completely outlawed or partially restricted under the laws of relevant jurisdictions, or whether notices to or consent from employees and/or external data subjects is required;
- Consider administrative or organizational measures that could help satisfy legal restrictions, such as enabling employees to configure and control those tools that are not primarily intended for monitoring (for example, spam filters);
- Prepare and maintain detailed notices and consent forms (for employees and external data subjects, company-owned devices and employee-owned devices), ideally supplemented by frequent, real-time reminders (such as log-in screens) and internal protocols regarding the use of the technologies deployed;
- Consult with works councils and collective employee representation where legally required outside the United States; and
- Submit notifications or requests for authorizations to data protection authorities, labor courts or other government authorities where legally required outside the United States.

5.30 *Investigations.* If and when a concrete need arises to investigate particular employees, employers should assess the legality of the contemplated measures under data privacy and employment laws and consider if and how any evidence gathered can and must be used.

If an emergency arises and the employer is primarily concerned about stopping harmful or illegal conduct (for example, an imminent danger of trade secret theft), an employer may decide that it has to act fast and cannot afford to wait for the outcome of complex legal analysis under privacy laws. In such cases, employers should be mindful of the fact that they may expose themselves to risks under data privacy or employment laws and they may not be able to use any evidence gathered in legal proceedings against the employees concerned.

When situations are less urgent, employers should carefully consider the costs and benefits of action and inaction. In some cases, a general reminder to all employees about company policies may be sufficient to address a particular concern and improve the company's legal position without creating exposure under employment or privacy laws. But, if circumstances warrant a decision on whether to deploy or utilize certain monitoring technologies or otherwise investigate an incident, companies should consider all potentially applicable laws in all jurisdictions affected and:

 **Action items**

- Verify that the potentially affected employees and external data subjects have received adequate notices or consented to applicable monitoring, as required;
- Determine whether collective employee representation consultation and government notifications/approval requirements have been satisfied, where required;
- Determine whether a legal basis for international data transfers has been established, as necessary; and
- Consider any evidence that could be generated by the contemplated monitoring or investigation that can be legally used in actions against the employees or external data subjects concerned.

*Whistleblower hotlines.* The Securities and Exchange Commission and  5.31 stock exchanges in the United States require publicly listed U.S. companies to establish hotlines that allow whistleblowers to report compliance issues anonymously. Also, many companies believe that they should implement such reporting programs to mitigate risks resulting from lax compliance attitudes by managers, employees and suppliers. Therefore, many U.S. companies – and increasingly also non-U.S. companies – operate whistleblower hotline programs, often via dedicated websites and call centers.

European data protection authorities, on the other hand, are concerned about the potential for abuse of hotlines and anonymous reporting, which can involve the processing and storage of potentially sensitive data that can harm employees without much transparency, access or opportunity to defend themselves, particularly if data is reported anonymously and decisions are made in other countries and subject to other laws. For example, a U.S. company might instruct its Canadian or German subsidiary to fire an employee because of an alleged violation of U.S. embargo laws that the employee was not even required or allowed to observe as a matter of Canadian or German law. Given the experience with anonymous reporting in fascist and socialist regimes in twentieth century Europe, some European data protection authorities require prior government approval before the implementation of hotlines and many have postulated a number of severe restrictions on whistleblower hotline compliance programs, particularly with respect to:

• The types of offenses that may be reported (crimes vs. violations of company code of conduct);

• Whether reports must relate only to managers or may also concern other employees and representatives of business partners;

• Whether some or all reportable offenses may be reported anonymously;

• How long companies may retain the reported information in case they do or do not follow through with an investigation (typically not more than two months).

U.S. companies with European subsidiaries have to carefully assess the obligations on the group under all applicable legal regimes. If the company determines that it is not obligated or interested in offering the hotline in Europe, it could exclude Europe from the program. If, however, the company determines that it will offer the program, then it needs to decide whether it can and wants to establish a uniform European version of its reporting program that complies with the stricter requirements in each European country (this allows some administrative efficiencies and savings but inevitably results in a severely 'watered down' program), or whether it will allow as much anonymous reporting as possible in each jurisdiction (which requires a country-by-country localization of the reporting program and significantly higher investment in legal review, and which will result in divergent reporting rules for each country). In any event, each participating European subsidiary will have to notify its employees about the data processing aspects of the program and how they can be affected individually by reports. Additionally, some entities have to obtain prior local government approvals before launching a whistleblower hotline program.

*Social media.* Employers are struggling to define policies on blogging  5.32
and social media by employees. In principle, similar concerns apply with respect to any other type of employee communications. If employees make statements and disclose their affiliation with the employer, then such statements are attributable to the employers – regardless of whether they are made in print media, press releases or social media. Such statements can affect the employer's reputation, and they can also be qualified as or conflict with advertisements, warranty statements, financial results forecasts, etc. Hence, in principle, employers should treat social media communications similar to more traditional forms of communications and ensure adequate review of such statements before they are published. The sheer volume of review requests can become overwhelming. Employers need to determine how valuable communications in social media are and either handle the review process restrictively or make additional review resources available.

When employees make statements concerning the employer's affairs (*e.g.,* products, services, financial health, etc.) without disclosing their affiliation, such statements can easily mislead the public. Employers have to ensure compliance with unfair competition laws regarding undisclosed endorsements, subliminal advertising, etc. Many employers simply prohibit such activities.

Recruiters and human resources personnel also tend to find information on candidates and employees particularly interesting. Social media platforms provide a rich source of information. As a rule of thumb, recruiters are advised to search only for information that they would also be allowed to ask the candidate directly. A number of U.S. states have expressly prohibited employers, colleges and certain other organizations from requesting candidates to provide their social media user account credentials, but even where such express laws do not apply, this practice usually violates the social media provider's terms of use and could therefore constitute a violation of computer interference laws (including the U.S. Computer Fraud and Abuse Act). Additionally, human resources professionals should consider the following points:

• If a candidate affirmatively consents to information access (*e.g.,* by referring to a profile in application materials), the research is generally permissible. The same should generally apply with respect to information that a candidate publicly posts or broadcasts without any restrictions, *e.g.*, on a completely public profile. More caution is advised when a profile is presented only to a limited circle on a social media platform. Then, human resources professionals should consider only using data on social media platforms that are dedicated to professional purposes and not purely private posts (even if they may be able to access these). Actively concealed research methods (*e.g.*, through anonymous accounts or, fake friends requests) constitute unfair business practices or misrepresentation under most jurisdictions' laws.

• Even where online research is generally legal, companies should carefully consider whether acquiring too much information is in their best interests. On social media platforms, companies can inadvertently find sensitive information that they would much rather not know, *e.g.*, information regarding candidates' gender, sexual orientation, ethnic background, disabilities, political opinions, union activities, religion, etc. To reduce the risk of discrimination claims based on such information, companies can task different employees with online research and candidate selection and instruct the researchers to refrain from passing on information categories that cannot legally be used in the selection process and could support discrimination claims. For similar reasons, particularly larger businesses should implement consistent rules and practices regarding the amount and methods of online research and be careful to verify the accuracy of research results.

Other topics to address in social media policies include the following:

• Confidentiality

• Restrictions on personal use during working hours or on employer equipment

• Ownership of information, accounts, etc. (*e.g.*, employee is required to assign Twitter account and list of followers in case of termination)

• Prohibition of harassment of co-workers

• Disclosures regarding employer monitoring

• Anti-spam law compliance.

# Financial information

People are particularly concerned about financial data. Lawmakers and   5.33
industry associations have created a number of specific legal requirements that companies have to observe with respect to financial data,
including the following:

+ Companies have to notify data subjects about security breaches and
  loss of certain types of financial account information under the laws
  of most U.S. states and an increasing number of other countries,
  unless the data was encrypted.

+ Companies must not transmit or store U.S. social security numbers
  under some states' laws, unless the data is encrypted.

+ Under the standards of the Payment Card Industry (PCI standards),
  banks, merchants and other companies involved must encrypt certain credit card and transaction-related information and apply
  other data security standards.

+ Credit bureaus have to provide data subjects with access to one free
  credit report per year and process corrections, under the laws of
  many jurisdictions.

+ Companies may not use credit reports for certain decisions under
  some jurisdictions' laws and they may have to notify data subjects
  of adverse decisions made on the basis of credit report information,
  so that data subjects can take actions to protect themselves.

Additionally, financial services providers are subject to industry-
specific data security and privacy laws in many jurisdictions, including
the Gramm–Leach–Bliley Act (GLB) in the United States.

# Government investigations, information requests

5.34   Companies should document and follow clear guidelines as to what data they routinely provide to governments and how to process extraordinary information requests, e.g., in the context of investigations. Applicable law usually defines specific duties for companies to disclose data to governments for certain purposes, but data privacy laws also limit what companies are permitted to disclose. Just because the police want certain data does not mean that you are legally permitted to produce it.

This is particularly true in a cross border context where a company may be required under the laws of one country (say, the United States) to provide data while the laws of another country (say, Switzerland) prohibit such disclosure. Such situations can warrant a thorough jurisdictional analysis. If conflicts of law cannot be resolved, companies have to make a risk-based decision as to which law to follow and which to break. For example, European airlines were caught between a rock and a hard place when U.S. authorities demanded certain passenger data under penalty of law and European data protection authorities prohibited the disclosures. Other examples resulted when U.S. tax authorities cracked down on SWIFT (a worldwide banking network organization) and banks in Switzerland to release information on foreign bank accounts held by U.S. taxpayers. In these cases, the airlines and financial institutions in Europe caved in to U.S. pressure and disclosed personal data in apparent violation of European data protection laws, bank secrecy laws and blocking statutes, as applicable. European authorities responded with administrative and criminal proceedings. Such cases, where companies are prohibited and required to provide data under conflicting laws of two countries, are relatively rare. In many cases, companies can avoid or mitigate conflicts by planning ahead. For example, companies can maintain copies of databases in jurisdictions where they are likely to receive government access requests; this will eliminate the need for international transfers triggered by government requests, which is restricted under blocking statutes in some jurisdictions. Also, companies can seek advance consent from customers for disclosures under certain circumstances. And, companies can carefully plan their corporate structures to minimize jurisdictional exposure, e.g., by separating databases and business lines in separate legal entities and jurisdictions.

But, even within one jurisdiction, companies can receive information requests from government authorities that they must not respond to based on data privacy laws. Companies that release data pursuant to informal requests, or faulty subpoenas, warrants and court orders are occasionally sued by the affected data subjects and can also be sanctioned by other government authorities for the unlawful data disclosure. Good faith reliance on the legitimacy of the government request is usually not an absolute defense. Companies that frequently receive such requests should develop clear protocols on conditions and processes for disclosures. For infrequent types of requests, companies should at least define a basic process; for example, data shall not be disclosed until in-house legal counsel or the data protection officer approves the disclosure.

Within the legal limits of disclosure obligations and prohibitions, companies tend to have some discretion, which they should exercise consciously based on business objectives. For example, a company that has been defrauded by a customer or receives complaints from some customers about fraud by another customer will probably want to disclose as much personal information about suspects to the police as legally permissible. On the other hand, a financial institution would probably want to disclose as little customer data as possible to foreign tax authorities due to the likely impact on customers, customer relations and business. Telecoms, Internet Service Providers and social media companies tend to get caught in the middle of disputes between users, government agencies and courts because these companies have evidence and information on user identities and whereabouts. Depending on the particulars of their business, these companies may generally lean towards or against disclosure or have different preferences on a case-by-case basis (*e.g.*, prefer disclosure to help police catch child molesters and fraudsters on the site, but oppose disclosure requests in the context of celebrity defamation lawsuits or campaigns against political dissidents). Another important factor that companies need to consider when shaping their policies is the cost and resource drain associated with the processing of government information requests. In business-to-business dealings, data processing service providers (*e.g.*, cloud computing companies) can try to contractually shift costs associated with government inquiries to their corporate customers. But, in a consumer business context, indemnification and reimbursement clauses in click-through terms and conditions can be unenforceable or even unlawful.

Based on these and other considerations, companies should consciously shape their internal protocols and also their external privacy notices, statements and contracts with data subjects. In privacy notices, statements and contracts, companies can set the stage for easy disclosures (*e.g.*, by obtaining consent or providing prior notice about the company's policy on disclosures, which will inhibit users' privacy claims vis-à-vis the companies and, by extension, also vis-à-vis the government) or for strong opposition of government requests (*e.g.*, by making strict promises to users regarding disclosures in privacy statements and contracts, which can help justify opposition to government information requests). Also, companies can decide to keep more or less data and for longer or shorter periods based on expectations as to what government agencies may request and what the company will want to disclose, while keeping in mind data retention and destruction requirements. When the company receives a government information request that raises concerns under the law of another jurisdiction, the company can try to negotiate a narrower scope. Occasionally, courts and government authorities are sympathetic to international comity considerations, especially where the requested information is held abroad, for example by a subsidiary company. But, U.S. courts have generally taken the position in the context of litigation-related discovery that information that is physically on U.S. territory or accessible by persons on U.S. territory has to be produced in accordance with U.S. law, without much regard for foreign laws.

If a company determines that it is legally prohibited from responding to a particular government request, or the company determines that it is not legally obligated to respond and based on business considerations does not want to respond, the company may be able to refer to data protection laws and privacy interests of the concerned data subjects in an objection to the government request. Or, the company may be able to notify the data subject of the government inquiry to give the data subject an opportunity to challenge the government directly. But, companies cannot typically assert their own privacy rights because companies tend to be excluded from data privacy protection, such as in the United States. On the other hand, a few countries including Austria, Italy and Switzerland also protect data relating to legal entities as 'personal data,' so in these jurisdictions, companies may also be able to assert their own original privacy rights against government inquiries.

In some scenarios, companies may be able to protect their information by referring to trade secret protection laws or data privacy laws. They may also contest requests for information on the grounds that the requests are unduly burdensome or that the data requested is not relevant to the purpose for which it is requested.

# Health information

Companies have to observe specific restrictions applicable to 'sensi-  5.35
tive personal data' under European data protection laws with respect
to health-related information, given its special importance and risks
of disclosure (*e.g.*, potential discrimination by employers and insurance companies based on health-related information). In particular,
companies have to obtain express consent before processing health
information and other sensitive personal data under European data
protection laws.

In the United States, healthcare providers and their service providers are subject to sector-specific legislation under the federal Health
Information Portability and Accountability Act (HIPAA) and some
state laws. Companies that neither provide nor work with healthcare
or health insurance providers (*e.g.*, online consumer health-related
information services) may not fall under HIPAA at all, even if they
do collect and use personal health information. But, since 2015, they
may be covered by California medical privacy law, which also covers
providers of online services, software and hardware if their products
are used in connection with healthcare. Service providers that want
to work for U.S. hospitals, health insurance companies and other
'covered entities' under HIPAA have to assess whether this makes
them a 'business associate' under HIPAA and whether the resulting compliance burdens are economically acceptable. Data security
and retention requirements under HIPAA are usually manageable
for most service providers, but some companies find data access and
deletion obligations and the need to get all subcontractors to sign
business associate agreements challenging. As a practical matter,
companies in the service provider space (*e.g.*, cloud computing, software as a service, data processing) should carefully analyze their obligations as a 'business associate,' how they would tackle compliance
and what they can contractually promise their customers. Some have
argued in the past that they did not qualify as 'business associates'
even if they received health information because their role was one of
a 'mere conduit' (*e.g.*, telecommunications or email services provider,
data storage company, platform as a service, software as a service).
But, the U.S. government has never condoned this view and in fact
opposed it in 2013 guidance. Also, customers may not understand or
agree and the resulting confusion may delay or prevent sales. If service providers find it manageable to take on 'business associate' obligations under HIPAA and successfully tackle the healthcare sector,

they should prepare standard template agreements, data security program descriptions and checklists to review customer agreements and requirements.

As a practical matter, companies outside the healthcare sector should try to minimize the amount of health-related personal data they collect, due to the potential regulatory impact. Employers may have to collect some health information to administer benefits, accommodate disabled employees or process work-related accident cases. But, employers typically do not have to – and should not – share this information with affiliated or unaffiliated companies, except where legally required or under data processing services arrangements where the recipient company acts as a mere data processor (*e.g.*, shared services centers, general data storage solutions, etc.). Employers should try to keep health-related information out of global human resources information systems (where they can track days of absence, but they should not track 'sick days' specifically). Also, if employers want to occasionally offer healthcare services or wellness programs (*e.g.*, flu shots, massages or health and fitness trackers), they should consider ways to organize the service so that providers deal directly with employees and employers do not have to collect or share any personal health information.

# Internet of Everything, big data, data brokers

Manufacturers have added connectivity features to more and more 5.36
products for various purposes as cellular and wireless communication connections have become omnipresent and economically viable.
Autonomous cars, drones and other devices can and must be tracked
and communicate with each other as well as third parties (including cyclists and pedestrians) for safety and loss prevention purposes.
The "Internet of Things," "Internet of Everything" or "machine-
to-machine" (M2M) commerce and communications spin off vast
amounts of data relating to devices as well as their owners, holders,
operators, passengers and persons close to their sensors. Aside from
concerns regarding notice, consent and accountability, regulators and
consumer protection authorities are particularly concerned about
data security risks associated with big data, and, more generally, with
large data bases. Citizens around the world are wary that not even the
NSA can keep data secure. Many industrial systems and consumer
products are far less secure and thus vulnerable to attacks. The U.S.
Federal Trade Commission brings legal action against companies that
sell devices with insufficient data security features, Examples include a
company that sold security cameras that transmitted data to be viewed
over the Internet with less data security safeguards than the Federal
Trade Commission expected and another company that sold software
updates with known vulnerabilities. Cybersecurity concerns also apply
with respect to cars, weapons systems, industrial complexes, energy
plants, airplanes and other machines that could be hijacked remotely
by hackers. Companies should consider cybersecurity carefully in every
product, system and premises design process.

The Internet of Everything also feeds big data. Information technology companies use the term 'big data' with excitement to describe
technologies, services and applications that can process large amounts
of often unstructured data, *e.g.,* to develop facial recognition systems
for authentication and security purposes, for new forms of predictive
analysis, urban planning, traffic forecasts and optimization, and medical research. Data privacy regulators and activists on the other hand
often use the term with a negative connotation to refer to situations
where companies or governments use excessive amounts of existing
data for new purposes without prior notice to data subjects and for
which data subjects have not granted valid consent, *e.g.,* harvesting
photos on social media pages for facial recognition systems to identify

persons for law enforcement or marketing purposes, GPS data to position radar controls to catch traffic offenders, browsing history to predict interests for certain products, etc.

Another source of big data analysis is online research. Companies use 'scraping' technologies to automatically collect data from Internet websites for myriad business purposes, including indexing websites to support search engine technologies, but also to gather data for big data analysis. Such data collection methods can violate privacy laws (if personally identifiable data is among the data collected), copyright laws (if the scraped websites do not permit copying via automated tools in their terms of use), trespass prohibitions and computer interference laws (including the United States Computer Fraud and Abuse Act) if the scraped websites expressly prohibit access by scraping technologies, such as robots, spiders and web crawlers. Under the laws of some countries, personal data is not protected if it is intentionally publicized, but European laws do not contain such broad carve-outs and would tend to prohibit collection of personal data via scraping unless the data subject consents. For example, if a data subject posts biographical information about herself on a personal home page without any restrictions, then others would be allowed to access this information via search engines and other technologies for their own purposes, based on a "legitimate interest exception" (or express consent – if the home page posts such consent). The difficulty in practice for companies engaging in scraping, however, is to determine which pages display personal data with permissive terms of use and which do not. If companies deploy 'scraping technologies' that ignore 'no robots' scripts and circumvent access restrictions, such as CAPTCHAs or registration requirements (by automatically creating webmail accounts and user IDs for the sole purpose of registering), then they run additional risks of violating laws prohibiting unfair business practices, online fraud and circumvention of technical protection measures (such as Section 1201-4 of the U.S. Copyright Act, part of the Digital Millennium Copyright Act, or DMCA).

Big data is traded by 'data brokers,' *i.e.*, companies that buy and resell information, including personal information. 'Data brokers' process information on data subjects with whom they do not have a direct business relationship. Such data subjects do not typically receive privacy notices and do not know much about the identities or practices of data brokers. This has recently raised concerns and regulatory interest in the United States. Under data protection laws in the EEA, data brokers are already subject to existing notice and consent require-ments; in some jurisdictions, they can also rely on "legitimate interest" exceptions, particularly with respect to data that data subjects make available without restrictions, *e.g.*, photos on public home pages and social networks.

## Jurisdiction

5.37 Every compliance effort and legal liability analysis begins with two questions: (1) what laws apply and (2) how can they be enforced? With respect to data privacy compliance, particularly in the international context, it is necessary to identify relevant laws and prioritize compliance efforts.

5.38 *Applicable law.* The answer to the first question – what foreign privacy laws apply – can be a long list. Under customary international law, every sovereign country is free to legislate regarding whatever it is interested in. Typically, countries apply their data privacy laws to you if you deploy employees or equipment in such countries' territory. Some countries go further and also apply their data privacy laws to companies abroad if such companies collect data remotely via local business partners, targeted websites (as indicated by languages, localized content, local phone numbers, etc.), or just on the basis that the foreign company collects data on residents or citizens of the legislating country. Therefore, many companies with some more or less direct business connection to other countries find on closer inspection that other countries' privacy laws apply to their data processing activities.

European Union law sets some limitations on EU member states' ability to apply their national data privacy laws extra-territorially against companies that are established in other EEA member states. An EEA-based data controller has to comply only with the laws of the EEA member state where it maintains a branch or other significant, physical presence, even if it collects data from other EEA member states. This privilege is not available to companies outside the EEA, however. Therefore, a U.S.-based e-commerce company with customers throughout the EEA may have to comply with more than 30 different national laws. If the U.S. company incorporates a subsidiary, however, in, say, Ireland (low corporate income tax rate) or Luxembourg (low VAT rate), to become the sole contracting party and data controller for all European customers, then the new subsidiary would have to comply only with the privacy laws of the one jurisdiction where it is incorporated. The significance of this advantage may be reduced by the harmonization brought by the EU General Data Protection Regulation, but companies may still want to consider this as many national data protection laws are expected to remain in place. Companies in the United States may be able to invoke similar protections under the U.S.

Constitution's 'Commerce Clause' against state laws that discriminate against, or unduly burden, interstate commerce.

*Enforceable law:* The answer to the second threshold question – how   5.39
can data privacy laws be enforced across countries' borders – tends to be more complex but usually quite helpful in prioritizing international compliance efforts. As a general matter, countries cannot easily enforce their laws against companies that do not have a physical presence, assets or employees on their territory. Customary international law prohibits countries from sending government officials across borders to issue warnings, collect fines or make arrests. Even mailing or emailing orders or official letters with warnings or threats across borders is not allowed without seeking consent from the home jurisdiction of the enforcement target. Some countries cooperate relatively closely on some topics (*e.g.*, EU member states), but more often than not it is difficult and burdensome to take enforcement actions against companies in other countries. Private plaintiffs (*e.g.*, data subjects) will often be able to convince a court in their home country to take jurisdiction over a foreign company; however, any resulting judgment is difficult or impossible to enforce across borders. Injunctions, penalties and other sanctions cannot typically be enforced across borders. Money awards (*e.g.*, judgments for damages) tend to be easier to enforce in other countries, so long as they do not involve punitive or penalty elements or invoke procedural principles that offend public policy. But, this leaves only compensation for pecuniary losses, which tends to be low and may not be worth pursuing in data privacy-related cases. For these and a number of practical reasons (including costs, difficulties of pursuing claims in other jurisdictions, languages, legal systems, etc.), the risk of enforcement of foreign data privacy laws tends to be much lower than the risk of applicability.

A number of noteworthy exceptions apply, though. Companies that have contractually agreed to comply with foreign data privacy laws (*e.g.*, in the EU Standard Contractual Clauses or free-form services agreements) may be forced to comply by their foreign business partners that have the means and motivation to press the issue, for example because they in turn are directly subject to governmental enforcement actions or consider compliance important to their business. Also, companies may have submitted to foreign laws and agreed to cooperate with foreign data protection authorities more or less voluntarily in connection with applications for permits, licenses or under the EU-U.S. Privacy Shield Program.

Based on these considerations, companies can create a priority list of jurisdictions whose data protection laws are particularly likely to apply and be enforced. Within this list, jurisdictions may be ranked based on the strength of connection (physical presence and data processing employees > targeted website > resident data subjects), whether the company has contractually committed or otherwise submitted to another country's laws or jurisdiction (*e.g.*, in connection with permits, licenses or the EU-U.S. Privacy Shield Program), and whether the company's home jurisdiction cooperates with the foreign country on data privacy or other law enforcement matters. If the remaining list of relevant jurisdictions is still overwhelming, companies tend to prioritize further by market considerations and turn first to countries with key markets, high sensitivity to privacy violations that can adversely affect business (*e.g.*, Germany) or particularly scary enforcement cases (*e.g.*, astronomical fines in Spain, publicized arrest of U.S. data privacy officer in Italy).

# K – Contracts

Companies have to take data privacy into account when they prepare 5.40
template agreements and review and negotiate contracts with others.
This can create operational challenges in larger organizations because
commercial contracts managers do not always have deep expertise in
the area of privacy compliance. Therefore, companies need to define
processes that involve privacy compliance gatekeepers in the contracts
drafting and negotiations process, as required, and provide the commercial contracts management group with template forms or clauses
that serve the company's needs in certain standard scenarios.

Contracts play a number of different roles with respect to data privacy
compliance, including the following:

- Contracts can allow companies to process personal data because
  they can either contain clauses in which the data subject permits
  the processing or clauses in which companies assume an obligation
  that necessitates the processing of personal data. Some companies
  intentionally include contractual duties into standard agreements
  that serve as a justification for processing of personal data, in lieu of
  seeking consent from the data subjects.

- Contracts are a means by which companies impose restrictions and
  data security obligations on employees, independent contractors
  and service providers in order to satisfy and pass on compliance
  obligations.

- Contracts enable companies to allocate commercial risks, liabilities, indemnification and cooperation duties in case of data security
  breaches, claims and lawsuits relating to data privacy compliance.

- Contracts with certain clauses have to be put in place to satisfy certain
  compliance requirements, for example, EU Standard Contractual
  Clauses, HIPAA business associate agreements and certain compliance undertakings under Payment Card Industry Standards.

- Contracts can invoke additional scrutiny and jurisdiction; therefore, companies need to think twice before they seek consent or an
  agreement from data subjects regarding a privacy notice or policy.

For more information on topics to consider and terms to include, see
Chapter 3.

# Location data

5.41   Location data is not (yet) included in the definition of 'special categories of personal data' (*a.k.a.* 'sensitive data') under EU General Data
Protection Regulation, but it is specifically called out in restrictions
on "profiling" and receives increasing attention as a valuable asset and
source of risk for privacy and individuals. A number of jurisdictions
have passed laws to restrict location tracking via RFID tags and other
technologies except with express consent of the person in possession
of the tracking device (*e.g.,* vehicle, computer, smart phone) or a judicial warrant for law enforcement. Mobile app platforms require app
providers to expressly seek standardized permissions regarding location data, and regulators have taken action against companies that
gathered location data without sufficient notice and consent (*e.g.,* the
U.S. Federal Trade Commission launched a complaint against the provider of a flashlight app that collected location information from users).
Companies have to assess and address compliance requirements when
they implement location-based behavioral advertisement programs,
company fleet management tracking devices or lost or stolen computer
location software.

# Minors

Children generally do not have the legal capacity to grant valid consent 5.42
or conclude contracts. Therefore, parental consent to contract formation or data processing is necessary in most countries, even without
any special legislation protecting children.

In the United States, where consent and contracts are not generally
required under data privacy laws, lawmakers opted for specific legislation to protect children against Internet companies. Under the
Children's Online Privacy Protection Act (COPPA) of 1998, website
operators have to comply with specific requirements if they knowingly
collect data from children under age 13 or because their website is
directed at children under 13. The Federal Trade Commission recently
clarified that companies must obtain parental consent even if they collect data on a no-name basis via persistent identifiers, such as cookies.
Whether a site is directed at children depends on an assessment of
the website's topics, graphics, model ages, etc. A clause in the website
terms of use according to which users have to be 13 years or older does
not suffice to avoid the applicability of COPPA. If COPPA applies, the
website operator has to address one privacy policy to children and
one to parents, and obtain parental consent. Website operators find
it difficult to establish with certainty whether the consenting person
who registers as the child's parent is in fact a parent (and not the
child herself under a different email address or user ID). If the website
operator follows self-regulatory guidelines that have been approved by
the Federal Trade Commission, the website operator will be deemed to
be in compliance with COPPA.

Under the EU General Data Protection Regulation, online service providers have to obtain parental consent before they collect personal data
from children under 16 years, and individual EEA Member States may
lower the threshold age to 13 as in the United States.

# Notification of data security breaches

5.43   Companies in California have been required since 2003 to notify data subjects without undue delay if unauthorized persons accessed certain unencrypted, sensitive information (originally including health information, social security numbers and credit card information - now also online account credentials and automated license plate scanner data). Data processors (such as cloud computing and other service providers) are typically required to notify the data controller but not the data subjects.

Good faith access by unauthorized employees is typically exempt. Other U.S. States and countries have followed suit and enacted similar laws, some including additional data categories, 30 to 60 day notification deadlines and requirements to notify government authorities in particularly serious cases.

5.44   The EU waited until 2016 to update its data protection laws and then enacted extremely broad and stringent requirements to become effective in May 2018. Under the EU General Data Protection Regulation, companies in the EEA are required to notify data protection authorities and individual data subjects within 72 hours of any breach of security leading to the accidental or unlawful destruction, loss, alteration, unauthorized disclosure of, or access to, personal data. As in other areas of EU data protection laws, companies can take comfort in the fact that extremely broad and stringent requirements are paired up with extremely broad and vague exceptions: companies do not have to notify breaches if risks to rights and freedoms of individuals are unlikely.

Some companies have also assumed notification obligations in privacy notices or in contracts with customers and other business partners.

5.45   *Preparing for a breach.* To prepare for data security breaches, companies should appoint a cross-disciplinary incident response team and train the entire workforce. All employees should receive a brief outline of protocol, perhaps in an employee handbook or separate one-pager, instructing them to report all incidents to the team immediately and confidentially. The protocol should define reportable incidents broadly in the interest of keeping the protocol simple and maximizing information intake. The incident response team should maintain a concise protocol outlining a process on how to respond to breach incidents. Such a process is best developed with particular scenarios in mind that are most likely or most severely going to affect a particular organization. Companies that make an effort to anticipate particularly likely and severe scenarios achieve two benefits: they both improve general compliance and also take a first step toward preventing incidents. For example, if you analyze the risks and liabilities arising from an incident of unauthorized access to employee social security numbers, you may decide to deploy additional encryption functionality, eliminate spreadsheets from HR staff laptops, etc. Or, a company that hosts significant amounts of data for other enterprises as a data processing agent may prepare an inventory of contractual notification obligations to determine quickly whether notices are required in case of certain incidents.

*Service providers* tend not to accept unlimited liability for security    5.46
breaches in cases of negligence or breaches of specific contractual commitments. Some companies obtain specific security breach insurance coverage, but premiums and deductibles tend to be relatively high. In the context of data processing services arrangements, companies tend to negotiate specific processes on how to handle data security breaches, including coordinating communications to the affected data subjects and possibly offering credit protection services to affected data subjects. Occasionally data controllers try to contractually shift notification obligations to their service providers, but this is not in either party's interest: The data controller has the primary relationship with the data subject, the most to lose from a botched notification and the statutory obligation to notify. Service providers are often not in a position to deliver notices and may need additional contact information from their customer, the data controller, which the data controller should be hesitant to provide right after a breach occurred. Also, the data subjects expect to hear from the data controller, not a service provider.

*Breach response:* In case of an incident, the team should try to gather    5.47
crucial information and take critical steps, including:

• Identifying the nature of the incident and the data affected,

• Preventing any further unauthorized use or disclosure of data,

• Preserving evidence that is relevant for the investigation and any subsequent actions,

+ Clarifying what data categories and systems were potentially accessed,

+ Determining who and where the potentially affected data subjects are,

+ Confirming who inside and outside the organization knows about the incident already,

+ Investigating any indications regarding a potential threat of abuse or harm.

5.48    Team members must be carefully selected to avoid compromising any investigations that may become necessary (in case of concerns regarding inside threats). The team should typically include an attorney and a data security or information technology specialist. Legal counsel should lead any investigations to preserve attorney-client-privilege where possible. Before a decision on notification is made, the number of informed persons should be kept to a minimum to avoid forcing public responses solely due to concerns about potential rumors. If disclosure is inevitable, a public relations or communications specialist and other stakeholders (for example, a member of the human resources department if employee data is affected, or account managers if customer data is affected) should be involved. The team needs to develop a timetable regarding possible notifications, for example, first to law enforcement officials where required or desired, then to affected data subjects, and finally to business partners and the public. Even if the company decides to keep the incident as secret as possible, it is often prudent to prepare a press release and talking points or scripts in case of media attention or inquiries.

5.49    Companies may be legally required to provide notice to law enforcement, data subjects or data controllers. What companies must and must not disclose in such notices often depends to a large extent on statutory requirements, which vary from jurisdiction to jurisdiction and can be conflicting. For example, in one jurisdiction, you may be required to disclose the breach to potentially affected data subjects as soon as possible, whereas other jurisdictions may require you to hold off on disclosures until you have consulted with law enforcement. If you have suffered a data security breach, you have to determine the exact nature of your disclosure obligations under all applicable statutes and plan your response. In larger incidents, it can be helpful to prepare a matrix to keep track of the different requirements. Given that breach notice recipients may talk to each other or go public, you may decide to use the most detailed format required under any applicable law for all necessary disclosures except to the extent that you are legally prohibited from including certain details in some jurisdictions.

Even where notices are not legally required, companies sometimes 5.50 issue notices anyway either because they are not sure whether a notice requirement applies, because they consider notification beneficial from a customer or public relations perspective or because they want to help potentially affected data subjects to mitigate risks, harm and damages claims. Such voluntary disclosures can be helpful, but they can also backfire and provoke over-reactions and unnecessary hassles for data subjects. For example, if a company issues a voluntary disclosure regarding weakness of systems hosting credit card numbers, credit card holders may be induced to cancel credit cards and make filings with credit bureaus, even if there is no concrete indication of an increased potential for abuse.

If other parties are involved (*e.g.*, corporate vendors or customers), 5.51 coordination, cooperation and allocation of costs and liabilities should be considered. If a data controller goes public with a notice that blames a vendor, and the vendor tries to shift blame back onto the data controller, such controversy can create additional media attention, harm and damages for all involved.

 **Action items**    5.52

Recommended action items for all companies include:

- Implementation of technical and organizational data security measures (such as encryption, physical premise safeguarding, systems access controls, service provider policing, and employee training);
- Routine self-assessments (or audits by specialized professionals) regarding data security, likely threats and preparedness for incidents;
- Assessment and audits of service providers and contracts;
- Concise protocols for all employees setting forth duties and processes to report security threats and breaches; and
- Appointment of a data security official or team that receives and processes reports pursuant to a protocol that ensures appropriate incident responses.

## Ownership

5.53 Data subjects do not own data concerning themselves in a property law sense. In most jurisdictions, facts and information are generally carved out and free from property rights to safeguard freedom of information and speech.

Companies can protect their investment in databases against wholesale, literal copying and use under unfair competition and copyright-like property law regimes. Even if a data base contains personal data, the creator of the database owns the property rights, not the individual data subject.

But, individuals own a right to publicity and the use of their name and likeness in commercial advertising. For example, companies need to obtain consent from data subjects before using their pictures in advertisements under torts and similar laws in many jurisdictions.

# Privacy by design

When companies design new products, services and operational pro-    5.54
cesses, they should take data privacy considerations into account early
and thus protect privacy 'by design.' For example, if a company devel-
ops employee-monitoring software for sale to enterprises, it should
not take the position that data privacy compliance is the customer's
problem, but rather plan ahead and add a feature that allows different configurations for different jurisdictions. If the software developer
includes such configurations, then the corporate users of such software
can better comply with different requirements under wiretap and other
privacy laws around the world. If not, the product may be deployed
in ways that violate applicable laws and result in liability for product
users or unsuccessful product launches. Also, companies are expressly
required to address "data protection by design and by default" under
the EU General Data Protection Regulation.

Companies that sell products with substandard data/cyber security
protections have been sued under warranty and consumer protection
laws. The U.S. Federal Trade Commission, for example, has taken the
position that offering smart phones, security cameras, hotel accommo-
dations or software products with insufficient data security protections
constitutes an unfair business practice. Also, software developers can
become contributorily liable for privacy violations by users of online
software-as-a-service solutions if the developer remains in control of
the servers on which data is processed. On the other hand, companies
that distribute software for users to host and operate do not typically
have to worry about contributory liability for violations of privacy laws
by users. To the contrary, companies that make and distribute products tend to be more concerned that if they represent their products as
being 'compliant by design,' this might trigger responsibility for legal
compliance by their customers. Nonetheless, all companies should at
least consider whether they can make their products, services and processes more usable and hence valuable by taking into account what
users have to do to comply with privacy laws.

In order to ensure that privacy law compliance considerations are
taken into account, some companies involve legal counsel early on in
the development process, *e.g.*, by requiring developers to fill out questionnaires that help counsel quickly determine whether further review
of the product concept is advisable.

## Questionnaires

5.56 When you send questionnaires to existing customers or prospects, you should confirm compliance with anti-spam laws (including opt-in/opt-out requirements) or that the questionnaire as worded, clearly falls outside the definitional scope of marketing communications under anti-spam laws. Also, questionnaires addressed to employees can fall under restrictions applicable to whistleblower hotlines if employees can or do use them to complain about co-workers or supervisors. You should clearly inform the data subjects if providing incomplete answers or failing to respond will have adverse consequences. If you want to promise that data subjects can respond anonymously, you should implement technical measures to minimize the risk of re-identification as much as possible and disclose all remaining potential risks of identification (*e.g.*, via IP addresses for online survey submissions). Consider also whether responses to certain questions will likely result in transmission of sensitive personal data (*e.g.*, political opinions, trade union membership, health, ethnic origin, religion, sexual orientation, or criminal records) and apply higher consent and security standards if required under applicable law. Finally, if responses are published, consider contributory liability for defamation based on user content and implement an efficient notice-and-take-down-process.

# Rights, remedies, enforcement

As part of prioritization and risk assessments, companies usually try    5.57
to determine the likely sources of claims and challenges, the probability of liability relating to particular practices or omissions and the impact on the business. Risk factors tend to be company-specific, such as the company's size, line of business, history of litigation and government charges, jurisdictional exposure and status of compliance efforts. Additionally, a few basic considerations are relevant for all companies, including the following:

• In which jurisdictions could claims and charges be brought?

• Who is likely to assert claims relating to privacy practices – government agencies, data subjects (customers, employees) or corporate customers and business partners?

• What could claimants demand? If demands have to be met, how would that affect the company's business?

• How easy will it be for claimants to establish violations of privacy laws and for the company to defend against those claims?

• What would be the reputational impact of privacy claims on customer and public relations?

Once a company has begun to prepare preliminary answers to these high-level questions, ideally for each key jurisdiction, the company will usually find a few sensitive areas of particularly high potential exposure. The company can concentrate its compliance efforts on those jurisdictions and sensitive areas. Here are a few related rules of thumb:

• Claims under data privacy laws can theoretically be brought in every jurisdiction where data subjects reside. But, usually companies are concerned only about jurisdictions where they maintain a physical presence, employees or data processing equipment. Data protection authorities rarely try to prosecute or fine companies outside their territory because it is virtually impossible to enforce administrative or criminal sanctions across territorial borders. Cross-border civil litigation is slightly more prevalent, but private plaintiffs and their lawyers also tend to shy away from cases that could in the best case result in judgments that will be difficult or impossible to enforce. See also Section 'J – Jurisdiction' in this Chapter 5.

- The party most likely to bring claims varies significantly from business to business and jurisdiction to jurisdiction. In most jurisdictions, businesses cannot bring claims of data privacy violations. Only living individuals are protected. Contractual claims based on breaches of agreements between businesses (*e.g.*, data security breaches under data processing agreements) are possible in any country, but such contractual claims tend to be indirectly affected by the level of exposure that the claimant expects from data subjects or government authorities:

  - In Europe, for example, data protection authorities take a relatively active role in enforcing data protection laws, requiring prior notifications and approval processes and conducting audits. Companies can expect increased levels of enforcement activity and scrutiny after the EU General Data Protection Regulation becomes effective in May 2018 and raises maximum fines to the greater of Euro 20m or 4% of annual worldwide sales for various offenses. Consequently, companies with presences in European countries are well advised to observe all formal requirements (filings, appointment of local representative and data protection officer, data transfer agreements, etc.) as formal compliance deficits are most easy to detect on audit. Another potential source of challenges under European data privacy laws are data protection officers and collective labor representation in Europe in the context of legally required consultations. Individual private lawsuits on the other hand are relatively rare in Europe because potential damages awards are seriously limited (no punitive damages and actual damages are usually limited to pecuniary losses) and lawyers are not allowed to take cases on a contingency basis. Most European countries do not permit class action lawsuits. But, in some European countries, consumer protection and civil rights watchdogs (like the German Center Against Unfair Business Practices) are quite active and bring lawsuits after an initial warning letter. Companies cannot protect themselves effectively via contractual limitations of liabilities, waivers or disclaimers because such clauses are largely invalid or unenforceable under European consumer protection laws. Companies that include U.S.-style disclaimers and limitations of liability in standardized consumer contracts governed by German law can be liable under unfair competition laws for confusing consumers with such clauses.

• In the United States, data protection authorities do not exist. The U.S. Federal Trade Commission and State Attorneys General bring charges based on consumer protection and unfair competition laws, but typically only in selected high profile cases and after individual data subjects complain. Private litigation on the other hand is very prevalent in the form of class action lawsuits and also individual litigation, because awards can be quite significant when punitive damages or damages for 'emotional distress' are awarded, even if plaintiffs cannot prove any significant pecuniary losses. Many plaintiffs' attorneys expect companies to settle even frivolous lawsuits due to the relatively high defense costs and the fact that in U.S. courts each party typically has to bear its own legal fees regardless of who wins the case. Companies can significantly limit their liabilities, disclaim implied warranties, obtain releases, pre-determine the dispute resolution forum (companies' home courts or preferred arbitration organization, so long as the consumer is not unfairly disadvantaged). Under U.S. laws, click-through agreements and other form contracts are largely enforceable as written.

• Other regions and jurisdictions have their own peculiarities that should be considered. More than 80 countries have enacted specific data privacy or data protection laws. Jurisdictions with strong labor or consumer protection laws may see data privacy law-like claims as one form of labor or unfair competition law claims. On the other hand, in many countries, there is still little or no enforcement or litigation relating to data privacy laws. Global businesses with limited resources usually focus their efforts on the jurisdictions with established data privacy laws and enforcement regimes.

• With respect to remedies that claimants may seek, consider the following:

  • Government authorities tend to focus on changes in practices, and sometimes impose penalties to discourage future incursions and as a warning to others. Therefore, government authorities will often issue injunctions and demand that companies stop processing data in a certain way and possibly delete existing databases. For example, French and German data protection authorities have prohibited local subsidiaries from transferring employee data to their U.S. parent company until adequate data transfer safeguards were implemented. This can be very disruptive. EU data protection authorities have stepped up their enforcement efforts and impose monetary fines in more and more cases every year. Often, they first provide warnings. Criminal enforcement is relatively rare and reserved to egregious offenses (*e.g.*, unauthorized wiretapping by private individuals).

- Private plaintiffs may seek access to data, and request correction or deletion, but usually private plaintiffs primarily seek damages. In European jurisdictions, where plaintiffs usually have to substantiate pecuniary harm and neither punitive damages nor class actions are recognized, companies tend to be less concerned about such lawsuits, as the amounts at stake tend to be small. In the United States, however, class actions and punitive damages claims cause much more concern for companies.

- Some kinds of claims are much easier to bring or defend against than others:

  - If companies fail to comply with formal compliance obligations under European laws, data protection authorities, data protection officers, works councils and others find it very easy to detect and act on violations. It does not require a lot of effort to determine whether a company has made required filings, obtained necessary authorizations, implemented data transfer agreements or issued notices. Also, it tends to be impossible to defend against such claims because the law is relatively straightforward on whether such formal steps are required.

  - A claim that private plaintiffs find easy to bring and often assert is that a company did not comply with its own data privacy statements or notices. Website privacy statements in particular are often full of over-promises and marketing fluff and lend themselves to assertion of misrepresentation claims, without a need to go into too much statutory interpretation or complex lawyering.

  - Class action lawyers have found it more difficult, however, to substantiate harm in the aftermath of data security breaches because it is challenging to show that a uniform class of individuals suffered the same actual harm, given that usually only some data subjects, if any, immediately fall victim to identity theft and other fraud. Also, consumers are often in different situations with respect to express or implied consent because of their individual level of awareness, understanding and time taken to read notices.

•  Another question that concerns companies is the impact of publicity related to assertions of privacy violations. A cloud computing service provider's business will suffer greatly if it has to disclose a data security breach, particularly if it hosts sensitive information for corporate customers. A small business outside the IT sector, however, such as a construction company that does not process any sensitive information for its customers, would probably not be too concerned about publicity regarding unauthorized access to employee data.

## Social media

5.58   Like many other online services, social media and social networking sites require certain information from users to set up an account. In this respect, such sites are not particularly special from a data privacy law perspective. General rules apply – see Sections on 'Advertising,' 'Tracking' and 'Unsolicited Communications' in this Chapter 5.

Social media-specific privacy concerns center around user-generated content: what an individual discloses about him- or herself and about others. In this respect, European-style data protection laws largely do not apply. Similar to blogs and bulletin boards, individuals upload data and content onto social networking sites and similar platforms at their own discretion for personal purposes. Individuals tend to be free to share data about themselves and also to process data about others for private household purposes. For example, the EU Data Protection Directive expressly states that it does not apply to the processing of personal data by a natural person in the course of a purely personal or household activity. So long as the network and platform operators do not exercise control over user activities, much of the user-generated and user-processed data remains outside the scope of data protection laws.

If users commit torts (defamation, invasion of privacy, infringement of publicity rights, etc.), the platform operator can become contributorily liable. In most jurisdictions, platform operators are exempt from liability if they take down content on request (for example, under the European Electronic Commerce Directive and under Section 230 of the Communications Decency Act in the United States).

Employers do not enjoy similar liability privileges and have to train and instruct their employees on how to use social media in compliance with applicable laws, including labor and employment laws on workplace privacy and communications, confidentiality duties and general business interests. Employers also have to be careful with online research, see 'Employee Data and Monitoring' in this Chapter 5.

5.59   *Testimonials and consumer reviews* on social media websites, social networks, blogs and other websites must disclose if they are directly or indirectly paid for by companies, *e.g.*, written by employees of the company whose products or services are covered in a review or testimonial. Employers have to instruct their employees accordingly and set rules on if and how employees may communicate about business matters in private, anonymously or otherwise.

# Tracking

5.60   When individuals use computing and communications devices, they create, store, process and transmit vast amounts of data. Much of this data is not stored in relation to a particular person's name but can be linked to a named person relatively easily. For example, if you type in a particular website address into your web browser, then your computer sends a request with certain information about the computer and its software and hardware to the server that hosts the desired website. This server processes the data received to respond to your request with whatever the website operator makes available to website visitors – pictures, text and usually also cookies, *i.e.*, small software files placed on the website visitor's computer that track information on the user for future access by the website operator. If the website operator finds out the user's name (because the user registers for a service or orders a product for delivery), the website operator can combine the actively submitted data (name, address) with the passively tracked data (websites visited before or after, time spent on websites, software/hardware information, etc.). Much of this data is collected at the data subject's initiative for purposes of communicating and providing information, and to that extent the data processing tends to be permitted under data privacy laws. However, any secondary uses or data collection beyond what is necessary to fulfill contractual obligations to the data subject requires consent under European laws and notification and opt-out rights under many other jurisdictions' laws.

5.61   *Cookies*, web beacons, tags and software are sent with web content in response to inquiries from web browsers. When an Internet user types an Internet address (*e.g.*, www.example.com) into her browser (*e.g.*, Microsoft Internet Explorer), the browser sends information about the inquiring computer's address and configuration to the server (the hardware that physically hosts the website information) at the chosen Internet address, which then returns the requested information and typically also some cookies or other tracking mechanism. Some companies store data collected through the use of cookies linked to user names while others only link to IP addresses, mobile device identification numbers or other numeric identifiers; either way, the user profiles usually constitute personal data under many data protection laws because they relate to an individual who can be identified. Many website publishers with third-party advertising also allow the third-party advertisers to send cookies in response to inquiries. The cookies are intended to gather and report back certain information about the requesting computer and are principally used for three purposes:

(1) Some cookies support site functionality. For example, cookies store what an online shopper has placed in the shopping cart before the shopper logs into a secure account. Also, cookies can store the user's name, language preferences and other configuration choices. Cookies can be used to gather information regarding websites that users visit before and after coming to a publisher's site to improve and further customize the website and measure each page's effectiveness. Internet users must be notified about data processing via cookies in this category, but if and to the extent the cookies are necessary to deliver services to the data subject, the publisher typically does not have to obtain affirmative consent or offer opt-out choices.

(2) Some cookies support website traffic analytics, site improvements and targeted advertising by the publisher (on its own websites or on third party sites, for retargeting purposes). Such cookies are placed by the publisher or its service providers to measure how long the user spent on a particular page, whether users clicked on ads or closed pop-up screens, etc. These cookies do not result in sharing of personal data between data controllers, and they are therefore often referred to as "1st party cookies" to differentiate them from the "3rd party cookies" described in the next paragraph. In many jurisdictions, 1st party cookies that are not essential for service delivery can be placed based on a unilateral notice (*e.g.*, in the website privacy statement). Under European laws, website publishers may have to offer users a choice to opt out of such cookies or even seek prior opt-in consent. Under the laws of Germany, for example, data controllers have to obtain affirmative consent before they may use any personal data for marketing purposes, regardless of whether such data is collected via cookies or otherwise. Where website publishers have to give website visitors an opportunity to opt out, it is often unclear whether the publisher has to allow users who opt out to nevertheless use the services or whether it is sufficient to inform users that opting out means opting out of using the website or service altogether. One possible implementation approach is for website publishers to offer free or discounted services to those users who accept cookies and/or charge others a fee (similar to free and pay TV).

(3) Some cookies support targeted advertising and related tracking by third-party advertisers. Publishers that allow third-party data controllers to place cookies when users visit the publishers' website not only engage in sharing data, but also enable third parties to collect data directly. Publishers often have little control or even knowledge over what type of data third-party advertisers gather. The third-party advertiser typically does not have the opportunity to provide notice to the consumers or obtain consent and must therefore work with the publisher to ensure that consent is obtained where legally required and that all required notices are provided. Since the third-party advertiser does not provide a service to, or have a contract with the website visitor, having the publisher obtain consent from the data subject is usually the only way to legitimize data collection, sharing and other processing via third-party cookies under European laws.

5.62 *Browser feature settings* and security software configurations allow Internet users to reject or delete most types of cookies. Users can check a box in most browsers to reject tracking and the browser will then communicate a 'do not track' (DNT) signal to the website publishers with each request. The Federal Trade Commission recommends in guidance – and California requires by statute – that web publishers and other online service providers expressly disclose in their privacy notices whether they honor 'do not track' signals. California law does not require companies to actually honor 'do not track' signals or obtain specific consent from users. But, data protection laws in some jurisdictions generally require that companies obtain voluntary, informed, express and specific consent from data subjects. If users actively select or passively accept browser configurations that allow cookies, they indicate consent. It is controversial, however, whether users can be deemed to consent by inaction merely because they do not configure their browser to send 'do not track' signals. It is fairly easy for Internet users to configure their browsers and users typically visit websites voluntarily, which involves the user's browser sending a request for information to the website. To support an assertion that users consent informedly, website publishers can disclose the details of their cookies and similar tracking programs in their website privacy notice. Implied consent through browser settings is not very specific or express, however, unless browser manufacturers deliver browsers with cookies rejected as a default (as some browser manufacturers have recently started doing), or take steps to prompt users to make conscious and affirmative choices with respect to different types of cookies and websites (for example, in the context of registration for an online account or via a pop-up window or conspicuous notice on sites that do not contemplate or require registration).

*Ad networks, ad exchanges* and other intermediaries place cookies on 5.63 websites of numerous participating publishers and serve ads of numerous participating advertisers. Depending on the particular data sharing arrangements, the ad network operators and all participating publishers and advertisers assume roles of data controllers and therefore obligations to notify data subjects and obtain consent where legally required. This presents significant practical challenges, as participating companies change constantly. To achieve compliance with European data protection laws, website publishers and ad networks may have to cooperate to ensure that website visitors receive adequate notice and grant express, specific and written consent regarding the data sharing and the identities and privacy practices of every data controller in the ad network that receives their personal data.

*Ad servers* and similar service providers can also act on behalf of one 5.64 website publisher under a data processing services arrangement by which the service provider uses data collected in the process only on behalf of and under instructions from the one website publisher. This setup would not involve data sharing with other data controllers and therefore raises far fewer compliance challenges.

*The Internet of things,* machine-to-machine communications and facial 5.65 recognition technologies have greatly expanded tracking online and offline. Facial recognition systems can recognize and track persons on the street, in apartment buildings, at airports, in football stadiums and in any large crowds. Machines can track, record and transmit data to their owners or others. Telematics solutions can not only inform car rental companies or truck fleet operators of the location of their rental cars, but can also inform family members of a possible accident. Moreover, employers can monitor employee whereabouts and performance. Spouses could use telematics products out of jealousy. Criminals can observe victims. Some companies sell computers, software products and content files with mechanisms that collect and transfer information on product usage. For example, 'dongles' and 'software license compliance managers' detect and report – through a 'back door' in the software – data on software usage outside license agreements or attempts to copy, transfer or re-install the software. Digital rights management (DRM) features may block copying beyond a certain permitted maximum and may also report attempts to make additional copies. Some software products keep the manufacturer informed about defects and crashes, either automatically or only if users click to agree to send an error report. In many cases, such technologies collect personal data (because the device or software is registered in an individual person's name or because it can be linked to a person). In Europe, 'call-home' technology features in cars have been regulated in great detail. California has enacted legislation regarding RFID tags that requires consent and has already been asserted as a defense by a smart phone thief against tracking. More generally, notice and consent requirements continue to apply. Companies are well advised to consider privacy by design principles early on in the product development cycle and must ensure that customers understand and agree to the use of tracking and data reporting mechanisms (*e.g.*, by including conspicuous clauses in contracts) and that each data subject receives adequate notice (*e.g.*, by displaying warnings before collecting and transferring the information).

# Unsolicited communications (spam email, cold calls, etc.)

According to some estimates, more than 70% of all global email traf- 5.66
fic consists of unsolicited and largely unwanted communications.
Individuals, businesses, governments and other organizations are
annoyed and largely address the problem through technological means,
with spam filters on corporate systems, web mail platforms and individual devices. Legislatures around the world have also reacted with
different anti-spam laws, most recently in Canada with its extremely
complex new anti-spam legislation (CASL). Most spammers are criminals who cover their tracks, hide offshore and are not reached by laws
and law enforcement. But, legitimate businesses have to invest time
and resources to address compliance requirements under anti-spam
laws, even though their contribution to the spam problem appears
relatively minor and technical solutions are available and widely used.

Businesses that want to engage in direct marketing (directly or indirectly with business partners or through 'refer a friend' programs)
must assess applicable legal restrictions, industry standards and local
consumer expectations. Companies need to train and instruct sales
and marketing personnel carefully and ensure that each employee con-
firms for each campaign and individual marketing initiative that all relevant legal and business requirements have been considered, including
the following:

* Can you use the mailing list or other contact information for marketing purposes? In some jurisdictions, you may have to obtain
  prior consent, while in other jurisdictions you have to provide
  notice and an opportunity to opt-out before you send the first marketing communication. If you acquired contact information from
  third parties (*e.g.*, list providers), you should confirm that the third
  party was permitted to collect and transfer the contact information
  to you for purposes of your marketing use.

* Has anyone on your mailing list opted out? In most jurisdictions,
  you have to honor opt-out requests based on your own suppression lists. In some jurisdictions, you have to also check public "do
  not call/email/fax" registers. If you are working with business partners who commission, deliver or benefit from the ads at issue, you
  may also have to observe their suppression lists or require them to
  observe yours. Employees are often not clear on the fact that these

requirements apply not only with respect to bulk email but also to customized, one-off messages and new forms of social media, such as posts on users' walls, etc.

- What disclosures are required on calls, email subject headers or snail mail envelopes? In most jurisdictions, you have to identify the specific entities that send or commission the marketing initiative, possibly with a physical address. Additionally, you may have to conspicuously disclose the advertising character of a message in its subject header, even in connection with 'mixed messages' (*e.g.*, newsletter with ads, customer satisfaction survey with an up-selling agenda).

- How do you enable recipients to opt out? In many jurisdictions, you have to offer easy mechanisms by which recipients can request to be removed from your marketing contact list. Details vary regarding the technological implementation requirements, for example whether you have to accept return emails or whether you can direct users to an opt-out website, how many communication preferences you have to offer in addition to an 'absolute opt-out' and how many steps you can require.

- Are you observing all requirements applicable to cold calls, including day and time restrictions, disclosure duties regarding call monitoring or recording and limitations on the use of "robo calls" or call-back systems?

- Is the advertising content appropriate for your audience? Many countries have product- or content-based restrictions (*e.g.*, pharmaceuticals, pornography, alcohol, tobacco warnings). Restrictions apply also with respect to marketing to children; for example, effective January 1 2015, companies are prohibited from advertising a long list of products to minors in California, including alcohol, handguns, ammunition, certain paints and etching creams that are capable of defacing property, fireworks, and tattoos. Comparative advertising is allowed in the United States but restricted in many other jurisdictions.

5.67 *Jurisdictional differentiation.* Companies that want to go right up to the legal limits in every jurisdiction and advertise as much and directly as possible have to develop very granular protocols relating to particular communications topics, technologies, and target recipients. If a particular direct marketing campaign targets several jurisdictions, advertisers may have to further differentiate, as laws in this area are hardly uniform and most jurisdictions apply their laws to protect people in their territory even if the sender or caller is in a different country or state. Within Europe anti-spam laws are only partially harmonized, and in the U.S., states have different rules with respect to cold calling and call monitoring. In addition to the laws of the target country, advertisers have to comply with data privacy and other laws of the place where they and their service providers are acting.

*Globally uniform approaches.* Companies that are willing to restrict 5.68 their direct marketing efforts may be able to establish less granular and more global marketing policies. To achieve uniformity they must: be content with completely ruling out data sharing with unaffiliated companies for marketing purposes; generally require informed prior consent for all marketing communications (calls, emails, postal mail, faxes, text messages and other forms); designate all marketing communications conspicuously as such (*e.g.*, in email subject headers and on snail mail envelops); include easy opt-out mechanisms with every message; and comply with opt-out requests within a couple of business days. Companies are not required to implement all these restrictions for all countries though, and in many major markets it is common and therefore possibly necessary for effective competition to engage in some forms of direct marketing without seeking prior consent.

*Consent implementations.* In the context of implementing notice and 5.69 consent requirements, companies have to be careful to avoid reducing the spectrum of options to a mere opt-in versus opt-out perspective. In reality, the implementation alternatives and applicable requirements are far more nuanced and include, for example, the following:

- Affirmative, express, and separate prior opt-in consent for using personal data for marketing purposes, and email contact could be implemented via an unchecked box during an online registration process followed by a confirmation email that has to be accepted to authenticate the consenting target. German courts and data protection authorities have taken the position that companies have to implement such a 'double opt-in' process in order to meet their burden of proof that a particular consumer granted consent, even though German statutes do not specifically require such a tedious process. In practice, such mechanisms tend to result in a relatively low opt-in rate because the vast majority of consumers either do not take the time to understand the option or find the confirmation process too burdensome to follow through – even if they are open or indifferent to receiving marketing communications.

• A prior opportunity to opt into marketing usage and email contact via a pre-checked consent box displayed in a registration process, or an unchecked box to opt out, probably offer a similar level of privacy protection. Some jurisdictions ignore the specific diction deployed and qualify any set-up that defaults into consent as 'prior opt-out,' unless the consumer takes specific action (by unchecking the pre-checked 'opt-in' box or checking the unchecked 'opt-out' box). This mechanism gives consumers the option to avoid ever receiving any marketing emails, but it requires action on their part. Indifferent consumers will opt-in by default.

• For some jurisdictions that require affirmative opt-in consent (and would, therefore, not be satisfied with the pre-checked opt-in box or unchecked opt-out box), companies can offer a hybrid choice and force the issue (*e.g.*, display a "Yes" and a "No" box) to avoid losing the indifferent, or offer only an unchecked box but require the check mark to proceed with the registration or other process that the consumer is primarily interested in. Such mechanisms are not acceptable in all jurisdictions and they involve a risk of annoying many consumers who want to complete processes with minimal clicks and distractions.

• Prior notice or opt-in/opt-out mechanisms can be offered conspicuously or more or less hidden in lengthy privacy policies or terms of use that are referred to in a sign-up process (*e.g.*, in mobile registrations or call center scripts) or linked at the bottom of a website. Most jurisdictions that require prior opt-in consent do not accept notices that are too difficult to access, so some types of implementation may not be sufficient under applicable law.

• Some jurisdictions accept and require only notice and opt-out mechanisms that are provided with the first marketing mail, for example, the United States in the CAN-SPAM Act. Thus, in the United States, advertisers can spam anyone except individuals who have already received a marketing message from or on behalf of the particular advertiser and then opted out. Opt-out choices can be quite granular so consumers have a choice as to which types of communications they want and do not want to receive. Regardless, most laws, including the CAN-SPAM Act, require that at least one easily accessible option is absolute, *i.e.*, no further marketing emails.

• For more details and options, see Chapter 3.

*Mixed messages.* Some types of communications contain advertise- 5.70 ments as well as other content (*e.g.*, order confirmations, invoices, payment reminders, etc.). Such mixed communications are typically not exempt from anti-spam and similar laws, unless the non-advertising purpose and character of the message is legitimate and dominant. The Federal Trade Commission offers illustrative examples in the context of its guidelines on the CAN-SPAM Act. Companies have to be careful when wording opt-out mechanisms to avoid giving consumers the impression and right to opt out of any type of communication such as invoices and payment reminders.

*Bulk and individual emails and social media communications are cov-* 5.71 *ered.* Anti-spam laws tend to apply to any advertising emails, not only bulk emails. It is important to instruct and train marketing and sales personnel accordingly so that they include opt-out choices – and consider the risks of customers receiving opt-out requests – with respect to every email they make for sales or marketing purposes. Also, messages sent through social media platforms may be covered, *e.g.*, posting messages on boards and personal pages, which would require the same kinds of disclosures and opt-out mechanisms as emails.

*Sender, initiator and beneficiary can be held responsible.* Responsibility 5.72 for compliance with anti-spam and similar laws lies with every company that sends or commissions others to send the advertisements. In connection with 'refer a friend' campaigns (where consumers are encouraged or incentivized to send or forward marketing emails to their friends), joint promotions and engagement of marketing service providers, companies have to carefully consider which opt-out lists have to be observed ('scrubbed against').

# Vendor management

5.73   Companies have to carefully select and monitor their vendors for purposes of assuring compliance with data protection laws. Vendors are
a key part of the extended enterprise and companies are responsible
for the actions of some of their vendors. Therefore, companies should
consider as part of their data privacy law compliance programs standard vendor onboarding procedures, including a technical and organizational due diligence, questionnaires, standard contract forms and
recurring audits.

Internal or external experts should conduct a technical and financial due
diligence on a prospective vendor. If the vendor is a well-established,
large, publicly-listed company, a high level review and contractual documentation may suffice. With respect to lesser-known organizations, on-
site visits, technical audits, completion of technical questionnaires, third
party security audits and other measures may be required, based on a
reasonable risk assessment. Companies can refer to the same standard
data security questionnaires that they use for their own self-assessments
or audits when they conduct technical due diligence on vendors.

If the vendor makes it past the technical and financial due diligence
stage, it should be asked to contractually agree to comply with your
company's data security standards or policy documents. In this context, you have to make sure that you pass on to the vendor all obligations that your company has assumed with respect to its own corporate
customers and data subjects so that your company does not get caught
in between high customer expectations and low vendor commitments. For example, if your company has selected the EU Standard
Contractual Clauses to legitimize data transfers from Europe to the
United States, then you must insist that every vendor that would gain
access to such data also commits to these Clauses. Similarly, if your
company has accepted obligations as a business associate vis-à-vis a
covered entity for HIPAA compliance purposes, then you have to insist
that your vendors back you up in the same manner if they assist with
processing of covered data. Also, companies are well advised to secure
cooperation duties from vendors to accept additional requirements
and conditions (possibly subject to additional compensation) in case
privacy laws and compliance requirements change over time.

For more information on: international data transfer agreements, see
Chapter 2; agreements more generally, see Chapter 3; due diligence,

see Chapter 4; and data processing services, see the Section on 'Cloud Computing' in this Chapter 5.

In checklist form, procurement managers could work with privacy counsel or officers through the following requirements:

- Do you have a concise description of the purpose of the vendor engagement as well as a technical assessment of the vendor's data security and privacy protection measures?

- What data categories would the vendor collect or have access to?

- Does the vendor engagement trigger requirements to notify customers, data protection authorities, data subjects or others?

- Are legal requirements for cross-border data transfers at the customer's and vendor's side satisfied?

- Does the contract with the vendor meet applicable legal requirements for data processing and data transfer contracts?

- Has your legal department and data privacy officer been consulted?

# Wiretapping

5.74  Wiretapping and similar forms of interception of live communications are particularly intrusive invasions into people's privacy and freedom of communications. Therefore, many jurisdictions prohibit interception of calls and other communications unless all parties consent. Historically, laws prohibited interception of 'live' analog calls and postal mail. Some commentators have questioned whether email correspondence can be protected under wiretap laws, given that email is frequently stored as part of the transmission process and thus in some ways more akin to voice mail recordings than 'live' analog phone calls. But, many countries have updated their statutory definitions to also cover various forms of electronic communications, including instant messaging, online chat, SMS and email.

Companies engage in interception of communications for a variety of reasons, including quality control (sales call recording), network protection (spam and virus filtering), premises security (video surveillance) and employee conduct monitoring (keystroke logging, screen shot savings, email and web filtering, etc.). Companies can obtain consent from employees relatively easily. They have to be concerned about the validity of employee consent in some jurisdictions (predominantly in Europe), but face less significant obstacles elsewhere. Obtaining consent from third parties is much more difficult, however. With respect to inbound calls, companies can play scripts that inform callers that 'calls are recorded and monitored for quality control.' But, on outbound calls, many recipients will hang up if they are first greeted by such scripts, so companies can either opt to refrain from monitoring outbound calls altogether or turn the recording/monitoring on only after obtaining consent during the call at an opportune time.

Obtaining consent from external email, IM or SMS partners is even more difficult. Most companies rely on general notices automatically placed into outbound messages. Those technically come too late because the message is filtered before the recipient is informed of the interception. Yet, as a practical matter, most people are not concerned about such technical filtering and the technologies are in such widespread use that the risk exposure to an individual company seems fairly low. Good faith efforts to comply (via general notices) should suffice.

# X-rays, genes, fingerprints, faces – biometric data

Persons can be identified through various types of biometric authenti- 5.75
cation information, including fingerprints, retinal scans, voice recordings, x-ray images and gene sequences. Also, developers have greatly
improved the reliability of facial recognition technologies. Companies
find such authentication methods particularly attractive because they
focus on unique physical features of a person that do not require the
person or company to make particular efforts (*e.g.*, conceive/remember/
reset passwords, carry/disable/replace smart cards or badges) and that
cannot easily be forged. Also, law enforcement and companies can
use biometric authentication methods to investigate problems without
much cooperation from the data subject. Facial recognition technologies can be deployed even in a covert manner, without the data subject
being close to the data capturing device. Given the resulting sensitivities for data privacy, companies have to observe additional data security, notice and consent requirements in some jurisdictions or build a
strong case under the "legitimate interest exception," where available,
if they want to collect or use biometric data.

*Genetic information* is increasingly used by research institutions, hos- 5.76
pitals, businesses, law enforcement agencies and others for purposes
of medical research, diagnosis of diseases, decisions regarding treat-
ment of diseases, identification of suspects in criminal investigations,
paternity determinations, etc. Each individual has a unique genome.
Genetic information is just as much an identifier as a fingerprint or
social security number, even when not associated with a person's
name or address. Therefore, a biospecimen (*e.g.*, tissue sample), gene
sequence or test result connected to a genome contain or constitute
personal data. If a researcher can deduce information about a person's health by analyzing genetic information, then such information
constitutes health-related data, *i.e.*, sensitive data under European
laws (U.S. HIPAA legislation differentiates depending on whether the
genetic information is associated with certain additional identifiers or
not). Researchers find it difficult to de-identify test results containing full or partial genomic sequences and unexpectedly easy to re-
identify aggregate and pooled research results. Individual data subjects
can be harmed by processing genetic information because they can
be identified and discriminated against; for example, health insurance
companies, employers and others could disfavor persons with a higher
likelihood of suffering certain diseases based on genetic predisposition.

Some jurisdictions have enacted laws to reduce the risk of discrimination, such as the U.S. Genetic Information Nondiscrimination Act of 2008. Therefore, companies should carefully assess if they really need genetic information; if they do, companies should collect, secure, use and delete genetic information like other particularly sensitive personal data. When companies obtain consent from data subjects for the collection or use of genetic information, they need to inform the data subjects about the potential risks, in particular identification and discrimination.

# Y – Why protect data privacy?

This question is not just philosophical in nature but has to be consid-    5.77
ered frequently when navigating privacy laws and making decisions on
data processing activities in companies.

*Why do governments protect data privacy?* Governments typically pro-    5.78
tect data privacy for purposes of safeguarding human dignity and the
right of self-determination (also known as "the right to be left alone").
Under the shield of data privacy protection, citizens are more empow-
ered to exercise civil rights, such as the freedom of speech, religion and
assembly. This in turn helps secure the functioning of the democratic
process. In jurisdictions with separate branches of government, legislatures and courts primarily make data privacy laws. Some jurisdictions
also have an executive agency or data protection officer in charge of
defining policy objectives or monitoring other government institutions
with respect to data privacy protections.

*Why do governments sometimes not protect privacy and even intrude*    5.79
*into data privacy?* The executive branch of governments fulfills
many functions, most importantly law enforcement, that necessi-
tate data processing and tend to collide with privacy protection
agendas. Additionally, legislatures and courts also safeguard interests and policy objectives that conflict with data privacy, such as
freedom of information and commercial enterprise. One person's
right to gather and share information on another person can intrude
on the other person's interest in data privacy. Different jurisdictions balance these conflicting policy goals differently. The U.S., for
example, tends to hold freedom of speech, information and commercial enterprise in relatively high regard and therefore decided
against enacting the kind of omnibus data protection laws that are
prevalent in Europe. Also, after the terrorist attacks of September 11,
2001, the United States has been very focused on national security
and ramping up government surveillance programs. In Europe, on
the other hand, some people still remember what surveillance by
totalitarian regimes has done to them and fellow citizens. European
lawmakers have decisively acted to limit the automated processing of
personal data and carved out narrowly defined exceptions for press,
media and non-commercial activities. Anyone trying to understand,
interpret and apply data privacy laws has to consider the various
conflicting interests and their relative status in the applicable legal
system.

5.80  *Why do companies protect data privacy?* All companies have to protect data privacy as required by applicable law to avoid penalties and civil liability. Beyond legally mandated protections, some companies protect data privacy for the following reasons, among others:

- To differentiate themselves in the marketplace, protect their reputation and satisfy customer or employee demands;

- To streamline compliance programs, simplify operations, and save costs, global players may opt for privacy policies that exceed legal requirements in a particular jurisdiction to set regional or global standards;

- To reduce the risk of becoming contributorily liable for violations of privacy laws by employees and users of products and services (*e.g.*, by designing software to reduce the risk of abuse for spamming or hacking, or by limiting system access and usage privileges for employees to disable tools that lend themselves to privacy intrusions); and

- To reduce the risk of getting caught in the middle of the conflicting interests of data subjects and law enforcement or private plaintiffs, some companies consciously limit the amount of personal data they collect or data retention periods so that they cannot be compelled to produce data that they did not collect or retain in the first place.

5.81  *Why do companies sometimes not protect privacy and even intrude into data privacy?* Like governments, companies pursue a number of objectives that conflict with data privacy interests, including the following:

- To comply with laws, companies have to provide personal data to governments and private plaintiffs (*e.g.*, in response to pre-trial discovery requests and investigations by law enforcement authorities, and to comply with routine reporting obligations under tax laws and various regulatory schemes);

- Beyond legally required reporting, some companies are interested in providing personal data to courts, government agencies and other companies for various reasons, including to assert legal claims against individuals, collect debts, cooperate with the government to reduce the occurrence of fraud between customers;

- Companies must collect and use data to pursue various business objectives, serve customers, identify customer preferences, deliver tailored advertisements, pay employees, monitor compliance with law and company policies;

- Companies also collect data to build databases and commercialize them as intellectual property assets. Customer lists and profiles are key assets of many businesses and translate directly into shareholder value. The more flexibility a company reserves in its privacy policy and notices with respect to what it may do with data, the more valuable the data is to the company (*e.g.*, a database that can be shared with advertisers and marketers can be monetized better than a database of a company that promises its customers that it will never share or sell data; of course, companies that do not make certain promises and assume certain restrictions may attract fewer customers in the first place and thus build smaller databases); and

- To save costs, companies minimize data security and deletion efforts. Technologies, human resources and legal research are expensive. Data storage on the other hand is relatively cheap, particularly if it is not encrypted or otherwise secured. Often it is cheaper in the short run to do only the minimum required or react to complaints rather than plan proactively. Different companies place different values on the risk of non-compliance, security breaches and public relations fiascos.

No one size fits all. Every company has to assess these and other considerations FOR and AGAINST data privacy protections in light of its own situation. Companies should revisit their individual positions regularly in light of the ever-changing landscape in data privacy law, expectations and industry practices. Every company has to find what is best for itself – as opposed to relying on general notions of "best practices," which tend to be a poor substitute for individual legal and business analysis.

## ZIP codes, IP addresses and other numbers

5.82  The California Supreme Court decided that ZIP codes (U.S. postal codes) are 'personal data' under the Song Beverly Credit Card Act. According to this law, merchants in California may not collect and record any personal data from credit card holders, except as necessary to process transactions. An Appeals Court had previously found that ZIP codes applied to multiple people and could not therefore constitute 'personal' data. The California Supreme Court noted, however, that the ZIP codes could be used to identify individual mailing addresses in the context of other data that the merchants were collecting. Courts in another U.S. state, Massachusetts, have taken a similar view on ZIP codes. The Federal Trade Commission has clarified that it views any data correlated to persistent device identifiers as 'personal data.' The highest court in the European Union, the European Court of Justice, confirmed that Internet IP addresses qualify as personal data to the extent they relate to identifiable individuals.

ZIP codes and IP addresses illustrate well the definitional scope of 'personal data.' If you just store numbers without any contextual information, then such numbers do not relate to an 'identifiable' human individual. But if you add even a minimal amount of contextual information, you may quickly transform bare numbers into 'personal data' under some laws. For example, the data 94111 or 123456789 alone does not relate to an identifiable individual. But, if you add that 94111 is the ZIP Code of the home address of a particular person who made a purchase in a certain store, this 'enriched' data relates to an identifiable individual. Similarly, if you add that 123456789 is a phone number, credit card number, or other identifier that is issued to an individual, you may have 'personal data.' On the other hand, if 123456789 is the number of a public phone booth, you would need additional information to render the data 'personal,' such as that a particular caller made a call from or to this number at a particular time. Internet Protocol (IP) addresses can be statically assigned to routers and other devices (which may be owned by individuals, Internet cafes or other businesses) or dynamically assigned by Internet Service Providers (ISPs). If you store IP addresses of website visitors, you probably collect some amount of personal data because a fair number of IP addresses can be connected to individuals (either by you or in coordination with ISPs or telecommunications service providers).

As a threshold matter, companies should presume that data is 'personal' unless they can positively confirm that particular data does not relate to any identifiable individual. As a second step, companies should analyze whether the particular data they want to process is subject to any restrictions (many privacy laws apply only to certain kinds of personal data, *e.g.*, personal health information, credit card holder data, etc.). Under the broadly-worded European style data protection laws, companies will often find that a particular processing activity does involve personal data and is subject to restrictions. The final step is to analyze whether restrictions may be overcome if the data at issue does not concern data subjects significantly (*e.g.*, public phone directory information, job contact data, etc.).

# Checklist
# Data privacy and security compliance program

Checklists can be handy to create agendas for meetings, task lists for projects and guidance for a quick health check on an organization's compliance status. They should not create a false sense of completeness though. With the following checklist, you should be able to determine major gaps and get a discussion about compliance going.

1. **Who is in charge of data privacy and security compliance in the organization?**

✔ Determine whether your company should appoint a Chief Privacy Officer and/or local liaisons, and whether you are legally required to appoint data protections officers.

✔ Are all stakeholders instructed and trained regarding their responsibilities, in particular:

  ✓ Information technology department (regarding data security, retention and access restrictions),

  ✓ Premises security,

  ✓ Human resources department (regarding employee files, HRIS, monitoring, whistleblower hotline), and

  ✓ Sales and marketing personnel (regarding direct marketing)?

2. **What does the company do to keep data secure?**

✔ Do you have a security policy that describes sufficient physical, technical and organizational data security measures, *e.g.,* database access controls and device encryption?

✔ Are all employees familiar with the policy and actually complying with it?

✔ Are service providers carefully selected and monitored with respect to data security and are appropriate contracts in place?

✔ Are you prepared for a data security breach with respect to notice and compensation requirements under law and contracts?

✔ Do you have a data retention and deletion program in place that ensures that data is securely discarded after it is no longer needed or legal to store?

3. **Have all data subjects received appropriate notices and granted consent where required, and are all notice and consent forms accurate and up to date?**

✔ Most companies need employee privacy notices and website privacy statements; many companies will also need consent for website cookie placement, online tracking, employee and call center monitoring, direct marketing, and video surveillance.

✔ Consider requirements following from law but also from contracts and commitments in prior notices and privacy policies.

4. **Have all data protection authorities or other government entities been notified and granted approvals, where required? Have any relevant facts changed since the last notification or approval?**

✔ Confirm for each jurisdiction where your company has an office, employees or other physical presence whether the government has to be notified about databases or processing and whether any approvals or authorizations have to be obtained.

5. **Do you receive or send data on persons in other jurisdictions across borders, *e.g.*, employees, consumers, or individual representatives of corporate customers?**

✔ For compliance with European data protection laws, do you and your business partners have qualified data transfer agreements, Binding Corporate Rules, consent or other compliance programs in place?

6. **Do you operate a whistleblower hotline or monitoring technologies?**

✔ If you operate a whistleblower hotline, you usually have to issue notices to individuals, submit filings to government authorities, consult with works councils and make some tough decisions on what may and must not be reported, how it is reported and to whom.

✔ Most companies filter emails, record phone calls, secure networks, operate surveillance cameras or deploy other technologies for purposes of data security and compliance monitoring. Consequently, companies have to issue notices to employees and external data subjects and, under the laws of some jurisdictions, companies have to obtain consent, submit filings to government authorities, consult with works councils and modify the technology deployment to satisfy local law requirements.

7. **Are your marketing activities in compliance with applicable law?**

✔ Do you obtain prior consent where legally required, *e.g.*, for marketing emails and behavioral tracking under European laws?

✔ Do you offer and honor unsubscribe options?

✔ Do you share personal data for marketing purposes with other data controllers or do you allow others to collect data directly from your customers or website visitors (*e.g.*, via third party cookies on your websites)? If yes, consent from data subjects and various disclosures may be required.

✔ Do you buy information from third parties, *e.g.*, email list vendors, background check providers or data brokers? If yes, do you receive sufficient contractual assurances that you can legally buy and use the information for the intended purposes? Have you conducted and documented reasonable due diligence steps to confirm the legality of the sources?

8. **Do you design products, processes and standard contracts to allow or facilitate compliance with data privacy and security requirements by your employees, customers and product users?**

✔ Have you prepared sufficiently detailed records of your data processing activities, equipment, personnel, processes and compliance programs?

✔ Do you have a process for conducting privacy impact assessments before you adopt new technologies or design new products or services?

✔ Do you assess and consider your customers' and end users' data privacy and security compliance needs in developing new products and processes?

✔ Do you seek input from your data privacy officer and legal department early on in the product development process?

✔ Do you provide customers and end users with guidance on how they can use your products in compliance with data privacy and security laws, or how to avoid pitfalls, for example, in user manuals, whitepapers, and FAQs?

✔ Do your standard contract terms offer your customers all legally required and reasonably expected representations and terms relating to data privacy and data security?

# Resources

Everyone has their own research methods and preferences. In the following list of resources, I am providing suggestions that I believe will supplement this Field Guide well, but the list is not intended to be anywhere close to complete or constitute a review, ranking or evaluation of resources included or excluded.

On the **World Wide Web**, government agencies, law firms, Wikipedia, the Electronic Frontier Foundation (EFF), the American Civil Liberties Union, media companies and individuals publish alerts and updates. As a starting point for initial orientation on a particular topic, I usually enter a buzz word or short phrase into a general Internet search engine.

**Opinions by Data Protection Authorities in the EEA.** Fairly comprehensive guidance is available from individual data protection authorities as well as an EU institution comprised of representatives from all national authorities (historically known as the "Article 29 Working Party" and renamed "European Data Protection Board" under the EU General Data Protection Regulation).

These documents are available in English, free of charge on web pages of the European Union (the exact URL/address changes frequently). The working group was originally created pursuant to Article 29 of the European Data Protection Directive and consists of representatives of data protection authorities of each European Economic Area (EEA) Member State. Its papers are not legally binding and do not always reflect the views of all national authorities. However, national data protection authorities occasionally refer to the papers when they issue binding decisions. Companies should not feel obliged to slavishly follow guidelines from the Article 29 Working Party, but they should also not completely ignore them. At a minimum, companies should consider the positions and arguments that the Article 29 Working Party advances and either adopt the suggestions fully or partly, or prepare themselves for challenges. Many national data protection authorities also provide helpful guidance and information on their home pages, including the UK Information Commissioner.

**U.S. Federal Trade Commission Guidelines and Cases:** These are available in English, free of charge at the FTC's home page, at www. FederalTradeCommission.gov. The site has limited search functionality, but you can enter search terms plus "FederalTradeCommission. gov" into general search engines. Companies in the United States tend to closely follow FTC decisions and respect the FTC as a very effective enforcer of consumer rights. The FTC is also specifically tasked with enforcing the EU-U.S. Privacy Shield Principles and the CAN-SPAM Act. The National Conference of State Legislatures publishes an overview regarding U.S. state data security breach notification statutes at **ncsl.org.** The U.S. government publishes guidance and materials on **HIPAA** at http://www.hhs.gov/ocr/privacy.

My law firm, Baker & McKenzie LLP, publishes an annual **Global Privacy Handbook**. Other law firms also make a host of valuable resources available on their homepages and in newsletters.

Many paid resources are also available, including the following: The International Association of Privacy Professionals (**IAPP**) offers conferences, training and certification programs as well as daily, weekly and monthly newsletters. A number of academics and practitioners publish books, including **Privacy Law Fundamentals** by Daniel J. Solove and Paul M. Schwartz (4th Edition, 2017, 318 page summary of U.S. legislation with an introduction to EU and other countries' privacy laws), the Privacy and Data Security Law Deskbook, a loose-leaf treatise by Lisa Sotto; PLI's Proskauer on Privacy (1,658 pages, 2nd Ed., 2016), and a two- volume Global Privacy and Security Law Treatise by Francoise Gilbert (3,000 pages, regularly updated). For a practical guide and detailed commentary on U.S. federal and California privacy law, see California Privacy Law (2nd Ed., 2017) by the author of this Field Guide.

# Abbreviations

| | |
|---|---|
| APEC | Asia-Pacific Economic Cooperation |
| Article 29 Working Party | Committee of national data protection authority representatives in Europe |
| CAN-SPAM Act | U.S. federal law restricting e-mail advertising |
| CAPTCHA | Completely Automated Public Turing test to tell Computers and Humans Apart; automated challenge-response test to confirm that the response is generated by a person |
| CBPR | Cross-Border Privacy Rules |
| CDA | Communications Decency Act (U.S. federal statute with contributory liability privileges for Internet service providers) |
| CFAA | Computer Fraud and Abuse Act (U.S. federal law prohibiting access of computers without authorization) |
| CNIL | Commission nationale de l'informatique et des libertés; French data protection authority |
| COPPA | U.S. Children's Online Privacy Protection Act |
| CRM | Customer Relationship Management |
| DPA | Data protection authority |
| DPO | Data protection officer |
| E-Commerce Directive | EU Directive with contributory liability privileges for Internet service providers |
| EEA | European Economic Area (EU member states plus Iceland, Liechtenstein and Norway) |

| | |
|---|---|
| EU | European Union |
| EU Data Protection Directive | Directive 95/46/EC on the protection of individuals with regard to the processing of personal data and on the free movement of such data |
| EU | General Data Protection Regulation (EU) 2016/679 of 27 April 2016 on the protection of natural persons with regard to the processing of personal data and on the free movement of such data, and repealing Directive 95/46/EC; effective as of May 2018 |
| FCRA | Fair Credit Reporting Act |
| FIP(P)s | Federal Information Processing Standards or Fair Information Practices Principles |
| FTC | Federal Trade Commission; U.S. authority tasked with consumer and privacy protection |
| GDPR | See EU General Data Protection Regulation |
| GLB | Gramm–Leach–Bliley Act, a U.S. federal privacy law, *a.k.a.* 'Financial Services Modernization Act of 1999' |
| HIPAA | Health Insurance Portability and Accountability Act, a U.S. federal law of 1996, as amended |
| HR | Human Resources |
| HRIS | Human Resources Information System, *i.e.*, employee database |
| IP Address | Internet Protocol Address; a number assigned to each device (*e.g.*, computer, router, server) in a computer network |
| ISO | International Organization for Standardization, non-governmental organization where representatives of national standards institutes (some governmental, some private sector entities) of 163 countries coordinate international standards setting |
| IT | Information Technology |

| | |
|---|---|
| Model clauses | See SCC, Standard Contractual Clauses |
| NSA | National Security Agency of the United States |
| PII | Personally Identifiable Information |
| RFID | Radio-frequency identification uses electromagnetic fields to track tags attached to an object, *e.g.*, products at retailers (to prevent theft), livestock and pets, automobiles (for bridge toll payments), etc. |
| SAS 70 | Auditing standard, replaced by SSAE 16 |
| SCC | Standard Contractual Clauses promulgated by the EU Commission for international data transfers |
| SOC Report | Service Organization Controls Report, under SSAE 16 standard |
| SOX | Sarbanes-Oxley Act, federal U.S. law specifying requirements for publicly listed companies in the U.S. |
| SSAE 16 | Auditing standard regarding internal controls of service organizations and entities that use service organizations |
| USA Patriot Act | Uniting and Strengthening America by Providing Appropriate Tools Required to Intercept and Obstruct Terrorism Act of 2001; federal U.S. law intended to combat terrorism; replaced by the USA Freedom Act, see Paragraphs 2.16 and 5.15 |
| ZIP codes | Zone Improvement Plan postal codes, used by the United States Postal Service since 1963 |

# Index

Access rights 0.35, 2.15, 3.29, 5.57
Access controls 1.38, 1.63, 5.12, 5.23, 5.52,
    *Checklist*
Access by employees in good faith 5.43
Access by governments 5.15, 5.34
Access as transfer 0.32, 0.33
Accountability 5.36
Advertising 3.08, 3.68, 3.78, 5.01–5.03,
    5.53, 5.61, 5.63, 5.66–5.72
Ad Networks 3.26, 5.63
Ad Servers 5.64
Aggregate, aggregation 0.25, 5.76
Agreements 2.22–2.27, 2.34–2.37, 2.42,
    3.66–3.73, 5.18, 5.23, 5.35
Alternative dispute resolution 2.62
Anonymous, anonymity 0.31, 5.31, 5.56,
    5.59
APEC 2.72–2.73, *Abbreviations*
Article 29 Working Party 0.36, 1.14, 2.29,
    *Resources, Abbreviations*
Asia-Pacific Economic Cooperation
    2.72–2.73, *Abbreviations*
Audits 1.34, 1.73, 3.20. 4.02, 5.08, 5.09,
    5.22, 5.23, 5.52, 5.57, 5.73
Autonomous car 5.36

Background checks 5.26
Beacon 5.61
Best practices 3.04, 5.81
Big data 0.13, 5.36
Biometric data 5.75
Binding Corporate Rules 2.29, 2.32–2.45,
    2.66–2.68, *Checklist*
Blocking statutes 5.34
Breach 0.17, 1.10, 1.61, 1.63, 2.38, 3.70,
    4.03, 4.05, 5.13, 5.21, 5.23, 5.24, 5.33,
    5.40, 5.43–5.49, 5.57, *Checklist*

Bring your own device (BYOD) 5.29
Browser settings 5.62
Business associate 0.34, 0.35, 1.45,
    1.55, 3.12, 3.73, 5.07, 5.23, 5.35, 5.40,
    5.73
BYOD 5.29

Canadian anti-spam legislation (CASL)
    5.66
CAPTCHA 5.36, *Abbreviations*
CBPR 2.72–2.73
Certifications 2.72, *Abbreviations*
CFAA, 5.32, 5.36, *Abbreviations*
Changing privacy policies, notices 3.22,
    3.32, 3.42, 3.56, 3.67
Checklists 0.03, 2.57, 5.35, *Checklist*
Chief Privacy Officer 1.11, 1.14, 1.23–1.24,
    1.26, 2.63, 3.88, *Checklist*
Cloud Computing 0.13, 0.15, 1.06, 2.27,
    3.20, 5.05–5.23, 5.34–5.35, 5.57
Codes of Conduct 2.32–2.33, 2.35–2.37,
    2.41, 2.43
Cold calls 5.66–5.67
Colocation provider 0.35
Common Market 1.51
Communications Decency Act (CDA)
    5.58, *Abbreviations*
Computer fraud 5.32, 5.36
Computer interference laws 5.32, 5.36
Consent 2.20, 2.24, 3.35–3.69
Contracts 2.21–2.45, 2.48–2.58, 3.66–3.73,
    5.18, 5.23
Control 0.34–0.35, 5.10, 5.20
Contributory liability 3.77, 5.55–5.56
Cookies 3.24, 3.35, 3.43, 5.04, 5.42, 5.60,
    5.61
COPPA 5.42, *Abbreviations*

Covered entities 1.45, 1.55, 3.73, 5.35, 5.73
Cross-Border Privacy Rules (CBPR)
2.72–2.73, *Abbreviations*
Crawlers 5.36
Cybersecurity 5.36

Data brokers 5.36
Data controller 0.09, 0.34, 0.35
Data handler 0.35
Data integrity 2.07, 3.79, 5.13, 5.28
Data processor 0.10, 0.33–0.35, 1.46, 2.06,
2.08, 2.10, 2.24–2.25, 2.27, 2.37, 2.50,
2.52, 3.20, 3.69–3.71, 3.84, 5.06–5.07,
5.10, 5.17–5.20, 5.23, 5.35, 5.43
Data privacy law 0.12, 0.14–0.21,
0.32–0.33, 1.43–1.56
Data protection authority 0.36–0.37, 2.35,
3.30, 5.18
Data protection law 0.15, 1.17, 1.20, 1.60,
2.01, 2.52, 2.72, 3.69, 5.17
Data protection officer 0.20, 0.37,
1.12–1.26, 5.34
Data retention 5.24
Data room 4.07
Data security breach notification 0.17, 1.61
Data transfer agreements 2.22, 2.24,
2.34–2.35, 2.42, 2.44–2.45, 2.54–2.55,
3.82, 3.84, 5.07, 5.57
Digital rights management (DRM) 5.65
Discovery 2.37, 5.34, 5.81
DMCA 5.36
DNT 5.62
Documentation 3.01–3.88
Do not call list 5.66
Do not track (DNT) 5.62
Double opt-in 3.52, 5.69
Drafting 3.01–3.88
DRM 5.65
Due diligence 2.35, 3.15, 3.80, 4.03, 4.05,
4.07, 4.09–4.10, 5.07, 5.23, 5.73,
*Checklist*

Employees 5.26–5.32
Encryption 0.17, 0.25, 1.27, 1.38, 1.63, 3.74,
4.07, 5.33, 5.45
Enforcement 1.01, 1.39–1.40, 1.52, 1.54,
1.59, 2.35, 2.37–2.39, 3.26, 3.73, 5.15,

5.24, 5.36, 5.39, 5.41, 5.48–5.49, 5.57,
5.66, 5.75–5.76, 5.79
EU Data Protection Directive 0.19–0.20,
0.36, 2.15, *Abbreviations*
EU General Data Protection Regulation
0.20, 0.36, 1.12–1.14, 1.18–1.19,
1.22, 1.51, 2.15, 2.33–2.36, 3.30,
3.80–3.83, 5.04, 5.38, 5.41–5.42,
5.44, 5.57, *Resources,
Abbreviations*
EU-U.S. Privacy Shield 2.13–2.14,
2.17–2.18, 2.25, 2.30, 2.33–2.45,
2.56, 2.59–2.61, 2.71, 3.15, 3.17–3.23,
3.80–3.81, 4.01, 5.04, 5.17–5.18, 5.39,
*Resources*
Export control compliance 0.29

Facial recognition 5.36, 5.65, 5.75
Fair Credit Reporting Act 3.50,
*Abbreviations*
FCRA 3.50, *Abbreviations*
Filtering 5.29, 5.74
Financial data 1.45, 5.33
Fingerprints 5.75–5.76
FOIPPA 5.15
Forgotten, right to be 5.25

Genetic information 5.76
General Data Protection Regulation 0.20,
0.36, 1.12–1.14, 1.18–1.19, 1.22, 1.51,
2.15, 2.33–2.36, 3.30, 3.80–3.83, 5.04,
5.38, 5.41–5.42, 5.44, 5.57, *Resources,
Abbreviations*
Good faith access 5.43
Government information request 5.34
Government filing 0.33, 1.55, 1.67, 2.07,
3.18, 4.09
Gramm–Leach–Bliley Act (GLB) 1.55,
3.19, 5.33, 5.35, *Abbreviations*

Health information 1.55, 3.27, 3.35, 5.15,
5.23, 5.35, 5.82
Hessen 0.15
Household 0.24, 1.45, 5.58
HIPAA 0.17, 1.24, 1.45, 1.55, 3.12, 3.19, 3.35,
3.50, 3.73, 5.07, 5.23, 5.35, 5.40, 5.73,
5.76, *Resources*

Human Resources Information Systems (HRIS) 3.19, 3.38, 5.15, 5.21, 5.28, *Checklist*
Hotline 3.19, 3.84, 5.26, 5.31, 5.56

Internet of everything 5.36
Internet of things 5.36, 5.65
Interoperability 1.54, 2.13, 2.42, 2.72, 5.06
Investigations 0.29, 1.05, 1.63, 2.37, 3.17, 4.10, 5.26, 5.30, 5.34, 5.48, 5.76
IP address 0.24, 5.56, 5.61, 5.82
ISO certification *Abbreviations*

Jurisdiction 5.66–5.67, 5.69

Key concepts 0.14–0.38
Key Terms 0.05–0.13

Lawful access by governments 5.15, 5.34
Legitimate interest exception 0.20, 1.54, 2.10, 3.30, 3.35, 5.28, 5.36, 5.75
Litigation hold 5.24, 5.29
Location data 3.28, 3.59, 5.41

M&A, mergers and acquisitions 4.01, 4.03, 4.05–4.07
Machine-to-machine (M2M) 5.36, 5.65
Maintenance 4.01–4.02
Making available transfer 0.32
Marketing fluff in privacy policies 3.04, 3.17, 3.33, 5.57
Mere conduit 0.35, 5.35
Minors 5.42
Mobile 3.59–3.60, 5.41, 5.61
Model Clauses (*a.k.a* Standard Contractual Clauses) 2.22–2.29, 2.32–2.44, 2.49–2.54, 2.71, 3.73, 5.04, 5.18, 5.23
Monitoring 0.37, 1.22–1.24, 5.26–32
Multi-tenant 5.13, 5.22

National Security Agency (NSA) 0.37, 2.16, 5.15, 5.36, *Abbreviations*
Networking 0.15–0.16, 3.24, 3.68, 5.58
Notices 3.18–3.32, 5.49–5.51
Notifications to data protection authorities 1.20, 1.84, 5.49
NSA 0.37, 2.16, 5.15, 5.36, *Abbreviations*

Onward transfer 2.13, 2.15, 2.32, 2.37, 2.58, 3.84, 5.07
Opt-in 3.59, 3.78, 5.04, 5.56, 5.69
Opt-out 2.32, 4.03, 5.02, 5.04, 5.60–5.61, 5.66, 5.68–5.72
Outsourcing 2.33, 2.40, 3.07, 3.38, 5.09, 5.15, 5.23
Ownership 5.53

Pareto Principle, 80–20 rule 1.37
Patriot Act 2.16, 5.15, *Abbreviations*
Payment Card Industry (PCI) 5.23, 5.33, 5.40
PCI Standards 5.23, 5.33, 5.40
Permissions 3.12
Personal data 2.57–2.58, 2.70–2.71, 3.11, 3.19, 3.30, 3.43, 3.72–3.73, 5.08–5.09, 5.11, 5.18, 5.23
Personal use 5.29, 5.32
Platform 0.16, 2.27, 3.59–3.60, 3.68, 5.05, 5.20, 5.32, 5.58, 5.66
Privacy by design 3.60, 5.54
Privacy Officer 0.01, 1.11, 1.14, 1.23–1.24, 1.26–1.27, 3.12, 5.39, *Checklist*
Privacy policy 2.47, 3.17
Privacy Shield 5.04
Privacyville 3.59
Private cloud 5.13
Private household use 1.45, 5.58
Protocol 3.05, 3.13, 3.74

Questionnaires 3.14, 3.13, 3.17, 3.74–3.75, 5.45, 5.52

Records of data processing activities 1.33
Redacted 0.25, 4.08
Remedies 3.63, 5.57
Retention 3.28, 5.24
RFID 3.24, 5.29, 5.41
Rights and remedies 2.54, 5.57
Right to be forgotten 5.25
Robots 5.38

Safe Harbor 2.14–2.15, 2.25, 2.28, 2.39–2.40, 2.57, 2.71, 5.04

SCC (*a.k.a* 'Model Clauses') 2.22–2.29, 2.32–2.44, 2.49–2.54, 2.71, 3.73, 5.04, 5.18, 5.23
Scraping 5.36
Search engine 5.36, *Resources*
Secondment 2.10, 2.21, 5.28
Self-assessment 2.13, 2.35, 2.42, 2.57, 2.65, 3.15, 5.52
Sensitive data 0.06, 0.20, 0.27–0.29, 1.15, 1.62, 5.31, 5.41, 5.76
Service Providers 0.10, 0.33–0.35, 1.17, 1.45, 2.08, 2.25, 2.33, 2.37, 2.40, 2.44, 3.20, 3.26–3.28, 3.65, 4.09–4.10, 5.01, 5.06–5.10, 5.14–5.23, 5.35
Smartphones 3.60
SOC 5.23
Social media 3.59, 5.32, 5.58
Social media passwords 5.32, 5.58
Social networking 0.15, 0.16, 3.24, 3.68, 5.58
Song-Beverly Credit Card Act 1.55, 3.35
Spam 1.45, 3.78, 5.01, 5.29, 5.32, 5.56, 5.66
Spam filtering 5.29, 5.66
Spiders 5.36
SSAE 16 5.23, *Abbreviations*
Standard Contractual Clauses, SCC (*a.k.a* 'Model Clauses') 2.22–2.29, 2.32–2.44, 2.49–2.54, 2.71, 3.73, 5.04, 5.18, 5.23
Subprocessor 2.24, 2.52

Tags 3.24, 5.29, 5.41, 5.61, 5.65
Task list 1.27–1.68
Telematics 5.65
Tracking 3.19, 3.24, 3.34, 3.65, 3.68, 5.02, 5.29, 5.41, 5.60–5.65
Trade compliance screening 0.29
Transfer 0.32, 0.35, 2.01–2.81

Unsolicited calls, emails 5.66–5.72
Updating notices, privacy policies 3.22, 3.32, 3.42, 3.56, 3.67
USA Patriot Act 5.15, *Abbreviations*

Vendors 4.09–4.10, 5.13, 5.20–5.21, 5.51, 5.73
Virus filtering 5.76

Web crawler 5.36
Whistleblower hotlines 3.19, 3.84, 5.26, 5.31, 5.56
Wiretapping 5.74
Why protect privacy? 5.77–5.81

X-rays 5.75

ZIP Codes 5.82, *Abbreviations*

*'Lothar Determann is Silicon Valley's go-to data privacy expert.* Determann's Field Guide to Data Privacy Law *is a practical and accessible guide for non-experts. I use it any time I encounter a new data privacy issue.'*

**Josh Faddis**
Vice President, General Counsel, Veeva Systems Inc., USA

*'*Determann's Field Guide to Data Privacy Law *allows privacy professionals to see the light at the end of the tunnel. The overview, practical advice, methodical organization and thoroughness distill down the complex world of international privacy, while also providing the necessary context behind these requirements. A must-have.'*

**Jeremy Livianu, Esq.**
Healthcare Compliance Officer, Associate Director, Legal Affairs,
Nevro Corp, USA

*'Understanding and navigating the complexities of data privacy is of paramount importance for companies. Many in-house practitioners, who graduated from law school before data privacy was taught, feel left behind on this trending area of law.* Determann's Field Guide to Data Privacy Law *demystifies data privacy by providing practical and sound advice in an easy to navigate format. A must-have reference book for all legal departments.'*

**David Tognotti**
Vice President and General Counsel, Monster Inc., USA

What readers have said about the first edition:

*'The proliferation of electronic commerce and the unprecedented volume of data stored by businesses have made data compliance programs for most businesses a priority. Therefore, the creation and regular audit of an efficient program intended to minimize data thefts and manipulations has become a need of the hour.* Determann's Field Guide *addresses all these issues in a comprehensive manner. Dr. Lothar has also taken a lot of effort to collate the concepts and practices of international data privacy law in a most lucid manner. The* Field Guide *is the reflection of Dr. Determann's finesse towards details and accuracy, which is associated with all of his works. Focusing on the global regulatory regime of data privacy norms compliance requirements, the* Field Guide *comes with startling clarity through concise and up to date checklists essential for data compliance audits. The* Field Guide *is thoroughly recommended for the lay and expert alike, especially for lawyers,*

*accountants and other professionals engaged in operations covering various jurisdictions.'*

**Anand Mehta**
Partner, Khaitan & Co., India

*'As the data stored by business entities globally increases at an exponential pace, the legal frameworks and regulations governing such data increase in complexity at nearly the same rate, creating an environment of conflicting requirements and unclear obligations. Determann's book* Determann's Field Guide to Data Privacy Law *offers a real-world, practical approach to dealing with the data privacy challenges that in-house counsel face on nearly a daily basis. In particular, I recommend it as a source of invaluable information for those of us operating in multiple jurisdictions.'*

**Scott Trainor**
VP and Regional General Counsel, APJ, SAP Asia Pte. Ltd.

*'With the proliferation and diversity of privacy risks and international regulatory controls, and the increasingly obvious intersection of data security and privacy, no company can afford to overlook the importance of an up to date and well-tailored global compliance program. For companies doing business in the cloud or transacting with consumers, a well-considered international data privacy compliance program is not only a critical legal and liability control – it is fundamental to earning and maintaining the trust of your customers. In this comprehensive yet concise "Field Guide", Professor Determann has managed to consolidate an enormous breadth of legal requirements and best practices knowledge into a single, definitive reference that should be quite accessible even to non-privacy professionals. As general counsel of a multinational public company, I consider* Determann's Field Guide to Data Privacy Law *to be a pragmatic and indispensable reference in improving our compliance program, and highly recommend it for anyone looking for clear, practical guidance on establishing or improving their data privacy program!'*

**Felix Sterling**
Senior Vice President and General Counsel at Trend Micro Inc.,
Silicon Valley, USA

'Lothar Determann has done a great service to the field of privacy by providing practical, workable advice for a dynamic and challenging issue. This Field Guide will certainly be a valuable and soon dog-eared, addition to any privacy professional's reference library.'

**J. Trevor Hughes**
President and CEO, International Association of Privacy Professionals
(IAPP)

'Determann's Field Guide takes the complicated subject of international privacy and breaks it down into helpful topics, checklists and suggestions. The focus on practical advice in an easy-to-use format makes it an ideal reference tool for in-house privacy professionals.'

**Rebecca Matthias**
Senior Corporate Counsel, Privacy and Data Protection, VMware,
Inc., Palo Alto, USA

'Determann's Field Guide to Data Privacy Law is an indispensable handbook for international privacy professionals. Written by a star lawyer, it explains how to develop and maintain a corporate privacy compliance program. The book manages both to explain the "big picture" of global privacy challenges and to point out relevant details in a clear and concise fashion.'

**Paul M. Schwartz**
Berkeley Center for Law & Technology, University of California,
Berkeley School of Law (Boalt Hall), USA

'Determann's Field Guide is an insightful practical guide which should be on every privacy practitioner's desk.'

**Daniel Blaettler**
Vice President and Associate General Counsel, Verisign, Geneva,
Switzerland